The SURGICAL HOSPITALIST

Program Management Guide

TOOLS AND STRATEGIES FOR EXECUTIVES AND PHYSICIANS

John Nelson, MD, FACP • John Maa, MD, FACS
Foreword by Robert M. Wachter, MD

HCPro

The Surgical Hospitalist Program Management Guide: Tools and Strategies for Executives and Physicians is published by HCPro, Inc.

Copyright © 2009 HCPro, Inc.

All rights reserved. Printed in the United States of America.   5 4 3 2 1

ISBN 978-1-60146-573-3

No part of this publication may be reproduced, in any form or by any means, without prior written consent of HCPro, Inc., or the Copyright Clearance Center (978/750-8400). Please notify us immediately if you have received an unauthorized copy.

HCPro, Inc., provides information resources for the healthcare industry.

HCPro, Inc., is not affiliated in any way with The Joint Commission, which owns the JCAHO and Joint Commission trademarks.

John Nelson, MD, FACP, Author	Janell Lukac, Graphic Artist
John Maa, MD, FACS, Author	Lauren Rubenzahl, Copy Editor
Robert M. Wachter, MD, Foreword Author	Karin Holmes, Proofreader
Karen M. Cheung, Associate Editor	Matt Sharpe, Production Supervisor
Erin E. Callahan, Executive Editor	Susan Darbyshire, Art Director
Bob Croce, Group Publisher	Jean St. Pierre, Director of Operations
Laura Godinho, Cover Designer	

Advice given is general. Readers should consult professional counsel for specific legal, ethical, or clinical questions.

Arrangements can be made for quantity discounts. For more information, contact:

HCPro, Inc.
P.O. Box 1168
Marblehead, MA 01945
Telephone: 800/650-6787 or 781/639-1872
Fax: 781/639-2982
E-mail: *customerservice@hcpro.com*

Visit HCPro at its World Wide Web sites:
www.hcpro.com and *www.hcmarketplace.com*

Contents

Figure List vii
About the Authors ix
About the Foreword Author xi
About the Contributors xii
Foreword xx
Preface xxiv

Chapter 1: Introduction 1
    Organization of the Book 2
    Suggested Uses of This Book.. 2

Chapter 2: Investing in a Surgical Hospitalist Program: Value, Structure, and Finance 5
    Financial Reasons to Start Up 5
    Structuring a Surgical Hospitalist Program 6
    Financial Considerations for a Surgical Hospitalist Program 9
    Creating a Budget for a Surgical Hospitalist Program 10
    Calculating a Return on Investment for Surgical Hospitalist Programs 13
    Key Traits to Look for in Surgical Hospitalists 14

Chapter 3: Calculating the Return on Investment for Your Surgical Hospitalist Program ... 17
    Assessment of the New Program 17
    Overview of ROI Calculation 18
    Estimation of Future Costs and Benefits—Pro Forma Development................................... 19
    Conclusion 37

Chapter 4: Management and Business Operations for Surgical Hospitalist Practices 39
    Hospital and Surgical Hospitalist Corporation 40
    Medical and Administrative Support Staff... 42
    Communication, Self-Evaluation, Recruitment, and Retention 45
    Medical Personnel 46

Chapter 5: Staffing a Surgical Hospitalist Program 51
    What Is Your Model? 51
    Demographics of Patient Populations 54
    Demographics of General Surgeons.. 55
    Are There Enough General Surgeons to Meet Our Future Needs? 56

Contents

Potential Pitfalls in Staffing a Surgical Hospitalist Program 58
Special Considerations 60

Chapter 6: Scheduling the Operating Room 63
Ideal Schedule Model 65
Classical Model 67
Trauma Center Model 69
Mosaic Model 72
Night Surgeon Model 76
OR Scheduling and Community 78

Chapter 7: Surgical Hospital Compensation Planning 81
Amount of Compensation 81
Models of Compensation 85
Special Consideration 92

Chapter 8: Surgical Hospitalist Scheduling 97
Challenges in Developing a Surgical Hospitalist Schedule 97
Specific Scheduling Issues 100

Chapter 9: Communication Issues in Surgical Hospitalist Practice 109
Communication with Patients, Families, and Significant Others 109
Communication with Physicians 112
Communication Between Surgical Hospitalists within the Same Practice 114

Chapter 10: Measuring Success 117
The Performance Measurement Process 117
Criteria for a Successful Performance Measurement System 118
What Aspects of Performance Should Be Measured? 119
Setting Performance Objectives 126
Analysis Considerations 127
Conclusion 132

Chapter 11: Trauma Coverage 133
The Role of EMS 133
Trauma Center Levels 134
The Role of the Surgical Hospitalist and Acute Care Surgeon 135
Benefits of Trauma Status 136

Chapter 12: Surgical Hospitalist Programs and the Academic Medical Center 141
Surgical Education of Surgery Residents and Medical Students 141
Promoting Clear Communication at an Academic Medical Center 143
Enhancing Resident Supervision and Continuity of Care 144
Complexity of Care 146
Collaborations 147
Conclusion 150

Chapter 13: Acute Care Surgery: The Evolution of a Specialty 151
Proposed Formats after Four Years of Core General Surgery 156

Chapter 14: Documentation, Coding, Billing, and Related Issues 161
Words 162
Codes 163
Present on Admission 166
ICD-9, or 10, and 11! 166
E&M Codes 167
Relative Value Unit 168
Hospital Observation 168
Consultations 169
ED Codes 171
Procedural Codes 171
Coding Education 172
E&M Coding Anatomy 173
History 174
Physical Examination 176
Critical Care and Time-Based Services 177
The Coding Bottom Line 177

Chapter 15: Case Study: Shady Grove Adventist Hospital, Rockville, MD 179
The Hospital 179
The Surgical Hospitalist 181
Other General Surgeons on the Medical Staff 183
Other Physicians on the Medical Staff 183
Follow-up and Outpatient Referrals 184
Conclusion 185

Contents

Chapter 16: Case Study: Anne Arundel Medical Center, Annapolis, MD 187
    Starting the Program 187
    Scheduling for Continuity of Care 188
    Outcomes 191

Chapter 17: Case Study: University of California at San Francisco, Department of Surgery 195
    UCSF Surgery Hospitalist Mission Statement 195
    Introduction 196
    Findings from the Surgical Hospitalist Model in Year 1 198
    Enhanced Efficiency and Value of Surgical Hospitalist Program 200
    Conclusion 204

Chapter 18: Case Study: Thomas Memorial Hospital, South Charleston, WV 205
    The Problem with West Virginia 206
    Now What? 206
    Why the Surgical Hospitalist Model Works 207
    Keys to Success 208
    Postscript 209

Chapter 19: Case Study: University of California, Irvine 211
    Background 211
    Stimulus to Create an ACS Program 212
    Lessons Learned 214
    What Is the Turf of the ACS Service? 215
    Staffing 215
    Cost and Caseload 216

Chapter 20: Case Study: Surgical Specialists of Spokane, Spokane, WA 219

Resources 223

Figure List

FIGURE 2.1: Sample Surgical Hospitalist Group Expenses: Community Hospital with Three Surgeons 12
FIGURE 2.2: Key Questions in Determining an ROI for Surgical Hospitalist Practice 13
FIGURE 3.1: Example of ROI Formula 18
FIGURE 3.2: ROI Calculation Using Summarized Financial Projections 20
FIGURE 3.3: Example Physician Recruiting Expense 21
FIGURE 3.4: Example of Outpatient Clinic Capital Costs 22
FIGURE 3.5: Example Capital and Startup Costs 23
FIGURE 3.6: Example Variables to Estimate Revenue 25
FIGURE 3.7: Example Revenue Forecast 26
FIGURE 3.8: Example Median Benchmark Physician Expenses 27
FIGURE 3.9: Example Physician Expense Projections 28
FIGURE 3.10: Example Operating Expenses Projections 29
FIGURE 3.11: Example Net Gains (Losses) 30
FIGURE 3.12: Overview of Potential Indirect Benefits 31
FIGURE 3.13: Call Coverage Stipend Benefit 32
FIGURE 3.14: Incremental Surgical Case Benefit 33
FIGURE 3.15: Surgical Coverage Alternatives 34
FIGURE 3.16: Review of Outsourced Arrangement 35
FIGURE 4.1: Conceptual Organizational Chart 1 40
FIGURE 4.2: Conceptual Organizational Chart 2 42
FIGURE 4.3: Conceptual Organizational Chart 3 46
FIGURE 4.4: Conceptual Organizational Chart 4 47
FIGURE 4.5: Sample Surgical Hospitalist Clinical Responsibilities 48
FIGURE 4.6: Sample NP and PA in a Surgical Hospitalist Practice Responsibilities 49
FIGURE 6.1: Ideal Operating Room Schedule 66
FIGURE 6.2: Classical Operating Room Schedule 68
FIGURE 6.3: Trauma Center Operating Room Schedule 71
FIGURE 6.4: Mosaic Operating Room Schedule 75
FIGURE 6.5: Night Surgeon Operating Room Schedule 77
FIGURE 7.1: Median General Surgery Compensation—Past Five Years 82
FIGURE 7.2: Quartile General Surgery Compensation—Past Five Years 84
FIGURE 7.3: Shift-Based Compensation Calculation 86
FIGURE 7.4: Salary-Based Model Compared to Market 87
FIGURE 7.5: Common Productivity Metrics 89
FIGURE 7.6: Tiered Productivity Compensation Plan 89

Figure List

FIGURE 7.7: Base Plus Incentive Compensation Plan 90
FIGURE 7.8: Sample Compensation Plan 92
FIGURE 8.1: Checklist for Evaluating a Surgical Hospitalist Schedule 101
FIGURE 8.2: Pros & Cons of Eliminating Fixed Start/Stop Times for Day Shift 106
FIGURE 9.1: Surgical Hospitalist Brochure 111
FIGURE 9.2: Ten Commandments for Effective Consultation 114
FIGURE 10.1: Checklist for Evaluating a Surgical Hospitalist Schedule 121
FIGURE 10.2: Sample Clinical Quality Metrics 122
FIGURE 10.3: Sample Operational Effectiveness Metrics 124
FIGURE 10.4: Sample Financial Performance Metrics 125
FIGURE 10.5: Sample Customer Satisfaction Metrics 126
FIGURE 10.6: Sample Report Card 131
FIGURE 11.1: Trauma Level Comparison Chart 135
FIGURE 13.1: The Essential Elements of a Career in Acute Care Surgery 154
FIGURE 13.2: Proposed Acute Care Surgery Formats 156
FIGURE 14.1: Consultation Rules and Description 170
FIGURE 15.1: Pros & Cons of Traditional vs. Block Schedules 182
FIGURE 19.1: Teaching and Administrative Responsibilities 216

About the Authors

John Nelson, MD, FACP

John Nelson, MD, FACP has practiced as a hospitalist since completing internal medicine training at the University of Florida in 1988. He is currently medical director of the hospitalist practice at Overlake Hospital Medical Center in Bellevue, WA, where he continues to provide patient care regularly.

Since the early 1990s, he has served as a consultant for more than 200 institutions around the country as they start or improve a hospitalist practice. He currently does his work through Nelson Flores Hospital Consultants, found at *www.NelsonFlores.com*. He has been an architect and leader in the evolution of "medical" hospitalist practice and is now on the forefront of the growth of surgical hospitalist practice through working with institutions to develop new surgical hospitalist practices.

In 1997, he teamed with a Massachusetts hospitalist to found the Society of Hospital Medicine (formerly the National Association of Inpatient Physicians), which is the professional organization for the nation's 15,000 hospitalists. He is a former president and board member of the organization.

John.Nelson@nelsonflores.com
425/467-3316

John Maa, MD, FACS

John Maa, MD, FACS, is a surgeon dedicated to improving the quality and access of emergency surgical care. He earned his MD at Harvard Medical School and served as a captain in the medical corps of the U.S. Army for nine years. During medical school, he was awarded the New York City Mayor's Prize for his research thesis, "Concomitant Mycobacterium tuberculosis and human immunodeficiency virus infection in New York City, 1986–1991."

About the Authors

During a general surgical residency at the University of California, San Francisco (UCSF), he was awarded a National Institutes of Health Gastrointestinal Research training grant and published numerous scientific articles on pancreatic and gastrointestinal inflammation.

Maa received a patent for his invention of a safer central venous catheter and is certified by the American Board of Surgery. After his residency, he completed a fellowship in health policy at the UCSF Institute of Health Policy Studies, exploring mechanisms to improve the overall structure and processes of general surgical care nationally. During the fellowship, he also helped create the UCSF Surgical Hospitalist Program, which seeks to enhance the quality and timeliness of hospital-based emergency surgical care. His current research focuses on applying the surgical hospitalist model to improve hospital-based emergency care, specifically through new processes and strategies that address the challenges of emergency department overcrowding, boarding, and ambulance diversion. Over the past year, he assisted in the creation of a multidisciplinary course in public policy and advocacy for the professional schools of medicine, dentistry, pharmacy, and nursing at UCSF.

Maa is a member of the board of directors of the American Heart Association and associate director of surgery clerkship at UCSF. He serves on several advisory boards and committees that focus on improving care in hospitals. He is currently an assistant professor in general surgery at UCSF and assistant chair of the department of surgery's quality improvement program.

John.Maa@ucsfmedctr.org
415/476-0762

About the Foreword Author

Robert M. Wachter, MD

Robert M. Wachter, MD, is professor and associate chair of the department of medicine at the University of California, San Francisco (UCSF), where he holds the Lynne and Marc Benioff Endowed Chair in hospital medicine. He is also chief of the division of hospital medicine and chief of the medical service at UCSF Medical Center. He has published 200 articles and six books in the fields of quality, safety, and health policy. He coined the term "hospitalist" in a 1996 *New England Journal of Medicine* article, is a past president of the Society of Hospital Medicine, and edits the field's first textbook, *Hospital Medicine*. He is generally considered the academic leader of the hospitalist movement, the fastest-growing specialty in the history of modern medicine.

Wachter is also a national leader in the fields of patient safety and healthcare quality. He is editor of *AHRQ WebM&M,* a case-based patient safety journal on the Web, and *AHRQ Patient Safety Network*, the leading federal patient safety portal. Together, the Web sites receive nearly 2 million unique visits each year. His book on medical errors, *Internal Bleeding: The Truth Behind America's Terrifying Epidemic of Medical Mistakes*, now in its fourth printing, has been a national bestseller. His new book, *Understanding Patient Safety*, is a leading textbook in the field.

Wachter has discussed patient safety and healthcare quality on *Good Morning America*, PBS' *NewsHour*, *Imus in the Morning*, CNN's *American Morning*, CBS *Sunday Morning*, and *The Big Idea with Donny Deutsch*. He received one of the 2004 John M. Eisenberg Awards, the nation's top honor in patient safety and quality. In 2008, *Modern Physician* magazine named him the 19th most influential physician executive in the United States, the highest-ranking academic physician on the list. He is on the board of directors of the American Board of Internal Medicine and serves on the healthcare advisory boards of several companies, including Google.

bobw@medicine.ucsf.edu
415/476-5632

About the Contributors

L.D. Britt, MD, MPH, FACS, FCCM

A native of Suffolk, VA, and graduate of Harvard Medical School and Harvard School of Public Health, L.D. Britt, MD, MPH, FACS, has had extensive surgical and critical care training. He is professor and chair of the department of surgery at Eastern Virginia Medical School (EVMS) and holds the Brickhouse Chair in Surgery.

Britt is the first African-American in the country to have an endowed chair in surgery and the first African-American in the history of the Commonwealth of Virginia to be appointed professor of surgery. He has been the recipient of numerous awards and honors that acknowledge his accomplishments in surgery and excellence in teaching, including the nation's highest teaching award in medicine: the Robert J. Glaser Distinguished Teaching Award, given by the Association of American Medical Colleges.

Britt is a distinguished member of several state, national, and international organizations and is actively involved in numerous church and community activities. He has authored numerous scientific publications and has been a reviewer and served on the editorial boards of several noted surgery journals. President George W. Bush recognized Britt's leadership role in medicine and nominated him to the Board of Regents of the Uniformed Services University of the Health Sciences. The U.S. Senate confirmed this nomination in August 2002. Community leaders have established a medical school scholarship and community service award in his name.

BrittLD@evms.edu
757/446-8950

Jason A. Brodsky, MD, FACS

Jason A. Brodsky, MD, FACS, completed his undergraduate studies at the University of Michigan in 1992. He then enrolled in the Hahnemann University School of Medicine, where he was awarded his Doctor of Medicine in 1996. Following this, he trained in general surgery at The George Washington University Medical Center. During his residency, Brodsky spent a year in the Minimally Invasive Surgery Center at the Cleveland Clinic Foundation as a research fellow. He returned to the Cleveland Clinic after his residency to finish his training as the advanced laparoscopic digestive fellow. He currently practices acute care surgery at Shady Grove Adventist Hospital in Rockville, MD, where he is the medical director of the surgical hospitalist program.

JBrodsky@adventisthealthcare.com
240/403-0621

Gaurov Dayal, MD

Gaurov Dayal, MD, works at Adventist Health Care, a health system based in Rockville, MD. He serves as the chief administrator for Adventist Physician Services, a multispecialty physician practice, as well as the chief medical officer at Shady Grove Adventist Hospital in Rockville. Prior to his current roles, Dayal created and led a pediatric hospitalist group. He is a graduate of Johns Hopkins University and received his medical degree from Northwestern University. He completed his residency training at Washington University in St. Louis.

GDayal@adventisthealthcare.com
301/279-6247

M. Tray Dunaway, MD, FACS, CSP

M. Tray Dunaway, MD, FACS, CSP, is not a coder. He doesn't even like coding. He is a physician who personally developed a physician-friendly algorithm to help other physicians who want to make money, save time, not have to understand arcane coding rules, and never have to fear an auditor. His documentation system, available on his Web site (*www.TrayDunaway.com*), has been sold to physicians nationwide since 1997, comes with a money-back guarantee, and instructs physicians and their employees how to solve the E&M coding conundrum. Dr. Dunaway still conducts entertaining and enlightening "documentation seminars" by invitation, but now primarily is an award-winning keynote speaker for a wide variety of healthcare organizations and businesses that want to take care of patients, and each other, better.

Tray@traydunaway.com
803/425-8555

Joshua J. Felsher, MD, FACS

Joshua J. Felsher, MD, FACS, received his BA magna cum laude with high honors in biology from Brandeis University in 1995 before attending The George Washington University Medical School. In 1999, he began his surgical training at The George Washington University Medical Center in the general surgery residency program. During residency, he completed a research fellowship in minimally invasive surgery at the Cleveland Clinic Foundation. Following residency in 2006, he completed a clinical fellowship in bariatric and advanced laparoscopy at the University of Massachusetts. With more than 15 peer-reviewed publications, he has presented at numerous national and local meetings covering a variety of surgical topics.

JFelsher@adventisthealthcare.com
240/403-0621

Leslie A. Flores, MHA

Leslie A. Flores, MHA, is a healthcare executive and consultant with a wealth of experience in the healthcare industry. Graduating from the University of California, Irvine, with a BS in biological sciences, she obtained her master's degree in healthcare administration from the University of Minnesota. She has held a variety of executive-level positions in Southern California hospitals, where she has been responsible for clinical and support services, as well as for staff functions in strategic planning and business development, managed care, community benefit planning, and physician recruitment and practice development.

Since 1999, Flores has provided management consulting, training, and leadership development services for hospitals, physician groups, and other healthcare organizations. She currently serves as a partner with John Nelson, MD, FACP, in Nelson/Flores Hospital Medical Consultants, a consulting practice that specializes in helping its clients build successful new hospital medicine programs and enhance the effectiveness and value of existing programs (*www.NelsonFlores.com*). She also serves as director of the Society of Hospital Medicine's Practice Management Institute.

Leslie.Flores@nelsonflores.com
760/771-3323

Robert J. Gray, FACHE

Robert J. Gray, FACHE, is senior vice president of Thomas Health System, located in South Charleston, WV. This two-hospital system is made up of two acute hospitals with 415 beds. Gray has worked in healthcare for 32 years and in hospital operations for the past 27. He received his undergraduate and graduate degrees from West Virginia University. He has taught courses at West Virginia University, Marshall University Graduate School, and the University of Charleston. He has served his community on several health-related and civic boards. He is a fellow in the American College of Healthcare Executives.

Bob.Gray@thomaswv.org
304/766-3529

David B. Hoyt, MD, FACS

David B. Hoyt, MD, FACS, received a BA degree with honors from Amherst College, followed by an MD from Case Western Reserve University in 1976. From 1976 to 1984, he was a surgical resident and research fellow at the University of California, San Diego (UCSD), and Scripps Immunology Institute. He joined the faculty at UCSD and immediately became involved in their trauma service, where his role as director lasted from 1989 to 2006. In 1995, he was appointed professor of surgery and was awarded The Monroe E. Trout Professorship in Surgery at UCSD in 1996. In 2006, he was appointed chair of the department of surgery and received the distinct honor of being named the John E. Connolly Professor of Surgery at the University of California, Irvine. On October 1, 2008, he was also appointed executive vice dean of the University of California, Irvine, School of Medicine.

Hoyt has distinguished himself within the department of surgery, having delivered numerous lectures, received multiple significant awards from his colleagues and scientific organizations, and serving in positions of leadership. He continues to serve as an advisor for many graduate students.

Hoyt is a member of the American Surgical Association, Surgical Biology Club, Western Surgical Association, and Society of University Surgeons and holds membership in other prestigious surgical organizations. He is the immediate past president of the American Association for the Surgery of Trauma, past president of the Society of General Surgeons of San Diego, past president of the Shock Society, past chair of the American College of Surgeons Committee on Trauma, and past medical

About the Contributors

director of trauma at the American College of Surgeons. He has been a visiting professor at several institutions nationally and internationally and is an editorial board member of six journals. He continues to receive significant public research funding and is the author of more than 475 publications. He was recently awarded the American Heart Association Resuscitation Science Lifetime Research Achievement Award and The American College of Surgeons Distinguished Service Award.

DHoyt@uci.edu
714/456-6262

Michael E. Lekawa, MD, FACS

Michael E. Lekawa, MD, FACS, is an associate professor in the department of surgery at the University of California, Irvine School of Medicine, and has been trauma director for 12 years. He is an active clinician and teacher and has been awarded the Resident Research Award. He is actively involved in running the acute care surgery service.

Melekawa@uci.edu
714/456-5890

Darin E. Libby

Darin E. Libby is the senior manager at ECG Management Consultants, Inc.'s healthcare practice. His healthcare background and leadership skills give him the experience to solve complex problems in business/physician development, strategic planning, and business operations. He has more than 10 years of experience in healthcare strategic and business planning, hospital operations, and physician development. At ECG, he has worked extensively with health system, hospital, and medical group clients to address a variety of planning, business development, and operational issues. He has specific expertise in strategic planning, hospital-physician ventures, medical staff development, operational restructuring, and hospital and medical group financial management. He has successfully negotiated numerous physician development arrangements that have resulted in improved hospital-physician relations and increased business performance.

Prior to joining ECG, he worked at Overlake Hospital Medical Center in Bellevue, WA, where he led an effort to build a 120-bed, $210 million hospital, managed the physician practice division, and directed physician and business development activities. In addition, he served as the cancer service line administrator at The Methodist Hospital in Houston, where he managed the development of a comprehensive breast center and a urology institute.

DLibby@ecgmc.com
858/436-3220

Paul Lin, MD, FACS

Paul Lin, MD, FACS, is the trauma medical director of Sacred Heart Medical Center and the medical director of Sacred Heart Wound Care Services.

Lin served his general surgery residency at the University of Washington Hospital. He received his Doctor of Medicine at Northwestern Medical School and his BA at The Johns Hopkins University. He is an active member of the North Pacific Surgical Society, Henry Harkins Surgical Society, American College of Surgeons, Washington State Medical Association, and Alpha Omega Alpha Medical Honor Society.

PLin@inwhealth.net
509/747-6194

Paul M. Maggio, MD, MBA

Paul M. Maggio, MD, MBA, is an assistant professor in the department of surgery at Stanford University School of Medicine. He completed his general surgery training at Brown University and then supplemented his education with additional training in trauma/burns and surgical critical care at the University of Michigan, where he also obtained his MBA. He is board-certified in general surgery, with added qualifications in surgical critical care.

PMaggio@stanford.edu
650/723-0173

About the Contributors

David Matteson, MD

David Matteson, MD, is medical director of the surgical hospitalist program at Anne Arundel Medical Center in Annapolis, MD, where he has been on staff since 1987 after finishing his residency in general surgery with an additional year of training in colorectal surgery. After spending 18 years in private practice, he became one of the original members of the hospital's new surgical hospitalist program.

DMatte8854@aol.com
410/573-0383

R. Steven Norton, MD, FACS

R. Steven Norton, MD, FACS, was in private practice in Olympia, WA, for 21 years before he began working as a surgical hospitalist in California in 2008. He is the founder of SurgicalHospitalists.org, an organization devoted to developing the structure necessary to run a successful surgical hospitalist program, including recruitment and placement of surgeons in permanent hospitalist positions in nonprofit urban center hospitals. The organization also aims to ensure adequate compensation for surgical hospitalists and keep the compensation in the hands of those doing the work. Outcome data software development and education are areas of the organization currently in development.

SteveNorton@mac.com
503/930-3083

Leon J. Owens, MD, FACS

Leon J. Owens, MD, FACS, received his undergraduate degree from the University of Michigan in 1972 and his medical degree in 1976. He completed a general surgery internship and residency at the University of California, Davis, in 1981. That year, he joined his brother in a general surgery practice in Carmichael, CA. He developed a trauma program at Mercy San Juan Medical Center in 1998, where he continues to serve as medical director. From 2003 to 2004, he completed a critical care fellowship at UC Davis Medical Center. In 2008, he created Acute Care Surgery Medical Group, which provides a 24/7 surgical hospitalist program to Sutter Medical Center in Sacramento, CA. In his role as trauma director and father, Owens has also focused on the problem of alcohol-impaired driving. He championed a state law change in California for a pilot program in Sacramento County, which is currently studying this problem, in conjunction with UC Davis and the University of Michigan School of Public Health. He has created a 501(c)(3), The Teachable Moment Foundation, to facilitate this endeavor.

AOwens5931@aol.com
916/483-4748

David A. Spain, MD, FACS

David A. Spain, MD, FACS, is professor of surgery and chief of trauma/critical care surgery at Stanford University School of Medicine. He completed his general training at the University of Medicine and Dentistry of New Jersey–Robert Wood Johnson Medical School and then completed a trauma/burn and surgical critical care fellowship. He is board-certified in general surgery, with added qualifications in surgical critical care.

DSpain@stanford.edu
650/723-0173

Eva M. Wall, MD, FACS

Eva M. Wall, MD, FACS, is a freelance emergency general surgeon and surgical intensivist. She received her medical degree from The George Washington University and completed her general surgery residency at Geisinger Medical Center and her fellowship in critical care at Queens Medical Center in Honolulu. She is board-certified in general surgery and surgical critical care. Her interests have recently focused on the needs of urgent surgical patients, the needs of her family, and fitting the two together.

EWall67@mac.com
425/743-7065

Foreword

Robert M. Wachter, MD

The launching of a new specialty is exciting to watch. The idea often arises organically—a need is identified, a new technology materializes, a new patient population emerges. A few hardy physicians, often endowed with an organizational mind, a sense of plucky entrepreneurialism, and a sense of humor (and some Kevlar couldn't hurt) step in to fill the breach. Although some physicians decry this new specialty as heresy, others applaud the innovation. But most take a wait-and-see approach: "That's interesting, but show me the data."

Ultimately, all startups can survive and thrive only if they can answer (in the affirmative) a series of questions: Does this new field improve value—namely, quality divided by cost? Does the field successfully fill an obvious gap in clinical care? If so, the data and experience encourage others to try the new model, adapting it to their own local circumstances.

Meanwhile, the leaders of the new field, now convinced that their specialty will endure, begin mapping out the future. There are pragmatic questions: How should leaders organize these programs? Who should finance the field?

And there are more academic questions: How do we train specialists in this field? What types of new educational materials do the specialists need? What is the research agenda for the future?

Finally, there are social network questions: What are the best structures (conferences, e-mail list servs, etc.) to promote collegial exchange of dialogue? Is the field substantial enough to have its own society? Its own newsletter? Its own journal?

This is all near and dear to my heart, since it is precisely the path that John Nelson, Win Whitcomb, and I trod in the early years of the hospitalist field.[1] In 1996, I wrote an article, entitled "The Emerging Role of 'Hospitalists' in the American Health Care System," published in the *New England Journal of Medicine*, which coined the term "hospitalist" and introduced the concept to the healthcare community.[2] Soon after that article was published, Drs. Nelson and Whitcomb, two practicing hospitalists in community settings, called me. Within months, we met and—armed with the hubris of youth—began to address all of these issues.

The rest, as they say, is history: The hospitalist field has become the fastest-growing specialty in the history of American medicine—from a few hundred practitioners in 1996 to more than 20,000 today. The field's specialty society, the Society of Hospital Medicine, is thriving, with nearly 9,000 current members,[3] and there are fellowship programs, research networks, textbooks, a journal, and even upcoming board certification for members of this new field. Why? Because the field met an important set of needs, demonstrated its value,[4] and ultimately won over even the naysayers.

When I first learned of the concept of surgical hospitalists from my UCSF colleague, Dr. John Maa, I had a sense of déjà vu. Up until that point, when I thought of a surgical hospitalist, I had in my mind's eye an internist-hospitalist helping comanage surgical patients, which is another rapidly emerging trend. But, as Dr. Maa described the rationale for inpatient-focused generalist surgeons, it made all the sense in the world, and I guessed that the surgical hospitalist model, like medical hospitalists a decade earlier, would become an enduring trend in American medicine.

In the first two years of the program at UCSF, our surgical hospitalists virtually worked and lived in the hospital for a week at a time, without a day off.[5] For that week, they were constantly available to the emergency department (ED) for consults. As a result, the average time at UCSF between an ED consult request and a surgeon's appearance in the ED is—I hope you're sitting down—16 minutes. Until I saw those data, I didn't know the elevators were that fast! In response to surveys, UCSF ED doctors and nurses were nearly euphoric with this unprecedented level of responsiveness.

Dr. Maa and his colleagues care for patients with a wide variety of clinical problems, ranging from cholecystitis to bowel obstruction. When the patient needs an operation that the surgical hospitalists feel is within their comfort zone (more than 90% of the time, in our experience to date), they perform the surgery themselves, shortening the time from diagnosis to incision for appendectomies by half. When the case is super-specialized or the patient has a long-standing relationship with another surgeon, the surgical hospitalists hand the patient off to the appropriate colleague. Although the surgical hospitalist service does receive medical center support dollars, the program also generates substantial new revenue through a marked increase in consultations, easing the need for financial subsidy.

Foreword

The surgical hospitalist model extends our concept of a hospital-based generalist who offers full-time on-site availability, personally handles a wide variety of problems and coordinates the care of others, and focuses on improving both the care of individual patients *and* hospital systems. Like all healthcare innovations, the model has brought out the usual skeptics and naysayers. But with a huge shortage of surgeons—particularly general surgeons—available to cover hospital call[6] and a national crisis in ED overcrowding,[7] it is clear that the surgical hospitalist model addresses several critical problems.

Based on my experience with medical hospitalists, I predict that the surgical hospitalist model will grow and thrive. It will be critical to define the role better, in terms of schedules, training, reporting relationships, interactions with other surgeons, and more. Assuming that the model requires some institutional (usually medical center) support, hammering out the finances will also be crucial. If hospitals do chip in to support the program, key organizational questions arise: Should surgical hospitalists work for the hospital, or for medical groups, or for large regional or national companies? These questions are complex, and there is unlikely to be a single correct answer to any of them.

Because so many hospitals and medical groups are considering surgical hospitalist programs, the need for a resource like this book is compelling. The book offers information on the background, the business and clinical case for the innovation, and the nuts and bolts of implementation. This book represents the combined wisdom of many of the early physician and nonphysician leaders of the surgical hospitalist field, and it addresses the key questions. It will be a valued resource to those practicing in this field and those charged with organizing new programs. Although it is sure to find a large and enthusiastic audience among physicians and hospital administrators, my hope is that it also contributes to the ultimate goal of any new specialty—improving the care of patients.

REFERENCES

1. R.M. Wachter, "Reflections: The Hospitalist Movement a Decade Later," *Journal of Hospital Medicine* 1 (2006): 248–252.

2. R.M. Wachter and L. Goldman, "The Emerging Role of 'Hospitalists' in the American Health Care System," *New England Journal of Medicine* 335 (1996): 514–517.

3. Society of Hospital Medicine, "Members & Growing," The Hospitalist eWire, *http://xrl.us/oxsza* (accessed November 18, 2008).

4. R.M. Wachter and L. Goldman, "The Hospitalist Movement 5 Years Later," *Journal of the American Medical Association* 282 (2002): 487–494.

5. J. Maa, J.T. Carter, J.E. Gosnell, R.M. Wachter, and H.W. Harris, "The Surgical Hospitalist: A New Model for Emergency Surgical Care," *Journal of the American College of Surgeons* 205 (2007): 704–711.

6. T.E. Williams Jr., and E.C. Ellison, "Population Analysis Predicts a Future Critical Shortage of General Surgeons," *Surgery* 144 (2008): 548–554.

7. Institute of Medicine, "Hospital-Based Emergency Care: At the Breaking Point," National Academy of Sciences, *www.iom.edu/CMS/3809/16107/35007.aspx.* (accessed October 21, 2008).

Preface

We see a book like this as an effort to tap into the thoughts and ideas of people who have demonstrated a commitment to developing and optimizing a future model of inpatient surgery practice. The fact that so many talented people have been willing to contribute to this effort is very gratifying, and we want to thank them for taking the time to provide their insight.

We wrote and edited this book in the spare time outside of our usual professional commitments. We owe a special thanks to our families for their understanding and support as we worked on this book, since they gave up some time with us so we could do this work.

A special thanks to Dr. Nancy Ascher, chair of the University of California, San Francisco (UCSF), Department of Surgery, and Dr. Hobart Harris, chief of the Division of General Surgery at UCSF, for their vision and support of the development of the UCSF Surgery Hospitalist Program.

We would also like to thank Drs. Guilherme Campos, Jonathan Carter, Laura Goetz, Jessica Gosnell, Electron Kebebew, Eric Nakakura, and Wen Shen for their invaluable contributions to the UCSF Surgery Hospitalist Program.

In loving memory of Laura Maa.

CHAPTER 1

Introduction

John Nelson, MD, FACP • John Maa, MD, FACS

The hospitalist model of medical practice has grown dramatically since the mid-1990s. The largest and most visible segment of this practice model is physicians trained in internal medicine, family medicine, or pediatrics, who provide care for hospitalized patients. These doctors are known either as hospitalists or pediatric hospitalists.

A less visible development is that the hospitalist model of practice has been adopted, at least to some extent, by many specialties in American medicine. We are aware of practicing GI hospitalists, orthopedic hospitalists, psychiatric hospitalists, obstetric hospitalists (often called "laborists"), and hospitalists in nearly every field, including general surgery. Healthcare administrators and providers will need to become familiar with what a surgical hospitalist practice might offer in their setting, as well as its limitations and costs.

During the past decade, a crisis in access to emergency surgical care has emerged, jeopardizing the ability of patients to receive optimal care in a timely and safe manner in our nation's emergency departments (ED). Both patient volume and complexity have increased, as increasing numbers of uninsured and underinsured patients have sought treatment in an ED. The traditional models of surgical call coverage have proven challenging, and a need has arisen to define new methods for surgeons to provide 24-hour coverage, seven days per week, particularly in the middle of the night and on weekends. A key intent of the acute care surgery and surgical hospitalist models is to propose solutions to the national crisis of access to emergency surgical care that promote efficiency, safety, and quality outcomes.

A central goal of this book is to share the experiences, insights, and valuable lessons learned from several of these emerging programs that will likely point to future directions as the field of emergency surgery continues to evolve. As of February 2009, we estimate that there are more than 30 surgical hospitalist programs across the country, and we anticipate that there will be approximately 300 within the next three years.

Chapter 1

A key question is the required level of hospital financial support to a surgical hospitalist program. From our observations, this amount has ranged from about $400 to $3,500 daily, with most programs in the $1,000-per-day range. A particularly successful model has been the following: A multispecialty surgical group negotiates a daily stipend (perhaps $500) with the medical center leadership to provide timely and quality care consistent with the surgical hospitalist model. This additional funding allows the existing group to recruit a new surgeon (and often recent graduate) to join the multispecialty group and provide on-site dedicated coverage from 7 a.m. to 6 p.m. on weekdays. One of the more senior partners then rotates into the call scheme to cover the evening from 6 p.m. to 7 a.m. once his or her daily clinics and operating room (OR) schedules are completed. This method allows the junior surgeon an opportunity to build clinical skills, become familiar with the medical center, and have backup from senior surgeons on more challenging cases—while also providing a relatively balanced lifestyle.

This book is an effort to provide the collective experience of the 20 total contributors with this new and rapidly growing field. Each contributor has already had significant experience in this field, either as an administrator or as a clinician. In many cases, the contributors are the founding surgeons of their surgical hospitalist practice.

Organization of the Book

This book addresses the management of a surgical hospitalist practice. It is written for healthcare administrators and for surgeons and other caregivers involved in a surgical hospitalist practice. The first part of the book is a series of chapters that addresses specific operational and organizational issues, such as financial issues, staffing and scheduling, managing OR scheduling, etc. The second half of the book is a series of case studies. John Nelson is from a medical hospitalist background, and in the early evolution of that field, the case studies of individual practices in operation proved to be very useful and popular sources of information. We believe that the same will be true for surgical hospitalists.

Suggested Uses of This Book

We are confident that each chapter in this book will prove valuable to readers, and we have tried to sequence the chapters in a logical way. Yet we think that most readers will benefit by reading the chapters in any order that matches their interest. Some may choose to start with the case studies, and others may want to turn directly to a specific topic in the first section of the book.

One of the goals of writing such a book is to identify the contributors as potential ongoing sources of information. We encourage readers to contact the authors in this book if they have questions or would like to discuss an issue further. Each contributor's availability to respond to queries will vary, but all have significant interest in this emerging field and will be accumulating more information and experience that will allow them to refine their recommendations as the field evolves.

Using the CD

When you see the CD icon, you can find the figure (e.g., sample form, policy, chart, or further information) on the companion CD that comes with this book. You can then customize these documents for your own facility.

Terminology

We have used what we believe to be the most appropriate terminology throughout the book, but because this field is still evolving rapidly, we want to explain it here. We chose to use the term "surgical hospitalist" in the title and throughout the book because it can already be found in the existing medical literature and even when hearing it for the first time, most people in healthcare understand its intended meaning. We believe it is nearly universally understood to serve as a job description for general surgeons with a practice focused on the surgical care of hospitalized patients.

Other terms, such as "acute care surgeon" and "traumatologist," that have some overlapping meaning and sometimes are used interchangeably with "surgical hospitalist" have also appeared in the literature. But we believe there are meaningful differences between these terms. "Traumatologist" generally refers to a surgeon who is principally involved in the care of trauma patients, as might be the case in a Level I or Level II trauma center. (And confusingly, "traumatologist" is also used to describe a different group of caregivers, who provide mental healthcare to victims of physical or emotional trauma.) In Chapter 11, Drs. Maggio and Spain describe the acute care surgery model of practice.

When used without a modifier preceding it, the term "hospitalist" is widely accepted to refer to a doctor who provides nonsurgical medical care to hospitalized adults or children. To avoid confusion, we have used "medical hospitalist" to refer to these doctors to distinguish them from surgical hospitalists. We have chosen not to use "surgicalist" interchangeably with "surgical hospitalist," although the former occasionally appears elsewhere.

Chapter 1

The overarching intent of this book is to stimulate a wider discussion of new models of emergency surgical care that are patient-centered, humane, responsive, and readily accessible to all. We welcome your insights, feedback, and suggestions of new solutions to the national challenges in the delivery of optimal and timely surgical care for our patients.

Voice

In editing these chapters, we've leaned towards preserving each contributor's own writing style, which means some chapters are written formally, and others more informally or colloquially. The surgical hospitalist field is still new, and the pools of people with experience come from diverse backgrounds and experiences and express their ideas in various ways. The careful reader may find conclusions and recommendations in one chapter that differ somewhat from those found elsewhere in the book. This reflects the variety of opinions and approaches in use currently, and we think there is value in being inclusive so that readers can have a broader understanding and form conclusions about the best approach for their own setting.

CHAPTER 2

Investing in a Surgical Hospitalist Program: Value, Structure, and Finance

Gaurov Dayal, MD

The surgical hospitalist movement is a relatively new phenomenon. But just as hospitalists for general internal medicine and pediatrics are becoming the norm at many hospitals, many expect surgical hospitalists to become an integral part of hospitals in the next decade. There are several reasons that a surgical hospitalist program provides value to a hospital.

Financial Reasons to Start Up

A hospital may wish to pursue a surgical hospitalist program to improve:

- Call coverage

- Hospital throughput

- Compliance with quality measures

Call coverage

Emergency department (ED) coverage for general surgery has become an ever-increasing challenge. Declining reimbursements, coupled with increasing malpractice and overhead expenses, have placed significant financial strains on general surgeons. Additionally, many general surgeons prefer to serve at outpatient-focused practices because of their predictable hours and reimbursements, compared to the long hours and poor reimbursements typically associated with inpatient services. An explosion in ambulatory surgical centers (ASC), often with surgeon investors, has further separated surgeons from community hospitals, and as a result, the call that was once viewed as an obligation is now a burden that many surgeons are choosing to forgo. Numerous ED patients are uninsured, making ED call an even more difficult burden for surgeons to bear.

Chapter 2

The cumulative result is that many surgeons are unwilling to take voluntary call, and hospital pay for call is gradually becoming the norm. A national shortage of general surgeons has made ED coverage a problem even for hospitals that are willing to pay for call. A surgical hospitalist program is a sustainable way a hospital can provide ED coverage, as well as inpatient consult coverage.

Hospital throughput

Insurance companies, regulatory bodies, and hospitals are applying increasing pressure to treat and discharge patients quickly. The past model of the surgeon rounding—once in the morning and once more after finishing a day at the office—is no longer viable. Surgical hospitalist programs enable rapid evaluation, surgery (if necessary), and close inpatient monitoring and discharge—a tremendous value to today's overburdened EDs and bed-constrained hospitals.

Quality measures

Hospitals are obligated to participate in an increasing number of quality measures (e.g., CMS-mandated "Core Measures"). Lack of compliance with these measures not only puts a hospital's accreditation at risk, but also may be reflected in hospital comparison data, which patients are increasingly accessing through Hospital Compare (*www.HospitalCompare.hhs.gov*) under the U.S. Department of Health and Human Services. Therefore, it is important for hospitals to comply and perform well on these measures, not only for patient care, but also to maintain a competitive advantage over other hospitals.

A fragmented surgical staff, which may consist of low-volume providers, makes it difficult to ensure consistent, reproducible outcomes with patients. A small number of high-volume providers, as seen with surgical hospitalist programs, ensures compliance with quality measures, as well as collaborative development of evidence-based protocols for common surgical conditions.

Structuring a Surgical Hospitalist Program

Surgical hospitalist programs tend to be much smaller, with fewer staff members, than the larger medical and pediatric hospitalist programs. Much of this difference can be attributed to the smaller volume of surgical patients compared to medical patients. For example, Shady Grove Adventist Hospital in Rockville, MD, has 290 beds, 18 full-time-equivalent medical hospitalists, and only three surgical hospitalists. Concurrently, the office staff required for such practices also is lower. This program employs only one office staff member who manages the follow-up clinic for surgical hospitalist patients.

As a result, the overall logistics of staffing and running a surgical program tend to be significantly less complicated than those for their medical counterparts.

Surgical hospitalist programs often follow one of three models:

- Employment model

- Contracted model

- Collaboration with existing surgeons

Employment model

In the employment model, the hospital or a hospital-owned group practice employs the surgeons directly. If the hospital already has other employed physicians, it may prefer this model because it requires less work; that is, already-employed physicians more easily integrate with the existing staff with an HR infrastructure. Best practice in an employed model dictates that there is explicit understanding between program administrators and surgeons about schedules and productivity, and ideally there is a compensation plan that incorporates incentives for productivity, quality, and patient satisfaction. In the employed model, the hospital typically covers all overhead expenses, including office space, support staff, and malpractice. The hospital also usually oversees billing and collections, either by having hospital employees provide this service or by engaging an outside vendor.

The employment model has advantages and disadvantages. If a hospital already has employed physicians, a surgical hospitalist practice can be readily established. However, such a practice may be less productive if the surgeons have a guaranteed income—hence, the importance of incorporating productivity incentives into the compensation package.

Contracted model

In a contracted model, a hospital typically enters into an agreement with a group for coverage for surgical hospitalist services. This contract typically is linked with an income guarantee, which is an assurance by the hospital that the group, regardless of collections, will never have less than a mutually agreed-upon amount of income. Typically, the contracted group proposes a budget to the hospital that includes salaries and overhead costs, such as staff salaries, malpractice insurance, and rent. If the group collects funds in excess of this amount, it can keep them as profit. If collections fall short of this number, the hospital makes up the difference.

Chapter 2

In a contracted model, the group is usually responsible for all aspects of running the practice, including recruiting, managing the office staff, billing, and collections. This model may best suit the needs of a hospital that does not have an established hospital-employed physician practice and that may wish to avoid establishing one. The main advantage of a contracted model is that the hospital need not be involved in the management and setup of the hospitalist group. However, in this model, the hospital incurs costs that may be higher than those in a direct employment model. In addition, the stability of such a hospitalist program may be tenuous if the contracted group is not well managed.

Collaboration with existing surgeons

In this model, the hospital may contract with existing community surgeons to provide surgical hospitalist coverage on a rotating basis, in exchange for a per-diem stipend. Essentially, the hospital pays surgeons who are already on the medical staff to take call, although it may require some performance outcomes that are not usually part of most pay-for-call arrangements. Such performance metrics might be response times to the ED, patient satisfaction scores, etc. Refer to Chapter 10 for performance metrics.

Although this model may serve in launching a program, such programs have poor long-term viability due to misaligned interests. For example, if the surgeon has a private practice in addition to the hospitalist practice, this potential conflict of interest will be a point of tension between the hospital and the referring community surgeon, who may view the rotating surgical hospitalist as competition and may believe that the surgical hospitalist is simply mining for patients.

This model is best used as a stop-gap measure while setting up a true surgical hospitalist practice staffed by a cadre of surgeons who don't have a private surgical practice. As mentioned previously, the main disadvantages to this model are the political challenges that may arise between community surgeons and surgical coverage.

In summary, for hospitals that have a well-established physician group practice, an employment model may be the easiest way to launch a surgical hospitalist program. At Shady Grove Adventist Hospital, the hospital does not have a significant number of employed physicians and opted for a contracted service that has worked out well. The collaborative model should only be viewed as an interim solution.

Financial Considerations for a Surgical Hospitalist Program

The financial success of a surgical hospitalist program will depend on a variety of factors, ranging from the patient payer mix to a surgeon's resource utilization practices. Calculating a precise return on investment is difficult, but consider some key indicators, most or all of which usually support development of a surgical hospitalist program:

- On-call payments for general surgery

- High number of uninsured patients

- Aging general surgeons with few replacements

- ED overcrowding and bed shortage

- Collaborative work with other hospitalist programs in your hospital (e.g., the medical hospitalists)

On-call payments for general surgery

If your hospital is paying for general surgery call, the money may be better spent on developing a hospitalist program. On-call payments to existing surgeons tend to serve as stop-gap measures that may not fix the underlying issue about ED call—surgeons are less likely to take on-call coverage even with increased pay. Paying them to continue taking call is unlikely to improve such issues as their ED response times or involvement in hospital quality initiatives.

High number of uninsured patients

If your hospital has a poor payer mix, it may be especially difficult or expensive to find existing general surgeons to participate in ED call. Setting up a surgical hospitalist practice may be a good option.

Aging general surgeons with few replacements

Many hospitals face the dual threat of aging surgeons on the medical staff and increasing difficulty recruiting new surgeons. A surgical hospitalist program may be a means of bringing a crew of younger, dedicated surgeons who will be invested in the long-term success of your hospital.

ED overcrowding and bed shortage

Nationally, ED overcrowding is a growing problem. Pressure on the ED makes it increasingly vital for hospitals to improve patient throughput. As hospitalists become readily available for and focused on

Chapter 2

inpatient care, they are able and expected to improve hospital throughput. The key effects that a surgical hospitalist program can have on throughput include:

- Significant reductions in ED patient waits, because surgical hospitalists can usually respond to consults more quickly than non-hospitalist surgeons

- Shorter door-to-OR time, as the hospitalists are not tied up seeing patients in the office

- Reduction in patient length of stay postop, as hospitalists can discharge patients throughout the day, unlike community surgeons, who may round only once daily

A well-run surgical hospitalist program can serve as a key tool in your hospital's throughput improvement strategy.

Success with other hospitalist programs in your hospital

Has your hospital set up an internal medicine hospitalist program? What about pediatrics or obstetrics? What is your track record in setting up these programs, and how does your medical staff view them? If you have been successful with other hospitalist programs, you probably have a good environment to support a successful surgical hospitalist program. But be careful if your track record with your other programs is not so stellar.

Creating a Budget for a Surgical Hospitalist Program

Unlike medical hospitalist programs, surgical hospitalist programs tend to be much smaller and have lower overhead costs. Some key expense items to keep in mind are:

- Number of surgeons

- Malpractice expense

- Follow-up clinic

Number of surgeons

For medium-sized community hospitals, three surgeons should suffice, but the optimal number of surgeons will vary greatly from one setting to the next and is influenced significantly by how the surgical hospitalists are scheduled. For more details, refer to Chapter 5 on staffing and Chapter 8 on scheduling.

Malpractice expense

General surgery is one of the higher-risk specialties, and depending on the state in which you are based, mature premiums for general surgery can be very high, with costs of $40,000–$100,000 annually.

Follow-up clinic

The practice will need a follow-up clinic for postop patients. It may be based inside or outside the hospital, and the hospital usually provides and pays for the follow-up clinic. In most cases, patients are seen only once or twice following hospitalization, which means that the clinic may only need to be open for five to 20 hours per week. This clinic space could be shared with other specialties.

The follow-up clinic will need one staff member to schedule follow-up visits and answer phones, but this person could handle other duties at the same time. For example, the surgical hospitalists and another practice (e.g., another specialty) could share a telephone receptionist.

Refer to an example budget in Figure 2.1, to be used as a template for calculating annual expenses for a three-surgeon group, with one secretarial staff member.

Chapter 2

FIGURE 2.1 — SAMPLE SURGICAL HOSPITALIST GROUP EXPENSES: COMMUNITY HOSPITAL WITH THREE SURGEONS

Note: The budget does not reflect billing fees. A typical billing fee is around 7.5% of gross collections. The budget also does not reflect recruitment fees or hospital/practice management fees. Secretarial support cost could be lower if the clerical staff also supports another practice and both practices divide the cost.

Hospitalist salaries and benefits	Units	Unit cost	Total
Surgeon salary	3	$245,000	$735,000
Retirement plan	3	$6,000	$18,000
Health and dental, disability allowance	3	$14,000	$42,000
CME and dues	3	$5,000	$15,000
Licenses	3	$500	$1,500
Cell phone/pager	3	$1,200	$3,600
Subtotal salary and benefits		$271,700	$815,100
Overhead expenses			
Payroll taxes	3	$21,330	$64,000 (approx.)
Banking fees	3	$2,000	$6,000
Business insurance	3	$2,500	$7,500
Malpractice insurance	3	$55,000	$165,000
Subtotal overhead expenses		$80,830	$242,500
Office expenses			
Rent and utilities	1		$30,000
Secretarial support (including benefits)	1		$80,000
Office supplies	1		$7,000
IT and telecom expenses	1		$8,000
Subtotal office expenses			$125,000
Total expenses for program			$1,182,600

Source: Gaurov Dayal, MD, chief medical officer, Shady Grove Adventist Hospital, Rockville, MD.

Investing in a Surgical Hospitalist Program: Value, Structure, and Finance

Calculating a Return on Investment for Surgical Hospitalist Programs

As with other hospitalist programs, a precise return on investment (ROI) is difficult to capture and will vary from hospital to hospital. Refer to Figure 2.2 for a worksheet that provides a framework and can serve as a starting point for ROI calculations.

FIGURE 2.2 — KEY QUESTIONS IN DETERMINING AN ROI FOR SURGICAL HOSPITALIST PRACTICE

Question	What is it worth?
Will your hospital be able to reduce length of stay of patients if you have a surgical hospitalist program?	Reduction in LOS × Daily cost savings
Will you be able to increase throughput in your ED or OR?	Increased surgical cases × Average revenue/surgical case
Are you currently paying for ED call coverage for general surgery?	Daily stipend × 365 days
Will a surgical hospitalist lead to a reduction in your malpractice settlements?	Average surgical case settlement × Probability of reduction of case
Does more consistent surgical coverage help your community mission to provide care within your hospital (rather than transferring patients elsewhere)? Is this important to your hospital from a political and community benefit perspective?	Difficult to quantify but may be of tremendous value
Will you be able to attract more community surgeons to your hospital if they no longer have to take call *and* they have an additional resource to help with complex cases?	Increased surgical cases × Average revenue/surgical case

Source: Gaurov Dayal, MD, chief medical officer, Shady Grove Adventist Hospital, Rockville, MD.

Financial calculation of an ROI for such a program may be difficult and will entail subjective valuations for some intangible benefits. However, using the above questions may help with directional data regarding the costs versus benefits.

Refer to Chapter 3 for more information on ROI.

Key Traits to Look for in Surgical Hospitalists

Finally, let's discuss the most critical factor in a creating and sustaining a successful surgical hospitalist practice: the surgeons. Whether the practice is set up as a contracted or employed model, the relatively small and intense nature of these practices places a heavy burden of success on the surgeons who serve as hospitalists.

Think of recruitment as an investment. To increase the odds that your program will be successful, focus on the following traits when recruiting a surgical hospitalist:

- Practice experience

- Skill and competence

- Team work

- Customer-service focused

Recruitment costs for new surgeons can be substantial, including a fee of $20,000–$40,000 for a search firm, relocation expenses, and, potentially, a sign-on bonus. These expenses need to be included in the financial pro forma for a new practice.

Practice experience

Unlike recruiting medical hospitalists, recruiting a surgeon directly from residency may not be the wisest choice. Ideally, a surgical hospitalist has some experience in working in a private practice setting and understands the demands and expectations of a hospital-based practice. This experience will also enable the hospitalist to work with and better understand the needs of the community general surgeons. A small but important part of the practice is also based upon running a clinic, which is an experience that most surgeons do not gain in residency.

Investing in a Surgical Hospitalist Program: Value, Structure, and Finance

Skill and competence

The surgical hospitalist is likely to perform a variety of surgical procedures, and unlike community surgeons, who can pick and choose cases, the hospitalist will be expected to operate on "all comers" in the ED. They will also be viewed as a resource for community surgeons, who may request their assistance with complex cases.

A well-trained, highly skilled surgeon can best meet the demands of serving as a hospitalist. A high-caliber surgeon will not only be an asset to the development of your program, but also will gain the respect of your community physicians. Over time, he or she will be viewed as an asset, rather than as competition. Perform a thorough reference check to ensure that you are working with top-notch people in developing your program.

Teamwork

A surgical hospitalist's role is very team-oriented. The hospitalist is expected to work on a variety of multidisciplinary teams in developing protocols as well as quality and throughput initiatives for the hospital and the OR. The surgical hospitalist also works closely with ED staff, medical hospitalists, and community surgeons; therefore, a good team player is very important. Consider having various members of these teams participate in the process of interviewing and selecting surgical hospitalists.

Customer-service focused

Regardless of the surgical hospitalists' employment arrangement, your patients will view them as part of your hospital staff. The best hospitalists are the ones who understand that and who work their hardest to treat patients with courtesy, respect, and professionalism. Consider using behavioral interviewing techniques in the recruitment process to ensure the best match with your vision and mission.

CHAPTER 3

Calculating the Return on Investment for Your Surgical Hospitalist Program

Darin E. Libby

The traditional hospital medical staff arrangement for handling unassigned emergency admissions is transforming from a "professional obligation" between surgeon and hospital to a "business arrangement," in which the surgeon expects financial remuneration for taking call. Further, at a growing number of hospitals, surgeons are choosing to cease taking call, even if they are offered payment. These changes have forced numerous hospital executives to evaluate the costs and benefits of establishing a dedicated in-house surgery program, (i.e., surgical hospitalist program) in an effort to maintain surgical care for emergency department (ED) and trauma patients, as well as the growing number of unassigned patients. As a welcome benefit, these new programs offer several advantages in addition to resolving the call coverage issue, such as enhanced quality of care, improved patient flow, and increased surgical volumes.

Assessment of the New Program

The decision-making process required to start any new program involves a particularly complex set of issues and choices—strategic, political, operational, and financial—that must be addressed by hospital and medical staff leadership. In particular, the financial investment decision for a surgical hospitalist program requires careful consideration and detailed planning because this choice results in a long-term commitment, with limited ability to revert back to traditional coverage models.

The financial analysis underlying the decision must be carried out within a consistent framework, using an objective, unbiased review that considers the economic impact of the program from startup capital investment to ongoing costs and benefits. A senior member of the hospital's finance department should manage the process of assimilating data and information. This person should calculate the financial analysis in a manner that enables sensitivity analysis to be performed. Hospital and physician stakeholders should provide input for the most accurate assessment of financial performance.

Chapter 3

This chapter presents the framework and components for conducting a commonly used financial analysis, the return on investment (ROI), to evaluate the financial implications of starting a surgical hospitalist program. The financial information in the figures in this chapter should be regarded as only rough approximations for any particular setting. They are based on experience in nonacademic community hospital settings and will vary significantly from one hospital to the next.

Overview of ROI Calculation

ROI analysis is one of the most common approaches to building a financial business case for a new program and providing a framework that management can use to evaluate the appropriateness of investment decisions. The approach calls for decision-makers to evaluate the investment, such as the startup of a new surgical hospitalist program, by comparing the magnitude and timing of expected gains to the direct and indirect program costs. The simplicity and versatility of ROI analysis contributes to its popularity as a decision-making metric. Figure 3.1 illustrates the ROI formula.

FIGURE 3.1   EXAMPLE OF ROI FORMULA

The simple and versatile ROI calculation can be modified to summarize financial gains and costs of a project to measure profitability of an initial investment. It is also important to remember there is no one right answer.

$$ROI = \frac{\text{Gain from investment} - \text{Cost of investment}}{\text{Cost of investment}}$$

Source: *Accounting the Language of Business*, 9th Edition, Weil, O'Brien, Maher, and Stickney, Thomas Horton & Daughters.

The detailed data driving ROI calculation can be modified to suit the situation; it all depends on what is included as financial gains and costs. The financial analysis, in the broadest sense, merely attempts to measure an initial investment's profitability. As such, there is no one right way to account for and calculate the gains and costs realized through startup and ongoing support of the program.

This flexibility has a downside, as ROI calculations can be easily manipulated to suit the user's purposes, and the output can express different results depending on the financial analysis supporting the calculation. Therefore, it is important to have multiple review points of the numbers and to perform sensitivity analysis to test changes in key variables, such as volume, payer mix, physician compensation, and staffing levels.

When calculating the ROI for a new program, consider what inputs are used and how financial figures are derived. As a rule, the power of the ROI calculation is only as accurate as the supporting financial analysis and requires discipline when conducting an unbiased, objective accounting of costs and benefits.

Estimation of Future Costs and Benefits—Pro Forma Development

Although the ROI calculation is a simple math exercise, the real work is in creating a sufficient level of analysis and review of the underlying assumptions and data.

PRO FORMA DEVELOPMENT

The main components of the supporting financial analysis include:
- Estimated capital and startup costs
- Forecasted program income statement (i.e., direct program profit/loss statement)
- Estimated indirect costs and benefits

The major investment in the program is the capital and startup costs. The return on this investment will be determined based on the magnitude and timing of any gains or losses forecasted in the program income statement or identified indirect costs and benefits. A simple example of a new surgical hospitalist program shows the ROI calculation. The sample analysis illustrates financial projections as summarized in the ROI calculation in Figure 3.2.

Chapter 3

FIGURE 3.2 — ROI CALCULATION USING SUMMARIZED FINANCIAL PROJECTIONS

This is a sample ROI calculation using summarized financial projections. Projections typically include startup costs and five years of operating performance. The figures are for illustrative purposes. Actual program performance will vary, and variations may be significant.

	Startup	Year 1	Year 2	Year 3	Year 4	Year 5	Totals
Capital	$(485,000)	$ –	$ –	$ –	$ –	$ –	$(485,000)
Program operating gain or (loss)		(356,169)	(344,746)	(332,083)	(318,103)	(302,724)	(1,653,824)
Indirect benefits or (loss)		693,500	693,500	693,500	693,500	693,500	3,467,500
Total annual gain or (loss)	(485,000)	337,331	384,754	361,417	375,397	390,776	
Return on investment =		274%					

$$274\% = \frac{(\$3,467,500 - \$1,653,824) - \$485,000}{\$485,000}$$

Source: Figures represent hypothetical program performance based on experience of ECG Management Consultants, Inc., headquartered in Seattle.

Estimated capital and startup costs

Fortunately, surgical hospitalist programs do not require significant amounts of capital to start, compared to other program investment decisions that necessitate major equipment or facilities. The typical range for capital and startup is $50,000–$400,000, depending on the program's size and the availability of existing surgeons to staff the service, facilities, and equipment. The costs depend less on the size or location (e.g., urban or rural) of the hospital. The capital and startup costs are mostly attributed to physician recruiting and developing an outpatient clinic for follow-up care. For many hospitals, particularly large community hospitals, these assets already exist, requiring only the minimal transition costs that the hospital incurs with the startup.

Calculating the Return on Investment for Your Surgical Hospitalist Program

> **STARTUP COSTS**
>
> To calculate each of these costs, consider the following:
> - Physician recruiting
> - Outpatient clinic
> - Other potential costs (e.g., working capital)

Physician recruiting

Recruiting general surgeons is becoming increasingly competitive as patient demand rises, and an increasing number of surgeons are electing to pursue subspecialization. Consequently, the program requires funds to recruit physicians, including sign-on bonuses, relocation packages, and recruiting expenses (e.g., recruiter fees, travel costs, and advertising expenses). Based on industry data, these recruiting expenses, which include professional or in-house recruiter costs, travel costs, and advertising expenses, will range from $30,000 to $45,000 per surgeon[1]. Total startup costs for a program that consists of four new surgeons could amount to more than $150,000, as illustrated in Figure 3.3.

FIGURE 3.3 EXAMPLE PHYSICIAN RECRUITING EXPENSE

This example represents the recruitment costs for a program of four hospitalists. The recruitment costs per full-time equivalent (FTE) are based on the average recruitment cost per physician, as reported by Carson Kolb Healthcare, Inc., a physician recruiting firm.

Cost per FTE	$30,000
FTEs	4
Total recruiting costs	**$120,000**

Source: Detailed recruitment cost per physician as reported by Carson Kolb Healthcare Group, Inc., Dana Point, CA.

Chapter 3

Outpatient clinic

The surgeons will need to establish a clinic location to provide postoperative follow-up care or other outpatient services identified as part of the program. Generally, the program will need two or three exam rooms per surgeon working in the clinic, which, for all but the busiest programs, is no more than one surgeon at any given time. This translates into a clinic space of 1,120–1,875 square ft. for two or three exam rooms, a waiting area, and back-office support.[2]

Depending on the condition of the space, some leaseholder improvements and new furniture and fixtures may be required. Equipment costs are generally minimal and related only to the outpatient clinic, as a vast majority of the surgical hospitalist work will be performed at the hospital, where equipment already exists. Figure 3.4 offers a basic example of how to estimate capital costs of the outpatient clinic.

FIGURE 3.4 EXAMPLE OF OUTPATIENT CLINIC CAPITAL COSTS

This example represents the hypothetical capital costs for a sample outpatient clinic. Specific costs will vary based on the extent of the facility improvements, amount and type of equipment required, and geography. Actual numbers will vary, and variations may be significant.

Square footage	1,500
Leasehold improvements	$50 per sq. ft.
Furniture, fixture, and equipment allowance	$20 per sq. ft.
Total investment	**$105,000**

Source: Values based on client experience at ECG Management Consultants, Inc., headquartered in Seattle.

Other potential costs

Identify and factor in other one-time startup expenses in the total amount of capital required to start the program. These other costs may range from working capital to major expenditures associated with dedicated operating rooms and other assets. Working capital commitments are typically based on a range of 30–45 days of operating expenses. This money is set aside to ensure that the program has adequate funding to operate during the startup phase, during which there will be a lag in collections. The initial program investment is summarized in Figure 3.5.

> **FIGURE 3.5 EXAMPLE CAPITAL AND STARTUP COSTS**
>
> This example represents the overall costs of starting up a program with consideration to recruitment, outpatient clinic, and working capital. Working capital equals approximately 45 days of cash required to support the program.
>
> | | |
> |---|---|
> | Physician recruiting expense | $120,000 |
> | Clinic development capital | $105,000 |
> | Working capital | $260,000 |
> | **Total investment** | **$485,000** |
>
> Source: Values based on client experience at ECG Management Consultants, Inc., headquartered in Seattle.

Forecasted program income statement

In all but a few situations, surgical hospitalist programs fail to generate positive income, requiring financial support from the hospital to remain viable. The operating losses are primarily attributed to physician coverage needs, as well as to inefficiencies that exist in the system because volume fluctuates daily and physician coverage cannot be directly tied to volume. Estimating the annual operating support needed is important not only for gaining financial approval to proceed with the program, but also to establish an expectation for ongoing funding. At a minimum, the forecast should be for a five-year period, as such an analysis can reasonably project key changes and still provide an extended forecast. Any forecast beyond five years is difficult to predict due to market uncertainties and the inability to accurately project changes.

Given that the program is new, the process of forecasting five-year income statement performance will require using historical baseline data, industry benchmarks, and planning assumptions. The summation of these data items will estimate the net gains or losses of the program.

> **PROGRAM INCOME STATEMENT**
>
> This compilation of data will be used to forecast the following:
> - Professional fee revenue
> - Physician expenses
> - Direct operating expenses

Chapter 3

Professional fee revenue

Revenue projections for surgical hospitalist programs include professional fee revenue generated during the in-house coverage. Minimal additional professional fee revenue will result from the surgeon working in the outpatient follow-up clinic because visits there are often paid prospectively, as part of the global surgical fee. Ideally, to provide the core data for developing revenue projections, physician-specific data includes volumes, charges, and collections associated with ED admissions and consults, consults performed by the surgical hospitalists on patients admitted by other doctors, and operative procedures. However, in most situations, hospitals struggle to obtain highly reliable data for professional fee revenue generated by surgeons because surgeons can't separate in-house revenue from elective case revenue.

Without available detailed historical data, hospital executives estimate baseline professional fees using a combination of existing data and planning assumptions. For revenue baseline, use a combination of hospital-reported surgical case and procedure volumes and industry benchmarks for physician work activity.

PROFESSIONAL FEE REVENUE

The selection of the data source will depend on the availability of information. Calculate revenue projections by including:

- Physician FTEs
- Patient care
- Volume
- Relative value units (RVUs) by payer mix
- Revenue per payer

Refer to Figure 3.6 for a sample table of variables that affect revenue estimates.

Calculating the Return on Investment for Your Surgical Hospitalist Program

FIGURE 3.6 — EXAMPLE VARIABLES TO ESTIMATE REVENUE

This example represents variables that can affect revenue estimates. The revenue baseline should use both hospital-reported surgical case and procedure volumes and industry benchmarks for physician work.

Variable	Data source	Calculation
Physician FTEs	• Hours of coverage required • Annual hours per FTE	• Coverage hours/hours per FTE

Patient care volume	• Surgical cases
	• Surgical procedures
	• RVUs
	   – Total RVUs per FTE
	   – Work RVUs per FTE
		• RVUs per patient
		• RVUs per surgical procedure

RVUs by payer mix	• Payer mix • ED • Hospital • Surgery department	• Percentage of payer mix × RVUs
Revenue per payer	• Per total RVU • Per work RVU • Per case	• For each payer class – Revenue per RVU by RVUs by payer

Source: Values based on experience of ECG Management Consultants, Inc., headquartered in Seattle, and available market information.

This professional fee baseline will serve as the starting point by which future periods' performance can be projected. Incorporate inflation assumptions and growth rates to forecast revenue in future years. Figure 3.7 displays an example of five-year revenue projections.

Chapter 3

| FIGURE 3.7 | EXAMPLE REVENUE FORECAST |

This example represents a hypothetical forecast for a five-year program, with modest productivity and revenue per unit gains. Actual numbers may vary, and variations may be significant.

	Baseline	Year 1	Year 2	Year 3	Year 4	Year 5
Volume						
Clinical FTEs		4	4	4	4	4
Total RVUs per surgeon FTE	11,863	12,160	12,464	12,775	13,095	13,422
Total RVUs		**48,638**	**49,854**	**51,101**	**52,378**	**53,688**
Payer mix						
Medicare	45%	21,887	22,434	22,995	23,570	24,159
Medicaid	15%	7,296	7,478	7,665	7,857	8,053
Commercial	35%	17,023	17,449	17,885	18,332	18,791
Self-pay/charity care	5%	2,432	2,493	2,555	2,619	2,684
Revenue per RVU						
Growth rate		2%	2%	2%	2%	2%
Medicare	$38.10	$38.86	$39.64	$40.43	$41.24	$42.07
Medicaid	$15	$15.30	$15.61	$15.92	$16.24	$16.56
Commercial	$47	$47.94	$48.90	$49.88	$50.87	$51.89
Self-pay/charity care	—	—	—	—	—	—
Revenue						
Medicare		$850,582	$889,283	$929,746	$972,049	$1,016,277
Medicaid		$111,625	$116,704	$122,014	$127,565	$133,370
Commercial		$816,102	$853,235	$892,057	$932,645	$975,081
Self-pay/charity care	—	—	—	—	—	—
Total revenue		**$1,778,309**	**$1,859,222**	**$1,943,817**	**$2,032,259**	**$2,124,728**

Source: Values based on experience of ECG Management Consultants, Inc., headquartered in Seattle, and available market information.

Physician expenses

Direct physician expenses are composed of physician compensation, benefits, and malpractice. Compensation levels will vary based on the type of the compensation model implemented, with a range typically set between the 25th and 75th percentile of industry benchmarks. Hospitalist programs are predicated on coverage requirements, but patient demand may be highly variable and out of the surgical hospitalists' control; therefore, most compensation arrangements require a sizeable base compensation or minimum income guarantee, which is typically near median benchmarks. Benefits and malpractice expenses are calculated on a per FTE basis and typically amount to approximately 20%–25% of total individual compensation. Figure 3.8 illustrates median benchmark data for these physician expenses.

FIGURE 3.8 EXAMPLE MEDIAN BENCHMARK PHYSICIAN EXPENSES

This example represents median benchmark physician expenses, based on the *2008 MGMA Physician Compensation and Production Survey* and the *2008 MGMA Cost Survey*. Incomes for surgical hospitalists might vary significantly from these numbers. For example, if there is shift work with no on-call responsibility, the surgical hospitalist's compensation may be lower than shown here.

Physician compensation	Physician benefits	Physician malpractice
$316,909	$24,780	$38,467

Source: Values based on the *2008 MGMA Physician Compensation and Production Survey* and the *2008 MGMA Cost Survey*.

Forecasting physician expenses requires using an annual inflation assumption to calculate likely adjustments. Evaluating historical trends in expense data is the appropriate method for setting the assumption. Recent trends show annual increases of approximately 3.5%.[3] Figure 3.9 is an example of a physician expense forecast.

Chapter 3

FIGURE 3.9   EXAMPLE PHYSICIAN EXPENSE PROJECTIONS

Direct physician expense	Year 1	Year 2	Year 3	Year 4	Year 5
Physician compensation	$1,347,636	$1,385,665	$1,424,835	$1,465,180	$1,506,736
Benefits	121,540	125,186	128,942	132,810	136,794
Malpractice	158,483	163,238	168,135	173,179	178,374
Total direct physician expense	1,627,659	1,674,089	1,721,912	1,771,169	1,821,904
Total compensation per FTE	*$336,909*	*$346,416*	*$356,209*	*$366,295*	*$376,684*

Source: Values based on experience of ECG Management Consultants, Inc., headquartered in Seattle, and available market information.

Direct operating expenses

The operating expenses associated with programs are mostly related to purchased services, such as billing and collections, and the operations of the outpatient clinic, including occupancy and staffing. These expenses typically represent 25% or less of the total program costs.

To estimate these direct operating expenses, use industry benchmarks or actual physician practice cost data to forecast the operating expenses. Figure 3.10 is an example of a five-year forecast that is based on industry assumptions, with costs inflated over the time period.

Calculating the Return on Investment for Your Surgical Hospitalist Program

FIGURE 3.10	EXAMPLE OPERATING EXPENSES PROJECTIONS

This example represents a sample projection of operating expenses.

	Baseline Percentage of revenue	Year 1	Year 2	Year 3	Year 4	Year 5
Operating expenses						
Total support staff*	8%	$142,265	$148,738	$155,505	$162,581	$169,978
Billing and collections	7%	124,482	130,146	136,067	142,258	148,731
Occupancy	3%	53,349	55,777	58,314	60,968	63,742
Supplies	3.5%	62,241	65,073	68,034	71,129	74,365
IT	2.5%	44,458	46,481	48,595	50,806	53,118
Other	4.5%	80,024	83,665	87,472	91,452	95,613
Total operating expenses		$506,818	$529,878	$553,988	$579,194	$605,547

*Most surgical hospitalist programs require minimal support staff. This projection assumes that the practice hires some combination of nonphysician providers (nurse practitioners and/or physician assistants) and office staff members to work with patients in the follow-up clinic.

Source: Values based on the experience of ECG Management Consultants, Inc., headquartered in Seattle, and available market information.

Net program gains or losses

The bottom-line calculation should be audited on an aggregate level and on a per-physician FTE basis to test the accuracy of the overall projections. Current industry data illustrate expected losses of $75,000–$200,000 per-physician FTE. The magnitude of the gain or loss will be highly sensitive to patient volume, revenue projections, and physician compensation. Smaller hospitals generally experience higher losses.

For example, a hospital that requires 24/7 coverage with a high percentage of uninsured or underinsured patients may experience losses well over $200,000 per FTE. Figure 3.11 summarizes the gains and losses.

Chapter 3

FIGURE 3.11 EXAMPLE NET GAINS (LOSSES)

Although programs typically experience a loss on operations due to poor payer mix, operational efficiencies reduce the loss over the five-year period.

	Year 1	Year 2	Year 3	Year 4	Year 5
Revenue expenses	$1,778,309	$1,859,222	$1,943,816	$2,032,260	$2,124,728
Physician expense	1,627,659	1,674,089	1,721,912	1,771,169	1,821,904
Direct operating expense	506,818	529,878	553,988	579,194	605,547
Net gain or (loss)	$(356,169)	$(344,746)	$(332,083)	$(318,103)	$(302,724)
Loss per physician FTE	$(89,042)	$(86,186)	$(83,021)	$(79,526)	$(75,681)

Source: Values based on the experience of ECG Management Consultants, Inc., headquartered in Seattle, and available market information.

Estimated indirect costs and benefits

The surgical hospitalist program will produce several indirect benefits, including the reduction of existing costs and increased revenue. The argument to include these benefits in the ROI analysis is clear, as each benefit is attained once the new program is established. The range of benefits and the magnitude depend on the unique situation of the hospital and local market.

This subsection provides several typical areas that generate benefits for the program. It is not intended to be an exhaustive list but rather a starting point for accounting for indirect program benefits. Figure 3.12 summarizes the potential indirect benefits, including reduced costs, improved inpatient/ED throughput, improved quality and continuity of care, and increased medical staff satisfaction.

Calculating the Return on Investment for Your Surgical Hospitalist Program

---

FIGURE 3.12 — OVERVIEW OF POTENTIAL INDIRECT BENEFITS

This figure represents where the treatment of patients falls in the benefits that come with starting a surgical hospitalist program.

Benefits

Treatment of patients →
- Reduced costs
- Improved inpatient and ED throughout
- Improved quality of care
- Improved continuity of care
- Increased medical staff satisfaction

Source: ECG Management Consultants, Inc., headquartered in Seattle.

INDIRECT COSTS AND BENEFITS

A surgical hospitalist program may have indirect benefits, including:

- Eliminated call stipends
- Increased surgical cases
- Improved operating efficiency
- Enhanced quality of care

Eliminated call stipends

A growing majority of hospitals pay for ED unassigned patient call coverage arrangements. Establishing a surgical hospitalist program may eliminate these payments, except for rare occasions in which temporary or partial coverage is needed from a nonsurgical hospitalist. These payments represent a sizeable annual expense, as illustrated in Figure 3.13. In effect, some hospitals acknowledge that they will need to pay for surgical coverage, and the cost of paying call stipends to the existing surgeons may be similar to the cost of supporting a surgical hospitalist program that can provide the ED call coverage and yield additional benefits. Therefore, the latter option appears more attractive for many institutions.

FIGURE 3.13 CALL COVERAGE STIPEND BENEFIT

This figure represents the estimated reduction in annual call stipend payments that an organization would no longer have to pay after establishing the program.

Reduction in stipend payments	Range Low		High
Average daily stipend	$1,000	to	$2,000
Total days of call average	365	to	365
Total annual call stipend	$365,000	to	$730,000

Source: Values based on the experience of ECG Management Consultants, Inc., headquartered in Seattle, and available market information.

Increased surgical cases

With a dedicated surgical team covering the ED and unassigned patients, nonhospitalist general surgeons who practice at the hospital will gain new capacity to work more efficiently. Because they no longer need to save time in their schedules for ED call or to recover following a night of little or no sleep due to call responsibilities, they are often willing to increase their scheduled practice volume. Depending on demand for surgical services, this can amount to significant increased elective surgical volumes, resulting in incremental contribution that exceeds the direct operating losses of the program, as illustrated in Figure 3.14.

Calculating the Return on Investment for Your Surgical Hospitalist Program

FIGURE 3.14 — INCREMENTAL SURGICAL CASE BENEFIT

This figure represents the range of estimated incremental revenue for surgical cases that a startup program may earn. All data shown here are for illustration purposes only. Actual numbers will vary significantly from one institution to the next, and there are not standard or typical amounts for these metrics.

	Range		
Incremental surgical contribution margin	Low		High
Incremental surgical cases per day	0.5	to	2
Direct margin per case	$1,800	to	$1,800
Total annual new cases	182.50	to	730
Total new net revenue	$328,500	to	$1,314,000

Source: Values based on the experience of ECG Management Consultants, Inc., headquartered in Seattle, and available market information.

Improved operating efficiency

Improved operating efficiency also may occur through the following:

- Enhanced ED patient throughput that allows for higher patient volumes without expanding facility space or resources

- Savings from reduced hospital length of stay (LOS)

- Reduced costs due to supply standardization and increased purchasing power

Enhanced quality of care

Enhanced quality of care may also reduce costs and increase payments because of the following:

- Reduced surgical infection rates

- Improved rapid response times

- Increased continuity of care

Chapter 3

With the elimination of call stipends and with more surgical cases, more efficient operations, and enhanced quality of care, the annual indirect benefits that will offset the initial capital investment and direct operating loss range from $700,000 to $2 million, thus producing a favorable ROI.

Alternatives of investment decision

The calculated ROI should be used as a performance measure to evaluate the efficiency of the investment or to compare the efficiency of several different investments. In theory, if an investment does not have a positive ROI, or if there are other opportunities with a higher ROI, the investment should be not be undertaken. However, unlike most other industries in which an executive can divest a program or business, hospital executives face the challenge of maintaining operations in programs that generate less favorable returns because of community obligations, such as maintaining trauma coverage and other access to medical care.

The decision to start a surgical hospitalist program is not made in isolation. More often, hospitals are faced with several alternatives for providing surgical coverage and improving surgical services, including volunteer call panels and employed general surgeons. Figure 3.15 illustrates the common options.

FIGURE 3.15 SURGICAL COVERAGE ALTERNATIVES

This figure represents the common options for surgical coverage. Dedicated surgical hospitalist programs include an in-house surgical group or can be outsourced with ED coverage.

Voluntary call panels — Payment for call coverage — Employed general surgeons — Surgical hospitalist group — Outsourced surgical ED coverage

Dedicated surgical hospitalist program

Source: ECG Management Consultants, Inc., headquartered in Seattle.

Each of these surgical coverage options presents advantages and disadvantages in terms of operations, physician alignment, strategic positioning, and financial implications. It is important to highlight a comparison between "making" and "buying" (i.e., outsourcing a surgical hospitalist program). Although the specifics will depend on the hospital's unique position, common points include those shown below in Figure 3.16.

FIGURE 3.16 REVIEW OF OUTSOURCED ARRANGEMENT

This figure represents the pros and cons to outsourcing surgical coverage. In general, if local general surgeons are interested in serving as surgical hospitalists, the advantages of forming a local surgical hospitalist group with ownership outweigh the short-term benefits sometimes found with outsourcing.

Advantages	Disadvantages
• Eliminates conflicts among private practices in the community	• Is more costly due to markup of services provided by vendor
• Ensures coverage through contractual obligation with vendor	• Distracts from existing relationship with private general surgeons
• Enhances ability to recruit surgeons who have a specific interest in hospitalist work	• Has limited continuity, as vendor may experience high turnover of surgeons
• Enables private surgeons to increase elective surgical cases and admissions	• Startup can take time, and vendor will likely negotiate protective clauses that provide it with adequate recruiting time
• Improves private surgeon recruiting by offering no call requirement	

Source: ECG Management Consultants, Inc., headquartered in Seattle.

If outsourcing is a consideration, turn special attention to making equal comparison of the financial implications among the alternatives. For example, a vendor may offer quality and utilization programs that are above what the hospital currently provides. The cost of these programs will be included in the vendor's proposal, but the cost of the hospital performing the same function may be missing from the hospital analysis. If the surgical service is needed, it should be accounted for under both the in-house and the outsourced options.

Chapter 3

Improvements to the ROI

Hospital executives should continually look for ways to improve the ROI by reducing costs, increasing gains, or accelerating gains. Whether starting a program or managing an existing program, take steps to evaluate the program's financial performance and to identify specific changes that will improve the ROI. The surgical hospitalist program leadership should consider submitting a brief outline of opportunities for hospital executives to consider when attempting to make improvements. The outline should include reducing costs, increasing gains, and accelerating gains.

REDUCING COSTS

Management has the most control over program costs and therefore should take active measures to reduce or eliminate program expenses. Examples of cost reduction opportunities include:

- Colocate outpatient clinic with an existing clinic
- Recruit part-time physicians to augment coverage without the burden of adding excessive surgeon staffing
- Improve clinical coverage model to reduce FTE requirement

INCREASING GAINS

Successful program management will require a proactive approach to capturing new revenue sources. Several tactics are available to drive more patient revenue or new sources of income to the hospital. A few examples are:

- Establishing productivity-based surgical hospitalist compensation systems
- Capturing new elective surgery cases (usually managed by the nonhospitalist surgeons)
- Attracting new general surgeons to the medical staff due to lack of call coverage obligations
- Applying for grants and other outside funding to augment program support

> **ACCELERATING GAINS**
>
> The timing of financial gains is important due to the time value of money (i.e., a dollar today is worth more than a dollar tomorrow). The ability to delay or eliminate startup expenses and accelerate revenue generated by the program will improve financial performance. Several opportunities are present in most hospitals to make these changes, including:
>
> - Colocating outpatient clinic with an existing clinic
> - Enhancing ED throughput
> - Enhancing discharge planning process for surgical patients to shorten LOS
> - Building part-time elective surgery practice within surgical hospitalist program

Conclusion

The decision to start a surgical hospitalist program is fraught with numerous political, operational, and financial implications. Due to the increasing demands on capital and operating funds throughout the hospital industry, new programs, such as a surgical hospitalist program, require careful consideration. Now more than ever, a thorough financial assessment is required before investing in the development of the new program. In the case of evaluating the startup of a surgical hospitalist program, the analysis will form the basis of making a "go" or "no-go" decision on the initiative. The importance of this decision is paramount, because once management decides to transition from a traditional call coverage model to a surgical hospitalist program, reverting back is difficult to impossible, and it would certainly require significant costs. A thorough financial analysis carried out within a consistent framework using an objective, unbiased review will help hospital executives make an informed decision about whether to proceed and establish an expectation for future performance.

REFERENCES

1. American College of Surgeons. "New Health Care Reform Agenda, Emphasizes Need to Address Access, Surgical Workforce Shortage, News from the College, *www.facs.org/news/hcragenda.html*, (Dec. 4, 2008).

2. Based on *MGMA Cost Survey for Single-Specialty Practices: 2008 Report Based on 2007 Data,* reporting square footage per physician for all general surgery practices.

3. Based on annual increase in median compensation for general surgeons reported in the *MGMA Physician Compensation and Production Survey: 2008 Report Based on 2007 Data* and the *MGMA Physician Compensation and Production Survey: 2007 Report Based on 2006 Data.*

CHAPTER 4

Management and Business Operations for Surgical Hospitalist Practices

Leon J. Owens, MD, FACS

Well-designed practice management and business systems are critical if a surgical hospitalist practice is to effectively address the unanticipated challenges that are likely to arise. Although a coherent understanding and structural plan for the surgical hospitalist program will not guarantee its success, the absence of those elements will likely ensure its demise.

Developing a practice that provides acute inpatient surgical care in an expert, efficient, team-oriented manner requires:

- Developing a schedule that allows the individual surgical hospitalist to provide complete care to the patient, while also allowing clear handoff between surgeons and sufficient time off to maintain a rewarding lifestyle.

- Providing around-the-clock coverage and support for nonelective surgical consults. This allows the nonhospitalist surgeons to provide improved surgical care to their elective and established patients while allowing enhancement of their own lifestyles.

- Establishing an interdependent system of communication and professionalism between surgical hospitalists and referring physicians that achieves high-quality patient care.

- Creating a system of experienced case review that will stimulate evidence-based policies and procedures that are directed to safe, sensible, successful patient care.

- Intervening for surgical patients in an appropriate and expeditious fashion to shorten length of stay and decrease risk of complications, thereby decreasing cost and increasing hospital bed availability while improving resource utilization.

- Ensuring appropriate practice administrative support, billing and collection procedures, and financial management.

Chapter 4

Hospital and Surgical Hospitalist Corporation

The cooperation and support of a hospital or hospital system to develop a surgical hospitalist program is critical to success. No amount of physician enthusiasm, emergency care demand, or talk of quality and safety can replace the commitment of the hospital or hospital system. When the hospital commits to patient safety, best practices, and increased satisfaction converge, financial savings result; the published literature supports the value of surgical hospitalist practices.[1] Ideally, a hospital administrator and an experienced, respected general surgeon with administrative abilities should lead the construction of the surgical hospitalist program. The initial challenge is securing adequate financial support from the hospital, as well as adequate budgeting. For example, hospitals with 250–750 beds might require approximately 3.5 general surgeon full-time equivalents (FTE) and two nurse practitioner (NP) or physician assistant (PA) FTEs. A conceptual organizational chart is presented in Figure 4.1.

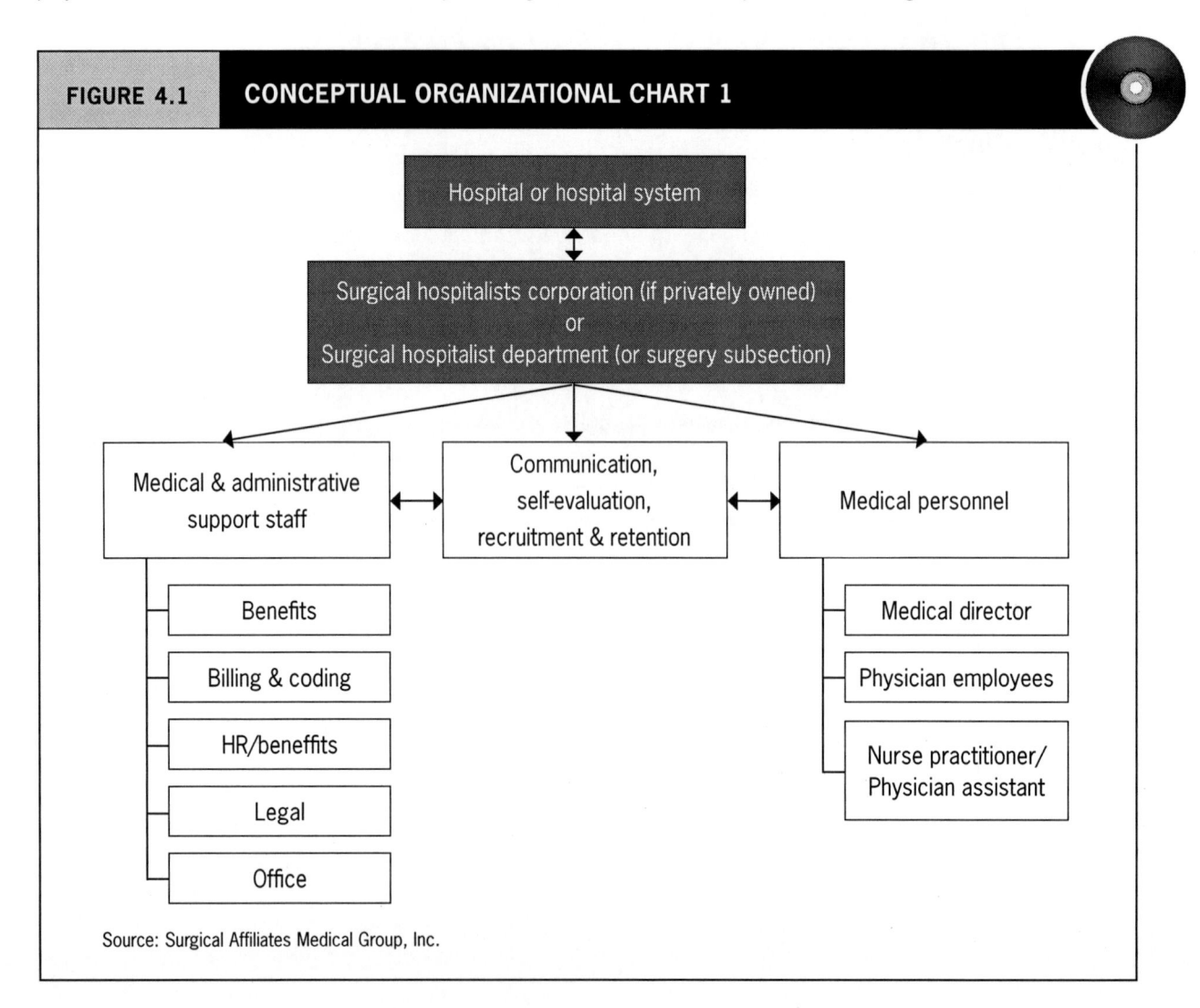

FIGURE 4.1 CONCEPTUAL ORGANIZATIONAL CHART 1

Hospital or hospital system
↕
Surgical hospitalists corporation (if privately owned)
or
Surgical hospitalist department (or surgery subsection)

- Medical & administrative support staff
  - Benefits
  - Billing & coding
  - HR/benefits
  - Legal
  - Office
- Communication, self-evaluation, recruitment & retention
- Medical personnel
  - Medical director
  - Physician employees
  - Nurse practitioner/Physician assistant

Source: Surgical Affiliates Medical Group, Inc.

Management and Business Operations for Surgical Hospitalist Practices

Do not underestimate the effect of a surgical hospitalist program on the operating room (OR) and its staff. The OR and anesthesia services are the bottleneck for throughput of surgical patients at nearly every general hospital and therefore, the anesthesia and the OR supervisors, and the staff members will be necessary. Emergent cases often are performed late at night and on weekends and, therefore, are likely viewed as disruptive and frequently unwelcome. Historically, convenience for the surgeon, OR, and anesthesia has played a significant role in the prolonged emergency department (ED) to OR time for both appendectomies and cholecystectomies (> 50% of the work of surgical hospitalists). Therefore, decreasing the time from the ED to the OR may result in the most significant cost reductions and length of stay reductions brought about by a surgical hospitalist program.

Ideally, an "urgent" OR should be designated for these urgent/emergent cases to increase throughput to surgery and reduce the effect on other elective, scheduled cases. (See Chapter 6 on OR scheduling.) Delaying or canceling the elective cases of nonhospitalist surgeons to meet the needs of the surgical hospitalist will likely cause antipathy toward this new program. The surgical hospitalists' dedication to the program, combined with a commitment to make available OR time, can result in significant patient satisfaction and financial reward for the hospital.

Likewise, strategic decisions about surgical hospitalist staffing will be delicate. Twenty-four hour, in-house dedication to the acute care surgical patient cuts across some subspecialty lines. The relationship of hospitalist and nonhospitalist general surgeons in the hospital may be a source of friction or resentment. If nonhospitalist surgeons rotate onto or moonlight for the surgical hospitalist program, they should dedicate their full attention to the service and reserve separate time for their other commitments, which temporarily come second. This is why a piecemeal approach to staffing may be less desirable than a service staffed with surgeons who do not have other responsibilities, such as elective or private surgical practice.

Define the role of the surgeon in admitting patients as part of initial contracting due to overlap between medical hospitalists and surgical hospitalists (e.g., small bowel obstruction admissions) or specialists' overlap (e.g., cellulitis of the extremities). This will preclude disputes in the ED over responsibilities for admitting certain types of patients.

Ensure adequate facilities for sleep, respite, and food for the on-call surgeon, as well as appropriate access to the hospital information system. Tracking of patients and recordkeeping can hamper the success of the program. (So much precious time can be wasted when a patient cannot be located.) Meticulous recordkeeping will be necessary to track your progress and ensure effective collection of professional fee revenue.

Chapter 4

Medical and Administrative Support Staff

The overhead for a surgical hospitalist practice is typically much lower than that of a traditional general surgery practice. However, it is still necessary to invest in office space for posthospital follow-up visits. This space should be available approximately four to six hours per week for every FTE surgeon. In many cases, it may be reasonable to share this space with other physician practices. Rental arrangements with local physicians, established medical groups (e.g., those whose patients benefit from surgical hospitalist service), or other physicians who benefit from subsequent referrals are all reasonable options.

Administrative office support and recordkeeping need to be streamlined. Front-office personnel may be shared. In many cases, the physician extenders (i.e., NPs or PAs) who serve the practice in the hospital can also function as office support and, with appropriate supervision, as clinical practitioners. Refer to Figure 4.2.

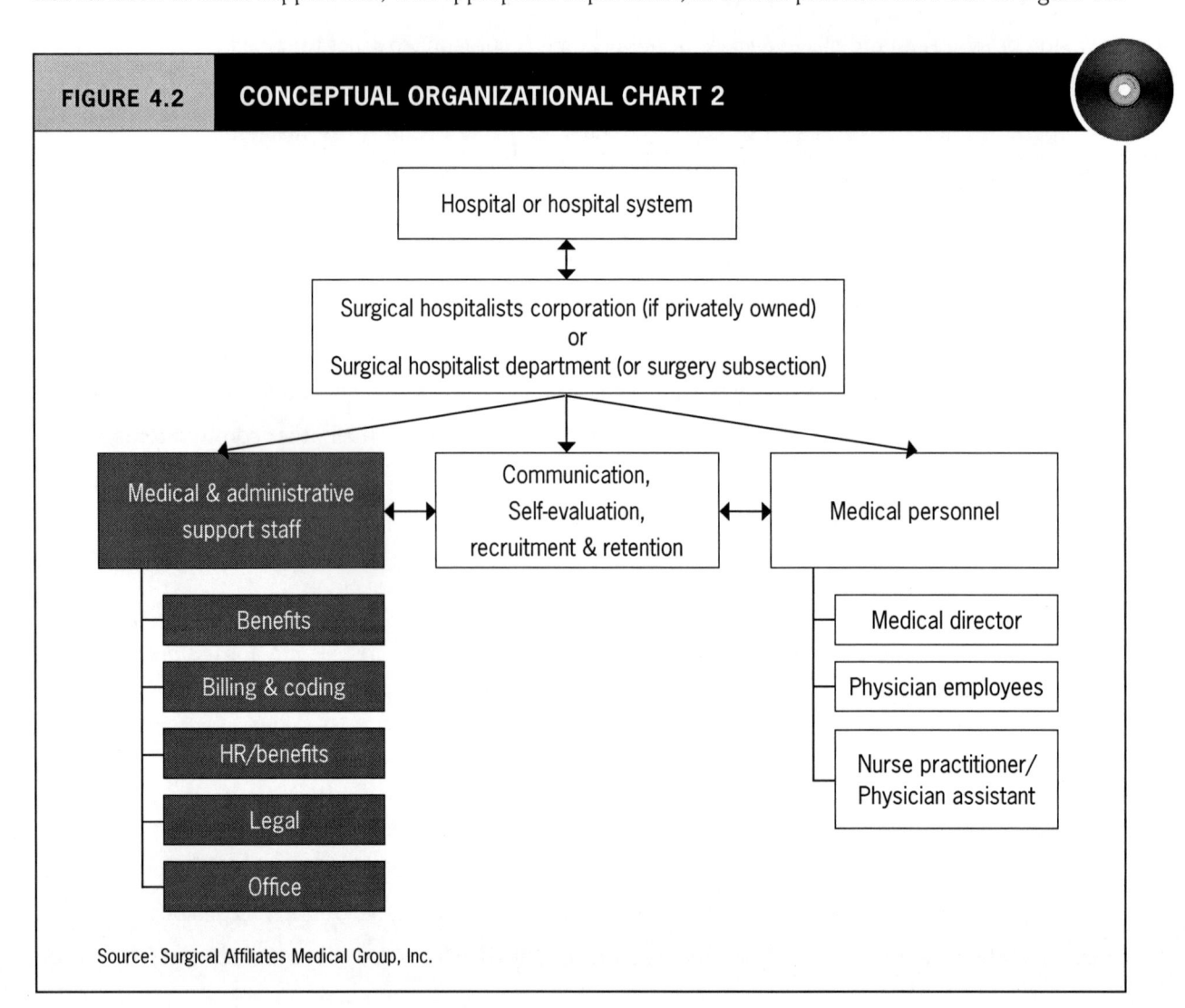

FIGURE 4.2 — CONCEPTUAL ORGANIZATIONAL CHART 2

Hospital or hospital system
↕
Surgical hospitalists corporation (if privately owned)
or
Surgical hospitalist department (or surgery subsection)

Branches:
- Medical & administrative support staff
  - Benefits
  - Billing & coding
  - HR/benefits
  - Legal
  - Office
- Communication, Self-evaluation, recruitment & retention
- Medical personnel
  - Medical director
  - Physician employees
  - Nurse practitioner/Physician assistant

Source: Surgical Affiliates Medical Group, Inc.

Billing and coding

An efficient billing and collection process is critical for the financial health and viability of a surgical hospitalist practice. It is usually best for the surgeon or NP/PA who performs the service to select the appropriate CPT codes for many reasons, including adherence to governmental mandates. This ensures that the provider becomes and remains well informed about documentation requirements and issues, such as bundling and unbundling of services. For ease of execution, a practice should develop preprinted billing forms listing the most common procedures, operations, and ICD-9 codes or use a commercial software product that supports electronic charge capture. Ideally, the provider should record billing codes on the day the service is provided. Once primary coding is complete, routine cases are sent to billers. For nonroutine cases, professional coders may need to assist with the coding. Routine audits of each surgeon's documentation and billing are important to ensure accuracy and compliance.

Computerized or preprinted forms for admission notes, pre- and post-op orders, progress notes, and discharge summaries help streamline recordkeeping and help ensure documentation that supports correct CPT coding. Ideally, these forms are available on the hospital information system for immediate use online or by printing a paper copy from any computer terminal.

Human resources/benefits

Surgeons who trained after the initiation of regulations that limit resident duty hours may not be attracted to a practice that requires frequent night call, in addition to daytime work. Valuable methods to address these concerns include defined work hours (e.g., two 24-hour shifts/week, or day and night shifts staffed by different surgeons each day), collaborative schedules, and equal sharing of holidays and weekends. Another option is to define a 48-hour week as the standard benchmark to determine the average surgeon's income. In addition, every effort should be made to off-load nonmedical responsibilities and to maximize the surgeon's ability to apply his or her surgical skills for maximal productivity.

Typical employee benefits for surgical hospitalists and NPs/PAs include:

- Workers' compensation insurance
- Malpractice insurance
- Life insurance
- Health/dental/vision insurance
- Short- and long-term disability insurance

- Retirement plans including 401(k) and pension and profit sharing
- CME allowance

In addition, a pathway for each new surgical hospitalist to become an owner or partner in the practice may strengthen an individual's commitment to the program as a result of pride of ownership.

Legal

Careful and attentive contracting among and between hospitals, physician groups, physicians, NPs/PAs, and billing companies are critical to success. As these contracts require specialization and intimate familiarity with federal and state laws, the enterprise may require healthcare, labor law, and business and benefit legal expertise. Therefore, don't expect a single legal practice to be sufficient for all of the new program's needs. The surgical hospitalist program's legal support may be a multispecialty dialogue, potentially requiring multiple legal specialists.

Office: Administrative/operational support

Dedicated administrative support is necessary on multiple levels of the hospital. Administrative supports include budgeting and financial management, recruitment, billing, HR, development and maintenance of employee handbooks, records of team meetings, physician practice management guidelines (PPMG), and policies and procedures.

Many administrative duties can be integrated with the hospital in states where hospitals can hire and employ physicians. This is economically wise because it avoids duplication of administrative services. Small practices (e.g., three or fewer surgeons) may share administrative personnel with other practices or hospital departments; even the largest practices can usually be managed by one experienced administrator with the help of an administrative assistant.

An administrative reference manual should integrate the employee handbook, physician handbook, job descriptions, and PPMGs. The manual also may include hospital-related information such as documents related to provider credentialing.

Communication, Self-Evaluation, Recruitment, and Retention

Few things improve care and decrease errors more than good communication. A valuable way to ensure good communication between members of the surgical hospitalist team is daily formal sign-out rounds between incoming and outgoing surgeons. An NP/PA who works multiple consecutive days can serve as the "living memory" of the service and help promote continuity of patient care. He or she may also be the primary point of contact for the case managers and discharge planners.

Plans for drains, anticipated culture results, length of antibiotic administration, and discharge planning information must be reviewed daily for each patient. The NP/PA who is on the service every day prevents overlooking this important information. As part of a daily review, highlight plans of all patients, particularly those patients shared with the medical hospitalists and other specialties.

There is also value in routine (e.g., weekly) meetings of the management team to review operational issues, including financial statements, cash flow, and recruitment, as well as to prepare for monthly meetings of the entire practice.

Full-team meetings should be held monthly and usually should include administration (e.g., administrator, administrative assistant, billers, and coders) and all physicians and NPs/PAs. The heart of these meetings is a review of quality data, including morbidity and mortality. A useful quality improvement model is contained in the American College of Surgeons' *Resources for the Optimal Care of the Injured Patient: 2006* guidelines.[2]

Monthly meetings between hospital administration and the medical director of the surgical hospitalist program focus on the surgical hospitalists' integration in the hospital environment, interpersonal challenges, and evaluations of formal surveys of nurses, ED physicians, OR personnel, medical hospitalists, and other specialists. This is also a useful opportunity to review the program's financial performance and progress toward addressing hospital goals and initiatives.

In addition to holding weekly and monthly meetings, there is value in holding monthly or quarterly meetings between all surgical and medical hospitalists to review cases of mutual interest, improve communications, and formalize mechanisms for sharing responsibilities. Refer to Figure 4.3.

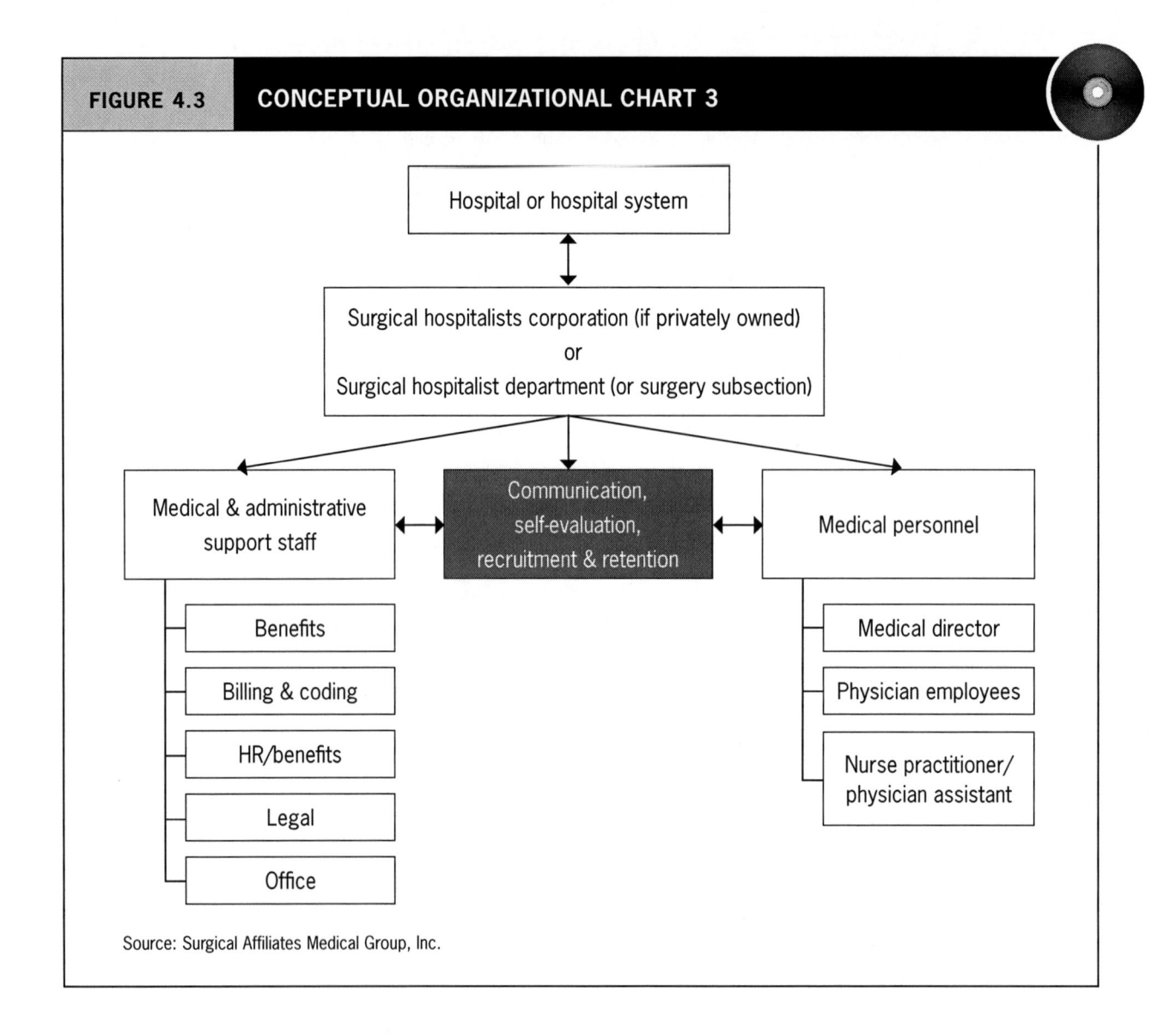

Chapter 4

FIGURE 4.3 CONCEPTUAL ORGANIZATIONAL CHART 3

```
                        Hospital or hospital system
                                   ↕
        Surgical hospitalists corporation (if privately owned)
                                   or
           Surgical hospitalist department (or surgery subsection)
                    ↙              ↓              ↘
   Medical & administrative   Communication,      Medical personnel
        support staff      ↔  self-evaluation, ↔
                              recruitment & retention
          ├─ Benefits                              ├─ Medical director
          ├─ Billing & coding                      ├─ Physician employees
          ├─ HR/benefits                           └─ Nurse practitioner/
          ├─ Legal                                    physician assistant
          └─ Office
```

Source: Surgical Affiliates Medical Group, Inc.

Medical Personnel

Medical director

The medical director is at the core of a surgical hospitalist program. The medical director will perform an important clinical and administrative role. Administratively, he or she develops and communicates policy, runs meetings, actively participates in recruiting, and is responsible for the group's performance on critical metrics such as quality improvement. The director also represents the surgical hospitalists on various medical staff committees. Refer to Figure 4.4.

Management and Business Operations for Surgical Hospitalist Practices

FIGURE 4.4	CONCEPTUAL ORGANIZATIONAL CHART 4

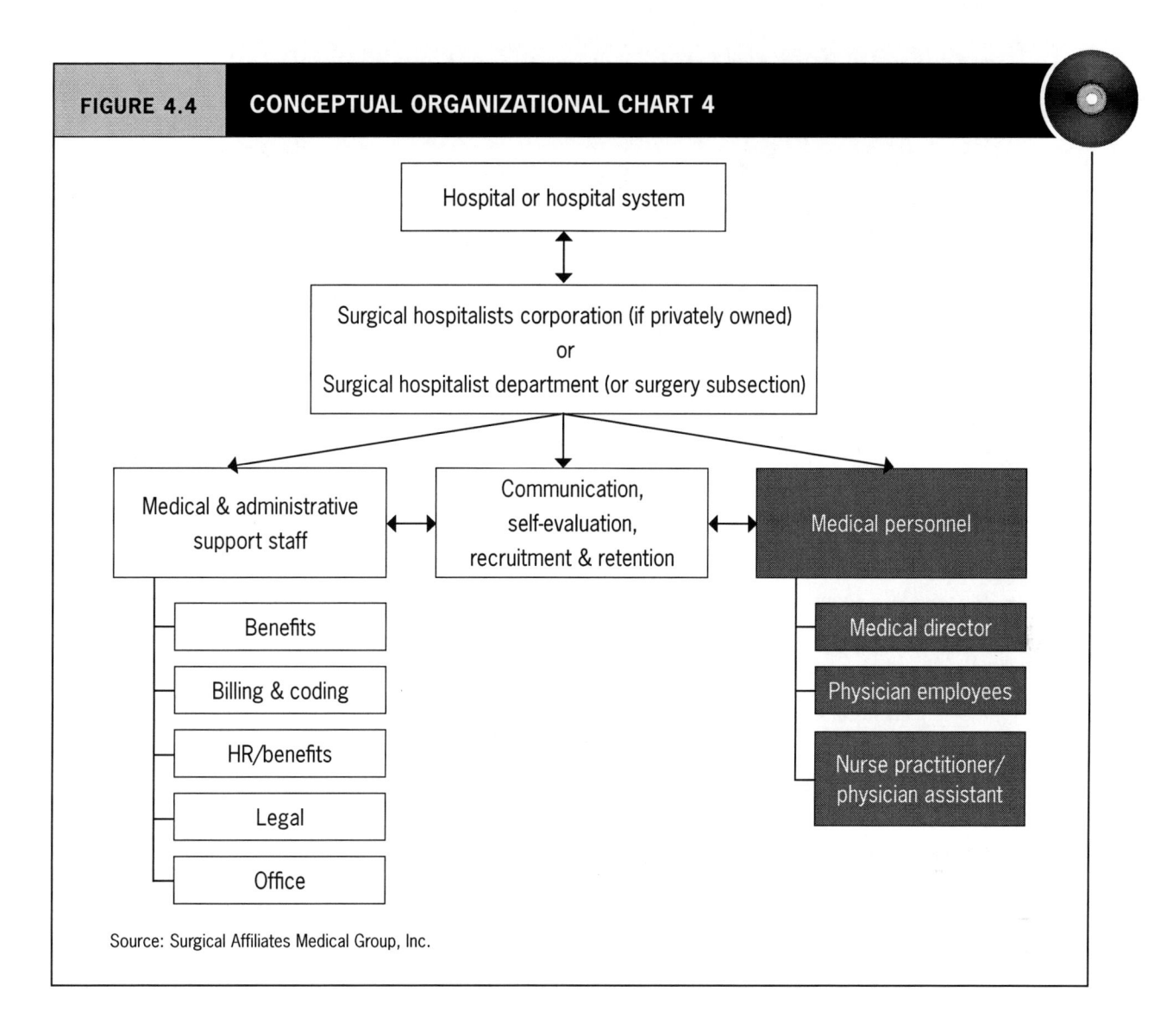

```
                    Hospital or hospital system
                              ↕
        Surgical hospitalists corporation (if privately owned)
                              or
        Surgical hospitalist department (or surgery subsection)
                ↓             ↓              ↓
    Medical & administrative   Communication,        Medical personnel
         support staff         self-evaluation,
                              recruitment & retention
                ↓                                     ↓
            Benefits                            Medical director
            Billing & coding                    Physician employees
            HR/benefits                         Nurse practitioner/
            Legal                               physician assistant
            Office
```

Source: Surgical Affiliates Medical Group, Inc.

Physician employees

The clinical duties of a surgical hospitalist vary from one setting to the next. The duties are typically listed in employment contracts and maintained in the practice policy and procedure manual, which is updated periodically. Successful surgical hospitalist programs involve a high level of cooperation, trust, and mutual respect. Careful selection of the physicians, NPs, PAs, and administrative support staff requires people who function well as team players. Refer to Figure 4.5 for a sample job description and list of responsibilities for surgical hospitalists.

Nurse practitioner physician assistant

Refer to Figure 4.6 for a sample job description for NPs and PAs.

FIGURE 4.5 SAMPLE SURGICAL HOSPITALIST CLINICAL RESPONSIBILITIES

Job description

- The surgical hospitalist will arrive promptly at 0630 hours. The previous surgeon on call will provide a report.

- If emergency duties preclude the outgoing general surgeon from attending 0630 report, it will be the outgoing surgeon's responsibility to arrange with the incoming surgeon the means and timing of report. Report must, in all cases, be given to the incoming surgeon.

- The outgoing surgeon will be responsible for assisting with any early morning operations that occur at the time of or shortly after report. The incoming surgeon will also be responsible for ensuring that appropriate coverage of these early morning operations occurs.

- The surgical hospitalist will make rounds on all consult patients, postoperative patients, and other patients admitted to the surgical hospitalist service.

- The general surgeon will respond to the ED or to an inpatient consult within 30 minutes unless prevented by other priorities, such as an ongoing surgery or management of an unstable patient. If unable to respond immediately, he/she will evaluate the patient at the first opportunity.

- The surgical hospitalist will evaluate all consults and ensure their disposition as appropriate, either admitting the patient for operation, admitting the patient for medical treatment or observation, arranging for discharge from the ED and follow-up for the patient, or deferring to a more appropriate physician service for care. Appropriate communication will be made with physicians who will assume primary or consultant care.

- The general surgeon will communicate personally with all referring and consulting physicians after completion of the patient evaluation.

- After all procedures, admissions, discharges, ICU evaluations, and daily notes are completed on patients that are not within the global period, the physician will complete the billing/coding sheet for each patient. Coding should be completed within 48 hours of service or sooner.

- The on-call surgeon will respond to all patient calls, such as those that come via an answering service (e.g., calls from recently discharged patients who have concerns such as pain or fever).

- The on-duty surgeon will see postdischarge patients in the outpatient clinic.

- Other duties will be assigned to the surgical hospitalist as appropriate to ensure fulfillment of the program goals.

Source: Surgical Affiliates Medical Group, Inc.

> **FIGURE 4.6**   **SAMPLE NP AND PA IN A SURGICAL HOSPITALIST PRACTICE RESPONSIBILITIES**
>
> ### Job description
>
> The NP/PA role is grounded in the understanding that they are physician extenders who must function under appropriate supervision, and should neither make the final decision about whether to operate nor perform operations in isolation. The NP/PA:
>
> - Completes and maintains a daily patient log, typically by using the hospital's computer system.
>
> - Rounds on hospitalized patients and provides hospital follow-up visits for general surgery patients in the outpatient clinic.
>
> - Orders and interprets laboratory studies and x-ray examinations to determine treatment.
>
> - Monitors ongoing problems of patients followed in outpatient clinic including counseling and coordination of resources. Answers phone calls from patients and documents a plan of care for physician review.
>
> - Assists with discharging patients, dictates discharge summaries, and ensures that referrals for patient follow-up are implemented.
>
> - Communicates with families regarding clinical conditions, expected course, prognosis, and plan of care.
>
> - Acts as first or second assistant to provide retraction, hemostasis, and closure of layers in the OR.
>
> - Completes billing in accordance with state and federal billing requirements.
>
> Source: Surgical Affiliates Medical Group, Inc.

REFERENCES

1. Michael S. O'Mara, MD, FACS; Timothy F. Daly, MBA; Cynthia C. Leathers, MPH, MBA; and Leon J. Owens, MD, FACS, *The Surgical Hospitalist: Aligning the Incentives of Patients, Hospitals, and Surgeons;* American College of Healthcare Executives. Paper presentation, Chicago, (March 2009).

2. American College of Surgeons Committee on Trauma. *Resources for the Optimal Care of the Injured Patient,* Chicago, American College of Surgeons (2006).

3. Kenneth G. Simone, DO, and Jeffrey R. Dichter, MD, FACP. *The Hospitalist Program Management Guide,* Second Edition. (Marblehead, MA: HCPro, Inc., 2008).

4. American College of Surgeons, *Bulletin,* "The Surgical Hospitalist: A New Solution for Emergency Surgical Care?" 82(11) (2007).

5. "Answers to ER Coverage Issue Cropping Up Across County." *General Surgery News* 35(5) (2008).

6. "Shortage of General Surgeons Looms as Patient Population Grows." *The Independent Monthly Newspaper for the General Surgeon* 33(12) (2008).

7. "The Surgical Hospitalist: A New Model for Emergency Surgical Care," *Journal of the American College of Surgeons,* 205(5) (2007): 704–711.

8. "A Longitudinal Analysis of the General Surgery Workforce in the United States, 1981–2003," *Arch Surg* 143, (4) (2008).

9. "Selling General Surgery to Today's Medical Students," *General Surgery News* 31(03) (2004).

10. "2005 Match Results: Success Depends on How You Look at It," *General Surgery News* 32(05) (2005).

11. "What's a Trauma Surgeon Worth? A Salary Survey of the Eastern Association for the Surgery of Trauma," *The Journal of Trauma Injury, Infection, and Critical Care,* 49(5) (November 2000).

12. American College of Emergency Physicians. *On-Call Specialist Coverage in U.S. Emergency Departments.* (Irving, TX: American College of Emergency Physicians, April 2006).

13. "Is Unplanned Return to the Operating Room a Useful Quality Indicator in General Surgery?" *Arch Surg* 136 (2001).

14. Michael B. Flynn, Dora Allen, "Getting Paid Fairly for Consultations," *General Surgery News,* December 2007.

15. Kate Johnson, "Shortage of On-Call Specialists Spreads Nationally & Acute Care Surgery Programs Emerging," *Surgery News,* 35(1) January 2008.

16. Vanessa Fuhrmans, "Surgeon Shortage Pushes Hospitals to Hire Temps," *The Wall Street Journal,* January 13, 2009, A1.

17. Joseph Ficsher, "The Impending Disappearance of the General Surgeon," *JAMA* 298(18) (Nov. 1990): 2191-2193.

CHAPTER 5

Staffing a Surgical Hospitalist Program

R. Steven Norton, MD, FACS

The intent of a successful surgical hospitalist program is to meet the trauma and emergency care needs of the hospital, the patient, and the community by delivering excellence in surgical care in a timely fashion, with the intent to reduce the length of stay, improve patient satisfaction, and minimize perioperative complications. There are several emerging surgical hospitalist models that can provide a solution that circumvents the national problems of access to emergency care. However, there is concurrently a diminishing supply of traditional general surgeons across the country, which may make it difficult for hospitals to recruit surgical hospitalists. Therefore, the surgical hospitalist program should provide an enriching experience for the surgical hospitalist, who should be appropriately compensated and will have a defined and balanced work schedule that may resemble the more regular hours of their medical hospitalist and emergency department (ED) physician colleagues. At a national level, current discussions suggest that the surgical hospitalist role might become one of the most popular models of practice for general surgeons, similar to the transformation of general internists and medical hospitalist practices.

What Is Your Model?

The major determinants of the required number of surgical hospitalists are the size of the hospital, its community, the local demographics, and the practice setting. Examples include:

- Academic medical centers

- Designated trauma centers

- Large urban centers with populations of more than 100,000

- Community and rural centers with populations of fewer than 100,000

Chapter 5

Academic medical centers

University or academic settings usually staff programs with a minimum of three to four surgeons, who are typically supported by a team of general surgery residents and medical students. These academic surgical hospitalist programs play a unique role by offering mentoring experiences to medical students as they consider possible future careers in general surgery. An important principal is to ensure that the general surgery resident at an academic medical center has a full general surgery experience, without competing with the surgical fellows in operative case management.

As a consequence of increased access to graduating surgical residents, surgical hospitalist practices in academic medical centers may grow more quickly than those in other settings. Please see Chapter 12 for more detail on considerations related to academic centers.

Designated trauma centers

The staffing needs will be greater at institutions with Level I and Level II trauma designations to fulfill the requirement that a surgeon be available either in the hospital 24 hours per day or within a 20-minute response time. These programs will likely require an additional backup surgeon who can respond to trauma alerts in the event that the primary surgical hospitalist is in the operating room (OR). Thus, they often require more full-time equivalents (FTE) of surgical hospitalist staffing than comparably sized settings that do not have a trauma designation. The new acute care surgery fellowship programs now being established at several university trauma centers will be valuable in providing additional FTEs trained to supply these designated trauma centers.

Large urban centers

Urban hospitals, generally of 300 or more beds, will typically require two to six surgical hospitalist FTEs. Because it may be difficult to find sufficient numbers of surgeons to perform this work full-time, many programs may be built around two or three full-time surgical hospitalists with the remainder of the FTEs provided by community surgeons who moonlight in the surgical hospitalist practice. The latter group could include general surgeons with an active elective outpatient practice who choose to work occasionally as surgical hospitalists because they find it professionally rewarding or seek the additional income. They could simply cover night call for the surgical hospitalist occasionally or work a weekend or series of consecutive days.

Another common configuration for a large urban center is composed of four surgical hospitalists to work 12-hour shifts: one surgeon is on service during the day, another works that night, and the other two doctors are off that day. The practice also might include physician extenders (i.e., nurse practitioners and physician assistants) who make rounds, provide timely consults, and then assist with emergency surgical care.

A local senior surgeon already on staff may be the ideal first surgical hospitalist, as he or she already understands the political landscape of that particular hospital and has existing relationships with other essential staff members and hospital leaders. A number of today's surgical hospitalists chose to leave private general surgery practices to become surgical hospitalists primarily to relieve the stresses of managing a private practice. And in many cases, surgical hospitalist positions allow a more predictable work schedule, sometimes arranged in shifts without call. In addition to being the first surgical hospitalist, such a surgeon can serve as the medical director of the program.

Smaller community and rural hospitals

Several smaller community hospitals are successfully developing programs that seek to fulfill the surgical hospitalist intent, although in many cases, these programs operate without dedicated full-time surgical hospitalists and, instead, ensure coverage of the service by having surgeons in the community provide most or all of the staffing. This may mean that no single surgeon regards him- or herself as a "real" surgical hospitalist or becomes as meaningfully invested in the management and operation of the program. This arrangement may more closely resemble a pay-for-ED-call" program than a true surgical hospitalist practice. But it may be the only feasible option for hospitals that are unable to recruit full-time surgical hospitalists.

Although staffing a particular surgical hospitalist program is largely dependent on the type and setting of the hospital, staffing is ultimately influenced by financial and recruiting capabilities and political considerations.

Recruitment incentives

As the supply of surgeons becomes limited, some hospitals in certain areas of the country may need to consider recruitment incentives for a surgical hospitalist. Some medical hospitalist programs have had to advertise outside of the United States to find additional internists to meet the needs of the expanding field. Recruiting from abroad will be more difficult to implement in surgical services, given the requirement of a foreign-trained surgeon to repeat a U.S. surgical residency before becoming licensed to practice surgery in the United States.

Chapter 5

Some practices have found value in offering recruitment incentives, such as loan repayment programs or a signing bonus, which is often equal to 5%–15% of expected annual income. A common method is to offer a minimum income guarantee for the first one or two years that the doctor practices in the program for surgical hospitalists, as for doctors in other specialties. The majority of programs pay new doctors' relocation expenses. One way to get a rough idea of what incentives other programs are offering is to simply review recruitment advertisements in various publications and on the Internet or to speak to recruiting firms. Recruiting firms quickly developed expertise in the recruitment and placement of medical hospitalists, and they are likely to become very involved in staffing surgical hospitalist practices as well.

Demographics of Patient Populations

When considering staffing models, surgical hospitalist practices should analyze the needs of their own patient population.

Consider these statistics:

- From 2010 to 2015, the elderly population will grow by 11.5 million

- Historically, there have been seven surgeons in the United States for every 100,000 individuals

- Rural areas are underserved by general surgery

- An increasing number of general surgery residency graduates are pursuing fellowship training in surgical subspecialties

- The American Board of Surgery (ABS) has recertified 13,861 surgeons during the past 10 years

- 10,227 surgeons have completed their first certification with the ABS; however, a comparable number of surgeons have retired over this same period

With an aging population comes a greater need for general surgeons and increased demands on the available work force.[1] The surgical hospitalist model is one way to meet this growing need.

U.S. census data and population statistics from 1995 indicate that the American population aged 65 and older will grow from 7 million to 11.5 million between 2010 and 2015. During this period, there will be an additional 4.5 million people who will be advancing from their mid-50s to their early 60s. Care of this advancing age population alone will require at least 800 additional surgeons. As the proportion of elderly people who require a disproportionately large number of surgical care providers increases, the time commitment to an individual surgical case may rise over time as surgeons are operating on more patients of advanced age. These increasing demands on general surgeons will intensify the need for surgical hospitalist programs and the numbers of providers needed to staff each.

Demographics of General Surgeons

In 1994, the number of practicing general surgeons in the United States was estimated to be 17,289, or approximately seven general surgeons per 100,000 population in the United States, according to data from the Fellowship files of the American College of Surgeons (ACS), the American Board of Medical Specialties, and the AMA. This number of surgeons does not include retired and military surgeons, but it does include surgeons from academic centers who may be involved in additional administrative or research activities. However, recent data indicate that the number of general surgeons has declined by 26% over the past 25 years and that the estimate of general surgeons in 2005 was 16,662.[2]

The 1994 data further indicated that more general surgeons were located in metropolitan than in rural areas and that few general surgeons practice in counties in which the whole county is designated as a PC-HPSA (Primary Care—Health Professional Shortage Area).[3] Nationally, the number of general surgeons per population of 100,000 varies from 6.53 in urban areas to 7.71 in large rural areas and 4.67 in small/isolated rural areas.[4] The average age of the surgeons in 1994 was 47, and it was estimated that most of these surgeons had practiced for 15 years after completing residency training.

There is a disparity in distribution of surgeons, with the rural surgeons tending to be an average of five years older than their urban peers. This disparity may lead to more staffing shortages in rural communities in the future as these surgeons reach retirement, which may be particularly acute in those counties defined as PC-HPSA. It has been suggested that up to 70% of rural community hospital revenues are derived from the elective practices and emergency cases performed by general surgeons at their institutions. In many cases, these rural hospitals need to fill their surgical staffing needs with nonlocal surgeons, usually through locum tenens companies.

Chapter 5

As an alternative to the surgical hospitalist model, recent media has discussed the possible recruitment of itinerant locum tenens surgeons to staff hospitals, particularly in rural areas. Some of the surgeons who have chosen this career path have discovered that the compensation offered may be greater than what they were receiving in their private practice, whereas others are finding it difficult to build a practice that can generate enough compensation to meet their financial needs and education debt. Thus, it is understandable to see these surgeons pursue such a pathway. But the positions involve travel and time away from family and are generally for only a limited period. A key concern is the lack of continuity in the care of postoperative patients after the locum tenens surgeon has rotated away to an assignment in a different city. Therefore, although more complicated to establish, a surgical hospitalist program is nearly always more effective in the long run than locum tenens coverage.

Are There Enough General Surgeons to Meet Our Future Needs?

Projections based on retirement of practicing surgeons and an aging population suggest that many rural residents will have increasingly limited access to surgical services. Hospitals must take steps to reverse this trend and preserve the viability of healthcare in many parts of rural America.[5] In addition, the average age of retirement for general surgeon Fellows of the American College of Surgeons has risen from 60.5 in 1984 to 63 in 1995.[6]

Because of increasing diversion of general surgery graduates into surgical specialties, total practice years are declining despite increasing length of practice time. According to the ABS, 10,227 surgeons were newly certified over the past 10 years by the ABS, and approximately the same number retired over that period. More significantly, in the past 10 years, 13,861 surgeons have recertified with the ABS. Because a proportion of these surgeons are board-certified and practice in other surgical subspecialties, the actual number of surgeons devoting their practice to general surgery may be much lower than was previously estimated. So what are the 13,861 general surgeons who have recertified over the past 10 years doing? In part, it depends on the practice location and the population, but primarily it consists of endoscopy, breast, cholecystectomy, hernias, and appendectomy.[7]

The younger general surgeon
Fortunately, the ACS is introducing new programs to solve these future staffing issues through leadership. Interviews with actively practicing surgeons at the 2008 ACS Clinical Congress were recorded and will be used to produce a recruiting video, which will be available on the Internet and is targeted at the medical student population to promote interest in careers in surgery. This younger population is more

interested in a balance between their professional careers and lifestyle than the previous generation, and they may be an excellent source of surgical hospitalists in the future. The best and the brightest of medical school graduates may be attracted to the surgical hospitalist model in this manner.

One drawback is that a recently trained general surgeon sometimes lacks the experience and skills to manage complex general surgical cases. The judgment and operative management skills of a recently trained surgeon may present special challenges to the delivery of optimal patient care until they build confidence through a track record of experience. The question of competency of the recently trained general surgeon has been a topic of discussion,[8] with the recurring suggestion that younger surgeons be mentored early in their clinical careers.

From 1992 to 2003, the operative caseload during the chief resident year at the University of Louisville (KY) School of Medicine declined from 375 to 200 cases.[9]

Similar experiences from residency programs nationally have raised concerns of the experience level of a recently trained general surgeon who is planning a broad-based general surgery practice.[10] Some suggest that an important reason so many recent general surgery residents pursue fellowship training is that they feel the need to obtain additional skills and hone their clinical judgment to achieve success in a surgical practice.

Can recently trained general surgeons be used as surgical hospitalists? Certainly they are eligible, as they are board-certified and have fulfilled the core competency requirements of their general surgery residency. But in the era of reduced work hours training, after the introduction of the 80-hour workweek, many might benefit from additional mentoring and access to a senior surgeon who can help develop additional judgment and critical thinking skills to provide optimal care for the patient. A large urban hospital can be staffed with two senior surgeons and two recently trained general surgeons who can work together in a collaborative way. Programs should strongly encourage having a senior surgeon available to recent residency graduates by phone to promote long-term successful patient outcomes.

Who is seeking to be a surgical hospitalist?

- Younger surgeons interested in a balanced lifestyle
- Senior surgeons whose children have graduated from high school and college

- Fellowship-trained surgeons interested in a more rewarding career

- Retiring military surgeons

Early anecdotal experience indicates that there are two groups who are most interested in surgical hospitalist careers. The first is the younger surgeon who desires a more balanced lifestyle that comes with a fixed schedule offered by some surgical hospitalist practices. The second is the senior surgeon who is later in his or her career, has children who have graduated from high school or college, and may be seeking relief from the burden of managing a private practice. Both groups have indicated interest in professional opportunities that are stimulating and well compensated.

Senior surgeons typically have previous experience in a broad-based general surgical practice that involved coverage of their hospital's ER and their private practice. The opportunity to apply their problem-solving skills as a surgical hospitalist in the evaluation of undifferentiated patients in the ED and in consult requests represents a welcome change of pace compared to the routine of an outpatient clinic.

Some senior fellowship–trained surgeons have chosen to switch to a surgical hospitalist career because it offers a more controlled work schedule and interesting work. The private practice business and office staffing requirements can place an undue burden on the fellowship-trained surgeon as a result of declining reimbursements. The alternative of becoming a surgical hospitalist has been a financial relief for some of these surgeons.

In addition, military general surgeons are often attracted to surgical hospitalist practice as they approach their 20th year of military service and are about to retire with a full military pension. Trauma surgeons have identified the surgical hospitalist pathway as an alternative to add additional operative opportunities and to use their trauma skills in a Level 2 trauma center.

Potential Pitfalls in Staffing a Surgical Hospitalist Program

- Communication with the patients and medical staff

- Organizational skills of the surgeon

- Code of conduct issues

- Sign-out rounds

- Length of the surgical hospitalist's shift

- Working in silos

Communication

Communication is a key component of a successful surgical hospitalist practice. If a surgical hospitalist does not respond to consults in a timely fashion or possesses poor communication skills, the ED and medical hospitalist staff will have difficulty working with that individual in the care of patients.

Organizational skills of the surgeon

Effective organizational skills for the surgical hospitalist are also critically important. With the potential of 20–30 hospitalized patients, five to eight patients located in the ICU, and an OR caseload of four to six cases in a 24-hour period, important patient care issues can be missed if the hospitalist is not organized in his or her thought process and approach to the day. The team approach and a good clear head can avoid this organizational problem.

Code of conduct

A clearly defined code of conduct is important in ensuring that expectations regarding the professionalism of the surgical hospitalist are met. A key requirement is that the surgical hospitalist continuously displays proper respect to all staff members at all times. If there have been conduct issues in the past with a potential surgeon, caution should be taken in hiring that individual and a 90-day trial employment period may be required to observe the interactions and communication skills of the surgeon. This can be supplemented with a quarterly or biannual confidential questionnaire to assess the performance of the hospitalist with other professional staff members such as the ward and ICU nurses and the OR staff, as well as the medical hospitalists.

Sign-out rounds

Daily sign-out rounds are one area that can be a potential pitfall if not done correctly. An effective surgical hospitalist program should establish a process to transfer information to minimize miscommunication of important patient care details and to mitigate possible patient harm associated with handoffs.

Chapter 5

The potential adverse effects on patient care can be significant if the surgical hospitalist is unable to communicate all of the critical issues during these sign-out rounds.

Length of shift

The shift length can be a potential pitfall for a surgical hospitalist program. There is no proven optimum shift length; the best arrangement will depend on local factors such as patient volume and whether the entire shift is in-hospital versus on-call from home. Working a 24-hour shift can be stressful and can potentially threaten patient care. A 48-hour shift that regularly involves on-site night work is probably untenable and risks burnout. In a busy practice, a 12-hour shift may be most appropriate. See additional comments in Chapter 6 and Chapter 8 on scheduling.

Working in silos

The surgical hospitalist must maintain a clear and quiet head at all times. When things get busy or there is an emergency situation, the surgeon will need to perform well under all conditions with a defined approach to solve the current crisis or emergency. There is typically no one else to lend a hand or give advice. However, the clear head may think to stop and see where the situation is heading when an urgent issue arises and help is needed. Perhaps another surgeon or consultant is available for advice or help.

Special Considerations

- Coverage of personal emergencies

- State licensure

- Termination of an unsatisfactory surgical hospitalist

- Communication with hospital administrators

Coverage of personal emergencies

If a staff surgical hospitalist has a personal emergency or illness, replacement coverage will be necessary to maintain 24/7 coverage. Although one or two days could be covered by another surgical hospitalist colleague, longer absences will need to be covered by a backup surgeon from the hospital staff.

State licensure

Another important consideration for staffing a new program is to ensure that the hospitalist surgeon has the appropriate state license to practice, especially in situations in which the hospitalist must relocate to a new state. The time required to complete individual state licensure can take four to six months, so the program and hospital leadership should anticipate credentialing needs well in advance to avoid delays in coverage.

Termination of an unsatisfactory surgical hospitalist

Proper education in a hospital code of conduct policy is an important foundation for the professional activity of surgical hospitalists. Maintenance of board certification with the ABS is essential to maintain the credentials to function as a surgical hospitalist. Monthly morbidity and mortality conferences where learning and discussion can take place amongst surgical peers can support the quality and transparency of the program. In some cases, it might be worthwhile to hold some of these meetings jointly with the medical hospitalists. Perioperative outcomes are typically followed by the hospital's quality assurance committee, and poor performance should be addressed; if not improved, termination of the surgeon might be appropriate.

Communication with hospital administrators

The hospital administration will be a key partner in seeking solutions to local systems challenges as they arise. A clear channel of communication is important to institute changes that may be required as a surgical hospitalist program is being developed. Initially, weekly meetings between hospital leadership and the director of the surgical hospitalist program are suggested, and as the program matures, monthly meetings may be scheduled.

REFERENCES

1. David A Etzioni, "The Aging Populations and its Impact on the Surgery Work Force," *Ann Surg* 238(2) (2003): 170–177.

2. Dana Christian Lynge, "A Longitudinal Analysis of the General Surgery Work Force in the United States, 1981–2005," *Arch Surg* 143(4) (2008): 351.

3. Francis A. Kawakwa, Olga Jonasson, "The General Surgery Work Force," *Am J Surg* 173(1) (1997): 59–62.

4. Dana Christian Lynge, "Rural General Surgeons: Manpower and Demographics, " *Surg Endosc* 22 (2008): 1593–1594.

5. MJ Thompson, DC Lynge, EH Lynge, et al., "Characterizing the General Surgery Work Force in Rural America," *Arch Surg* 140(1) (2005):74–79.

Chapter 5

6. Olga Jonasson, Francis A. Kwakwa, "Retirement Age and the Work Force in General Surgery," *Ann Surg* 224(4) (1996).

7. MF Brennan, HT Debas, "Surgical Education in the United States: Portents for Change," Ann Surg 240(4) (2004): 565–572.

8. Ibid.

9. Ibid.

10. William G. Cheadle, Glen A. Franklin, J. David Richardson, Hirma C. Polk, "Broad-based General Surgery Training in a Continued Utility for the Future," *Ann Surg* 239(5) (2004): 627–636.

CHAPTER 6

Scheduling the Operating Room

Eva M. Wall, MD, FACS

The hospitalist model first appeared in internal medicine, and the success of the model has led to its adoption by other specialties, including general surgery. In many ways, internal medicine hospitalist principles can be translated directly to the surgeon hospitalist paradigm. However, surgery differs critically in one regard—the activity in the operating room (OR). As no analogy exists in internal medicine, the management of the OR schedule deserves special attention when implementing a surgical hospitalist program. The schedule has significant implications on the viability of the program, and it affects the patient, anesthesiologists, and nonhospitalist surgeons.

A well-executed plan for OR scheduling prioritizes patient safety and satisfaction, as well as accommodating the needs of physicians, staff members, and the hospital facility. Given the relative novelty of the surgical hospitalist concept, adapting a hospital's routine to integrate an unplanned surgical case can pose challenges. How do you plan for the unplanned?

Efficiency is the goal. In the perfect world, all surgical cases would be scheduled weeks in advance. All the patients would show up on time, well prepared for surgery. There would be no difficult intubations. The surgeons would start and end as scheduled. Operations would always be standardized. Every room turnover would be 10 minutes, and finally, the emergency department (ED) would never call.

Yes, we all want to work at this "Perfect Medical Center." Unfortunately, in reality, we struggle on a daily basis to keep up with all the adversities that make surgical life exciting.

Unplanned surgical patients bring instability into OR proceedings. The challenge is to accommodate their needs in an efficient, fiscally responsible manner without detriment to the patient. Evaluation of the particular institution's operating costs, which include OR costs, staff compensation, and hospital bed availability, should govern that institution's method of scheduling unplanned surgical cases.

Chapter 6

There is no single solution to this challenge. The task can be viewed as a puzzle with many pieces: patients, surgeons, OR staff, hospital administration, and finance. There are several potential strategies to assemble the puzzle, so how does a hospital choose which OR scheduling model is best for its facility? The best method is determined by institution-specific data relevant to the patient population. Consider the following questions related to data:

- What portion of your institution's OR case volume is a result of unplanned surgical care, such as emergency cases from the ED?

- What is the distribution of unplanned cases in terms of acuity and necessity? What percentage are emergent, urgent, or otherwise unplanned?

- What are the comorbidities in this patient population? What are their special needs, such as large-volume blood loss, ARDS, chronic lung disease, coronary artery disease, renal failure, or extremes of age? What special resources are required for these cases, and do these unplanned cases then detract from resource availability for elective cases?

- At what time of day do these patients require surgery? What is the distribution of these patients over the course of a week?

- How efficient is the OR in managing elective cases? Are data available regarding case duration, based on surgeon and case type, to predict OR use?

- How are the surgical hospitalists to be organized? How long is a surgeon's shift? Is operating at 2 a.m. handled by the OR in nearly the same way as operating at 2 p.m.? Does one surgeon work primarily daytime hours but cover the evening hours from off-site, with the assumption that not as much work goes on?

- How efficient are the surgical hospitalists? If the surgical hospitalist estimates that the case will last 90 minutes, is the estimate reliable? Does the case usually run overtime, thus making the OR manager hesitant to open slots between elective cases? If the average laparoscopic appendectomy at the hospital takes 30 minutes, does the surgical hospitalist take 20 minutes or 60 minutes?

All of these independent factors influence what model is best suited to a particular institution to maximize unplanned surgical patient care.

Ideal Schedule Model

In the schedule for the hypothetical Perfect Medical Center OR, all cases are elective; there are no urgent or emergent cases. In this ideal schedule, the OR would include an even distribution of elective surgeries across all rooms. Each room would also include a standardized, most efficient turnover time. In this ideal day, no patients would require urgent or emergent surgeries, and physicians could go home at night. All cases would start on time. The room turnovers would be predictable. No case would run beyond its anticipated completion time. Refer to Figure 6.1 for an ideal operating schedule.

In reality, however, more demanding cases with the natural ebb and flow of a real OR require more sophisticated scheduling models. There are four potential ways to approach scheduling the OR to accommodate unplanned surgical cases, the classical model, the trauma center model, the mosaic model, and the night surgeon model.

Chapter 6

FIGURE 6.1   IDEAL OPERATING ROOM SCHEDULE

This figure represents an ideal schedule at the hypothetical Perfect Medical Center. In this ideal schedule, the OR would include even distribution of elective surgeries across all four rooms and balance workloads amongst elective surgeons. Each room would also include a 30-minute block between surgeries for cleanup and sterilization. In this ideal day, no patients would require urgent or emergent surgeries, physicians could go home at night, and no surgical hospitalists would be needed.

	Elective case	Urgent case	Emergent case
	☐	▨	■

Time	Room 1	Room 2	Room 3	Room 4
6 a.m.				
5 a.m.				
4 a.m.				
3 a.m.				
2 a.m.				
1 a.m.				
12 a.m. (midnight)				
11 p.m.				
10 p.m.				
9 p.m.				
8 p.m.				
7 p.m.				
6 p.m				
5 p.m.				
4 p.m.				
3 p.m.	☐	☐	☐	☐
2 p.m.				
1 p.m.		☐	☐	
12 p.m. (noon)	☐			☐
11 a.m.				
10 a.m.		☐	☐	
9 a.m.	☐			☐
8 a.m.		☐	☐	
7 a.m.				

Source: Eva M. Wall, MD, FACS, freelance emergency general surgeon and surgical intensivist, Lynnwood, WA.

Classical Model

The classical model of scheduling the OR is designed for an environment in which all surgeons care primarily for electively scheduled patients, with few urgent or emergent cases. For example, if a patient in the emergency department (ED) is diagnosed with appendicitis at 10 a.m. and has no stigmata of septic shock, that patient, typically, is scheduled in the add-on queue for surgery at the end of the scheduled day. The patient is put in a holding pattern until an OR opens and the surgeon, anesthesiologist, OR staff, and instrumentation are available at the same time. This often culminates in a mad rush for the OR at 5 p.m. when surgeons complete their office schedule, and it often results in a single OR running with add-ons late into the night. Cases are prioritized on a first-come, first-served basis.

An institution may find the classical model most effective if the number of unplanned cases is generally low. Refer to Figure 6.2 for a classical operating room schedule.

CLASSICAL MODEL

Advantages

- Elective cases are completed without delay
- Unplanned cases (low volume and not urgent) are completed in a reasonable amount of time

Disadvantages

- Increased volume of unplanned surgical patients can lead to long delays until an OR is available
- Some caregivers, such as the ER staff, might have to manage a patient for an uncomfortably long time, until the care is transferred to the OR staff and surgeon when a room becomes available
- Delays in elective cases when emergency cases take priority and resources

Chapter 6

FIGURE 6.2 — CLASSICAL OPERATING ROOM SCHEDULE

This figure represents the classical model of scheduling the OR. It is designed for an environment in which all surgeons care primarily for electively scheduled patients and not for urgent or emergent cases. Cases are prioritized on a first-come, first-served basis. An institution may find the classical model most effective if the number of unplanned cases is generally low.

	Elective case	Urgent case	Emergent case
	☐	▨	■

Time	Room 1	Room 2	Room 3	Room 4
6 a.m.				
5 a.m.				
4 a.m.				
3 a.m.				
2 a.m.				
1 a.m.				
12 a.m. (midnight)				
11 p.m.		Urgent		
10 p.m.			Emergent	
9 p.m.			Emergent	
8 p.m.		Urgent	Emergent	
7 p.m.		Urgent	Emergent	
6 p.m				
5 p.m.		Urgent		
4 p.m.		Elective		
3 p.m.	Elective	Elective		Elective
2 p.m.	Elective	Elective		Elective
1 p.m.	Elective	Elective		Elective
12 p.m. (noon)	Elective	Elective	Elective	Elective
11 a.m.	Elective		Elective	
10 a.m.			Elective	
9 a.m.	Elective			Elective
8 a.m.	Elective	Elective	Elective	Elective
7 a.m.		Elective		

Source: Eva M. Wall, MD, FACS, freelance emergency general surgeon and surgical intensivist, Lynnwood, WA.

The benefit to the classical model is that this schedule allows elective cases to proceed without delay. It also allows unplanned cases to be completed in a reasonable time frame without taxing healthcare staff members or threatening patient health—so long as the volume of unplanned cases is low and the acuity of the cases does not demand urgent attention.

The downside to the classical schedule is that unplanned surgical patients may have to wait hours before definitive treatment. With delays in transfer to the OR, the ED or ward healthcare staff members are then responsible for caring for the patient until an OR is ready. Emergency cases upset the proverbial applecart, placing delays in elective cases while resources are diverted to manage the emergency.

In facilities whose number of acute cases is low, anticipation of the ideal schedule model is possible and probably most cost-effective. However, if the number of unplanned cases increases, the burden they create by displacing elective cases requires forethought to minimize their negative impact. Institutions experiencing these higher volumes of acute cases should consider other strategies for integrating unplanned cases.

Trauma Center Model

Unlike the classical model, which best serves elective cases, the trauma center model caters to urgent and emergent cases, particularly for the acutely injured patient. The evolution of trauma centers has funneled high-acuity patients to regional hospitals that have specialized resources to manage them, and because of the increased numbers of these unplanned patients requiring urgent or emergent surgery, high-volume centers frequently reserve an OR and OR crew for unplanned surgeries only. Such surgeries can include trauma emergencies, ruptured aneurysms, and emergent cardiac cases, as well as add-on general surgery, orthopedic surgery, otolaryngology, or obstetrics.

Utilization of these resources requires careful consideration of the proportion of elective and emergent or urgent cases. It also requires accounting for the cost of providing reserved emergency operating services, as opposed to integrating these unplanned cases into the existing elective schedule.

> **TRAUMA CENTER MODEL**
>
> **Advantages**
> - No delay in addressing emergent cases
> - Little impact on the elective surgical schedule
> - Reputation as an acuity service that leads to recognition and distinction
>
> **Disadvantages**
> - Cost of resources, personnel, sterilization, and nonreimbursement.
> - Reputation and increasing emergency cases may lead to lower payer mix

The trauma center model presents some advantages. There are no delays in rendering surgical care to patients with emergent problems, such as exsanguinating hemorrhage and septic shock. Services that use this model have a capacity to provide specialty support staff for emergencies (e.g., critical care anesthesia or cardiac anesthesia, OR staff with proficiency in emergency surgery, and perfusionists). There is a negligible effect to the elective schedule because emergencies are functionally separated from the day-to-day function of the OR. Refer to Figure 6.3 for a trauma center schedule.

The trauma center model also may enhance the hospital's reputation. Hospitals that provide high-acuity services can rapidly gain distinction in their geographic area, thereby changing the demographic of the patients they receive. This can be either advantageous or detrimental. For example, a hospital that gains recognition for superior outcomes in high-profile cases can alter the perception of elective patients and increase the percentage of well-insured clients seeking care at that institution. This balance needs evaluation on the institutional level; not all hospitals will enjoy better payer mixes depending on the locality's demographics.

There are also disadvantages to the trauma center model—specifically, costs. First, underutilization of expensive resources and personnel may occur. Secondly, sterile instrumentation reprocessing requires investment when OR sets are left open and go unused. Thirdly, the service invests in expensive resources for a patient population without means for compensation for specialty care (i.e., the uninsured or underinsured). This factor may be perceived or real, but it requires determination by the institution.

Scheduling the Operating Room

FIGURE 6.3 — **TRAUMA CENTER OPERATING ROOM SCHEDULE**

This figure represents the trauma center model, which is appropriate for urgent or emergent cases. It is contingent on the number and acuity of cases and availability of surgeons and healthcare staff members. One room is reserved solely for these urgent or emergent cases.

Source: Eva M. Wall, MD, FACS, freelance emergency general surgeon and surgical intensivist, Lynnwood, WA.

Chapter 6

As a final consideration, trauma model institutions can gain recognition for excellence in emergency care. In that way, trauma centers can increase their percentage of emergency patients as other area hospitals and emergency medical services divert urgent and emergent patients to them. Whether this is an advantage or a disadvantage is difficult to predict. The effect on the bottom line depends on the hospital's locality and on the resulting change in clientele once the hospital's reputation becomes established.

Acute surgical cases generate stress, and in large volumes, care can only be rendered to this challenging population when it is recognized as a separate entity. The point at which separation occurs should be governed by case numbers and comorbidity assessment, with evaluation of the cost of such a stratification. Not all institutions can or should embark on this evolution; regionalization of care has naturally developed as a result of these issues. In this sense, an individual institution must consider the region's healthcare facilities and their capabilities and resources before deciding where a trauma model hospital should develop.

Mosaic Model

When a hospital's unplanned caseload becomes burdensome for community surgeons to manage without financial support, but the number of cases does not merit transition to a trauma center model, what alternatives are available?

In cases in which the elective schedule has openings over the course of a regular workday, there's another solution to integrating unplanned cases into the regular schedule, with minimal effect on the remaining elective caseload. Such a hospital may consider the addition of a single surgical hospitalist to act as a coordinator of acute surgical care. This model is termed the mosaic model: It rests on a classical model foundation, with community surgeons continuing to take call, but it takes the first step in appointing a specialized surgeon dedicated to the care of acute general surgical patients.

With the initiation of a mosaic surgical hospitalist model, a single surgeon is hired to augment the emergency capabilities of the general surgery community. Essentially, the general surgery community can be thought of as a group that hires a new member whose specialty is unplanned care. This single hospitalist surgeon works business hours providing unplanned surgical care in the same way that elective surgeons spend their weekdays caring for elective patients. Such a surgical hospitalist is often readily available when time slots open up in the schedule.

For example, if the OR schedule is organized into morning and afternoon blocks, and the morning surgeon's block is not completely filled, the afternoon surgeon often cannot start until his or her regularly scheduled start time. That is, they cannot "move up" because of time commitments elsewhere (e.g., scheduled office time). In this instance, the opening in the OR schedule goes unfilled because other elective surgeons likewise have their daytime hours committed. The result is an open OR with an anesthesiologist and an OR crew sitting in the lounge waiting for the afternoon block to start. However, with the advent of a surgical hospitalist working a mosaic model, the appendectomy in the add-on queue that would normally have gone at 5 p.m. or later in the classical model gets bumped up to the opening in the OR schedule. (Refer to Figure 6.4 for a mosaic operating room schedule.) Thus, the OR is in use during regular daytime hours, and the anesthesiologist and OR crew, already paid to work the day shift, are also put to use. The add-on list gets shorter. If the evening OR staff is compensated specially for working at night, OR staffing costs go down.

Frequently, the OR staff members are eager to get the case done because they are the individuals on call that evening. In this situation, everybody wins—the patient receives expedited care, the length of stay (LOS) decreases, and the surgeon, anesthesiologist, and OR crew are all likely happy to finish the case. The other elective surgeons in the queue also benefit by having one less case to wait for before they can start; the fatigue factor of the medical staff goes down.

MOSAIC MODEL

Advantages
- Expedited patient care
- Reduced LOS
- Less wasted time and increased productivity by the surgeon, anesthesiologist, and OR staff
- Decreased medical staff fatigue
- Reduction in the number of hours each surgeon is actually on call in a 24-hour period
- Decreased workload while on call
- Business hours become protected time for the elective general surgeons when they can carry on a regular workday without disruption from the ED

Disadvantages
- Can only be implemented when unplanned case numbers are sufficient to constitute a practice for the surgical hospitalist
- Does not account for a high volume of unplanned cases, at which point a different model may be more appropriate to provide care to the enlarging patient population

This mosaic model is best suited to situations in which the elective schedule has openings through the day, as, for example, the unfilled block or the case that got canceled because the patient contracted the flu. It is also contingent on an unplanned volume that remains relatively low. When the unplanned caseload fills every available slot and then goes on into the night, consideration must be given to the institution of a separately reserved room for unplanned cases; as the case volumes increase further, a different model for the surgical hospitalist service may be more appropriate.

The mosaic model is ideally suited to the hospital that has experienced an increase in acute care volumes that makes scheduling in the classical model unwieldy. Having all acute cases stacked up at 5 p.m. in one room, while daytime slots go unutilized because a surgeon is unavailable, is inefficient. The mosaic model allows for better use of facility resources, more satisfied patients, and happier surgeons and staff members. Although a community call system can stress the community's surgeons when volumes increase, the transition to hiring a minimum of four surgeons for a separate acute surgical care service line also can be difficult. The jump to four new surgeons may be unrealistic if surgical volumes do not support this number of additional surgeons. The mosaic model may offer a reasonable transition step for institutions experiencing this phenomenon.

Scheduling the Operating Room

FIGURE 6.4 — MOSAIC OPERATING ROOM SCHEDULE

This figure represents the mosaic model, which is best suited to situations in which the elective schedule has openings through the day, such as an unfilled block of canceled surgeries. This model has many advantages, including expedited patient care, reduced length of time, increased use of OR staff members, and reduced fatigue. However, it is contingent on an unplanned volume that remains relatively low.

Elective case ☐   **Urgent case** ▨   **Emergent case** ■

Time axis (top to bottom): 6 a.m., 5 a.m., 4 a.m., 3 a.m., 2 a.m., 1 a.m., 12 a.m. (midnight), 11 p.m., 10 p.m., 9 p.m., 8 p.m., 7 p.m., 6 p.m, 5 p.m., 4 p.m., 3 p.m., 2 p.m., 1 p.m., 12 p.m. (noon), 11 a.m., 10 a.m., 9 a.m., 8 a.m., 7 a.m.

Room: 1, 2, 3, 4

Source: Eva M. Wall, MD, FACS, freelance emergency general surgeon and surgical intensivist, Lynnwood, WA.

Chapter 6

Night Surgeon Model

As another possibility in the transition from the classical model to the trauma center model, a group of community surgeons or a hospital can hire a surgeon who only works the night shift, perhaps nine or 10 nights per month.

If the main impetus for starting a surgical hospitalist service is to reduce community general surgeons' night call, consider hiring a night general surgeon, or "surgeon nocturnist." Such an individual would be hired for the express purpose of replacing community surgeons in their on-call responsibilities and would not have routine daytime responsibilities. Refer to Figure 6.5 for a night surgeon operating room schedule.

NIGHT SURGEON MODEL

Advantages

- Easier access to the OR for surgeons when no elective cases are scheduled
- Fewer burdens on community general surgeons for night coverage
- Night surgeon does not need to flip from day to night shift

Disadvantages

- Overworked anesthesia and ancillary staff members
- Cost

The advantages to using the night surgeon scheduling model is that staff members can access the OR more easily at night, when elective cases are not scheduled. There is also decreased burden on community general surgeons for night coverage. There is no flipping from day to night shift for the night surgeon.

However, this model does come with some disadvantages. The expectation that an OR runs every night places new demands on anesthesia and ancillary staff members. They may be accustomed to being on-call for emergencies at night but have historically understood this to mean that actual work duties occur only from time to time, not every night, all night. Traditional night call responsibilities mean little actual work during the occasional emergency, whereas a nocturnist plan increases the amount of work being done at night significantly, not only for the surgeon but for all members of the OR team.

Scheduling the Operating Room

| FIGURE 6.5 | NIGHT SURGEON OPERATING ROOM SCHEDULE |

This figure represents the night surgeon model with the use of "nocturnists." Using this model may lead to easier access to the OR and less burden on community general surgeons, but it also may result in an overworked anesthesia and ancillary staff and expensive salary costs for surgeon salaries.

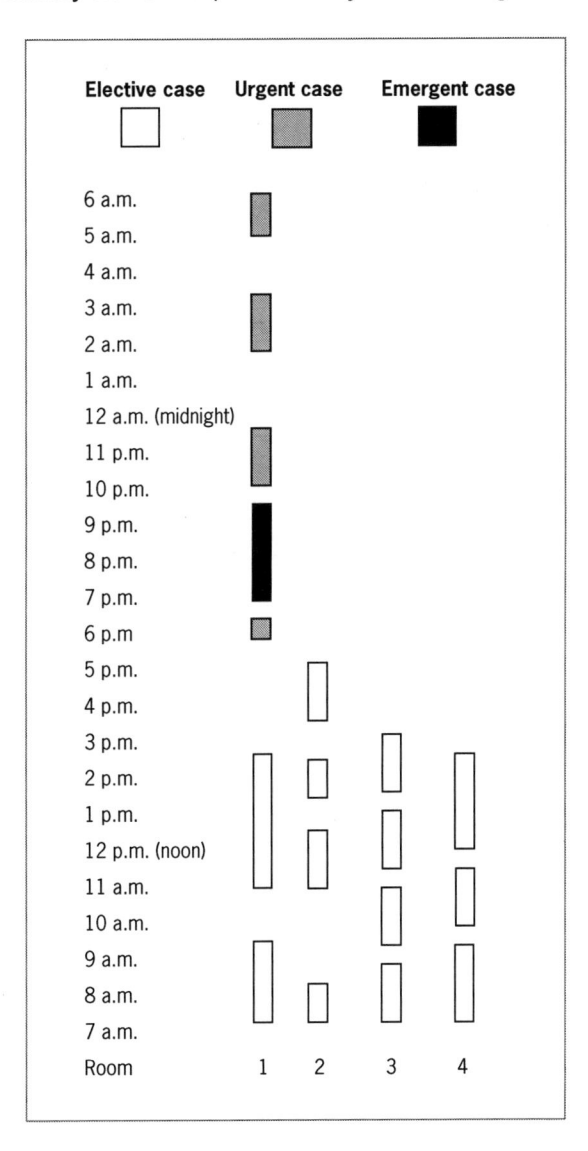

Elective case □   Urgent case ▨   Emergent case ■

Time	Room 1	Room 2	Room 3	Room 4
6 a.m.				
5 a.m.	Urgent			
4 a.m.				
3 a.m.	Urgent			
2 a.m.				
1 a.m.				
12 a.m. (midnight)				
11 p.m.	Urgent			
10 p.m.				
9 p.m.	Emergent			
8 p.m.				
7 p.m.				
6 p.m.	Urgent			
5 p.m.		Elective		
4 p.m.		Elective		
3 p.m.	Elective	Elective	Elective	Elective
2 p.m.	Elective	Elective	Elective	Elective
1 p.m.	Elective	Elective	Elective	Elective
12 p.m. (noon)	Elective	Elective	Elective	Elective
11 a.m.	Elective		Elective	Elective
10 a.m.	Elective		Elective	Elective
9 a.m.	Elective	Elective	Elective	Elective
8 a.m.	Elective	Elective	Elective	Elective
7 a.m.				

Source: Eva M. Wall, MD, FACS, freelance emergency general surgeon and surgical intensivist, Lynnwood, WA.

Chapter 6

In addition, costs may be a downside. A surgeon employed to work only at night would likely handle cases with limited compensation potential, such as abscesses or trauma. The surgeon would therefore likely need a salary guarantee or assurance of a stable pay grade. This arrangement may pose no benefit over paying community general surgeons for taking call, depending on the institution's individual needs and patient demographics.

One other important point to consider is quality of care in late-night operating. Some nonemergent surgical cases present challenges because of complexity or comorbidity that truly increase the risk involved if that case is undertaken at night. Each case slated for the OR must be individually assessed for appropriateness before being taken to the OR, keeping in mind that patient safety should always be the prime directive.

In conclusion, a nocturnal surgeon, conceptually, may offer benefits to a surgical community struggling to provide care during night and weekend hours. If, as a community, the surgeons at a hospital are able to devise a compensation strategy for a surgeon or nocturnist, this represents another potential way of bridging the gap between the small-volume (classical model) hospital transitioning to the large-volume (trauma model) hospital.

At this time, the model remains conceptual with respect to general surgery; although internal medicine hospitalist programs do incorporate nocturnists, there are no hospitals that have adopted this model for surgical care to date.

OR Scheduling and Community

These four approaches—classical, trauma center, mosaic, and night surgeon models—are not necessarily the only solutions to the problem of scheduling the unplanned surgical patient. What is crucial to the success of any plan for scheduling unplanned surgery is OR management that can adapt to changing circumstances.

This relies heavily on excellent communication skills of the surgeon and the OR staff in order to coordinate their efforts. To facilitate patient care in a constantly changing environment, identify a single individual with global oversight of the entire operating theatre. How many times in everyday practice has an urgent patient been put into the OR schedule, then brought to preoperative holding without being ready? Perhaps an EKG has not been done, or the patient is anticoagulated and surgery will have to wait until the anticoagulant effect can be reversed. Sometimes the patient never even makes it to preop holding because the ward nurse cannot send the patient as a result of incomplete ward-to-preop paperwork. In those instances, which regrettably occur in ORs throughout the country every week, if not every day, the facile OR manager can manipulate the schedule and available staff members and resources to make the puzzle fit together efficiently and still provide excellent care to unplanned and elective patients alike. A close relationship between the person in charge of the OR and the hospitalist surgeon provides the foundation for smooth work flow in the OR.

Each of the surgical hospitalist models provides quality of care, availability of care, and efficiency of care to an increasing patient population that suffers from diminishing surgical support from our current system of care. Regardless of the model, dedicated surgical hospitalists increase efficiency by actively engaging the OR "foreman," be that a charge nurse or an anesthesia charge, to expedite cases. In surgical hospitalist programs that are established, the OR may contact the surgeon to solicit cases when openings in the OR schedule arise, knowing that this surgeon is available when elective surgeons are not.

Surgical hospitalists can potentially increase patient safety and shorten LOS because of increased availability and based on their experience. They typically care for patients with comorbidities that require surgical intervention urgently. The surgical hospitalists can become better prepared to offer medical strategies to protect patients with cardiopulmonary disease, renal disease, liver disease, immunosuppression, and the like, whenever possible. Familiarity with accurate risk-benefit analysis in high-risk patients becomes a great advantage to the surgical hospitalist and, thereby, to the hospital and patient as well.

Surgical hospitalists are an invaluable resource because they are comfortable with difficult situations and are therefore well positioned to aid as backup surgeons when elective cases prove more challenging than initially anticipated.

The surgical hospitalist can become a point person in improvement projects, being ever-present in the OR. Whether the subject is care maps, order sets, preference cards, or quality improvement projects, the surgical hospitalist can be a wonderful resource for the hospital, the ER, the OR, the ICU, and the surgical ward.

Chapter 6

Perhaps the most important aspect to making OR scheduling work rests on the concept of community: The means by which a medical community provides care to patients requires the involvement and support of the entire community. In building a hospitalist plan, the hospital administration, surgeons, and OR staff ought to have input at the planning stage. There should be some form of two-way communication, such as meetings or regularly updated bulletins, throughout the process to delineate their perceptions of what deficits require correction and, basically, how to build a better widget. When everyone along the chain of patient care has the opportunity to voice concerns, the individual members can take pride in the plan when it is instituted. Ultimately, when the people taking care of the unplanned surgical patient feel that they have helped make the patient care process the best it can be, the net result will be a stronger, more confident OR community in which patients can be assured that they will receive the best care possible. The surgical hospitalist builds communication channels to realize this goal.

Consider the patient's point of view. Unplanned surgical patients never wanted to be where they find themselves. They and their families are anxious and frightened, sometimes for their very lives. They face possible loss of function, income, and independence. When the system they find themselves in is disorganized in its approach, or when they are pushed to the end of the waiting list, their fears are exacerbated. It becomes imperative, therefore, that the unplanned surgical patient's doctor and all the people that care for him or her have a well-thought-out, smoothly flowing process. It will help the patient and family cope, survive, and thrive as they advance through what is often the most difficult time in their lives. With a well-planned strategy for scheduling the unplanned surgical case, even the most hectic situations can seem predictable, and predictability is comforting. When an OR achieves this goal, the surgeons, physicians, hospital staff, OR staff, and hospital administration can all feel pride in a job well done, allowing patients to feel safe in their caregivers' hands and giving them hope for their future.

CHAPTER 7

Surgical Hospital Compensation Planning

Darin E. Libby

"Nothing focuses the mind like a discussion about compensation." —Anonymous

The amount of compensation paid and the method by which a surgical hospitalist earns his or her income are key elements for establishing a sustainable surgical hospitalist program. Setting the appropriate compensation level and model will assist in attaining recruitment and retention goals while simultaneously driving optimal physician behaviors. Numerous physician compensation models exist, ranging from fixed salary to 100% productivity-based salary, but there is not a universal approach. Each surgical hospitalist program will have specific objectives and should design a compensation model that meets the unique characteristics of the program.

This chapter presents an overview of compensation planning for new and existing surgical hospitalist programs. The chapter specifically reviews methods to determine the appropriate compensation amount, various compensation models, and special considerations.

Amount of Compensation

The amount of compensation offered to a surgical hospitalist should be based on industry benchmarks for general surgery. Although the economics and work schedule of a surgical hospitalist varies from the practice of a traditional general surgeon, compensation levels are comparable. Recruiting occurs within a defined pool of applicants, and hospitalist programs must match or exceed compensation packages offered for traditional general surgery practice opportunities. In addition, the lack of access to technical revenues through ambulatory surgery center ownership increasingly has required surgical hospitalist programs to offer more generous amounts to attract the best candidates. Over time, more specific surgical hospitalist compensation and productivity data will likely become available through industry surveys, as has occurred for data regarding internal medicine hospitalist compensation. Until more specific data are available, a reasonable approach is to use the general surgery benchmarks from several widely accepted industry surveys that report physician compensation. Several commonly used surveys are published by the following organizations:

Chapter 7

- Medical Group Management Association (MGMA)

- American Medical Group Association (AMGA)

- Sullivan Cotter and Associates, Inc.

- ECG Management Consultants, Inc.

- RSM McGladrey, Inc.

It is important to understand each survey's unique characteristics and to identify the most relevant survey or, in many situations, a combination of the surveys. For instance, using surveys that provide an understanding of national and local compensation trends will help set compensation levels that recruit and retain surgeons and ensure that these levels fall within market standards. When establishing a composite benchmark, calculate either a weighted average based on the respective survey's sample size or an equal weighting between surveys.

Across the industry, general surgeons have experienced a steady rise in compensation over the past five years, with annual gains averaging 5.3%, as illustrated in Figure 7.1.

FIGURE 7.1 MEDIAN GENERAL SURGERY COMPENSATION—PAST FIVE YEARS

This figure illustrates the rise of general surgery compensation over time due to multiple factors, including a growing demand for surgeons, short supply of surgeons, and increasing productivity gains.

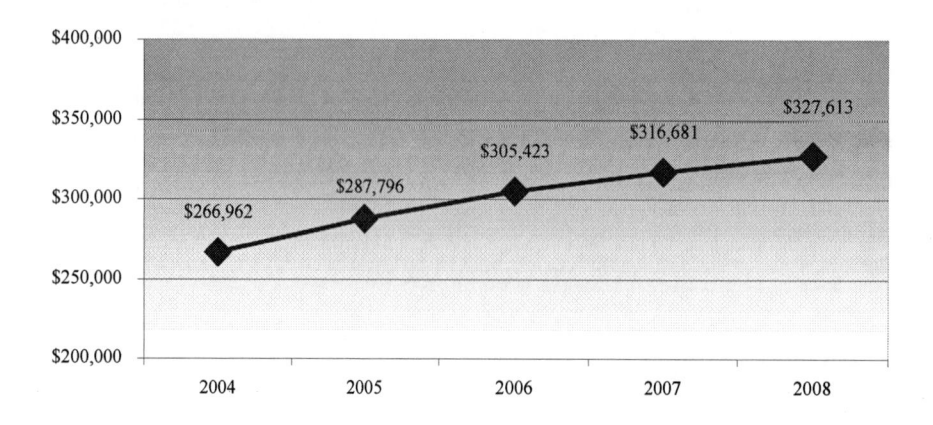

Year	Median Compensation
2004	$266,962
2005	$287,796
2006	$305,423
2007	$316,681
2008	$327,613

Source: Based on a weighted average of median in the annual MGMA and AMGA Physician Compensation and Production Surveys. Graphic by ECG Management Consultants, Inc., headquartered in Seattle.

Surgical Hospital Compensation Planning

Compensation levels are rising more quickly than in other physician specialties because of the growing demand for general surgeons and short supply of qualified general surgeons. This imbalance of supply and demand of general surgeons leads to increased productivity of surgeons and heightened competition for candidates, resulting in higher compensation to recruit and retain.

The Association of American Colleges (AAMC) reports that fewer medical school graduates are pursuing careers in general surgery and instead are electing to pursue subspecialty training. There is little indication that the trend in compensation increases for general surgeons will slow anytime in the near future.

The amount of compensation paid to individual physicians varies significantly based on several factors:

- Physician performance

- Physician experience

- Unique demands of the surgical hospitalist program (e.g., trauma center and night coverage)

- Regional recruiting trends

In all but a few situations, compensation levels will fall between the 25th and 75th percentiles of benchmark compensation, with a growing number of surgical hospitalists expecting to earn in the third quartile—approximately $325,000–$410,000 per surgeon, according to the most recent benchmark data.

> **TIP: HOW MUCH TO PAY A SURGEON**
> Most surgical hospitalists expect to earn approximately $325,000 –$410,000.

Figure 7.2 illustrates the compensation range for the most recent five-year period.

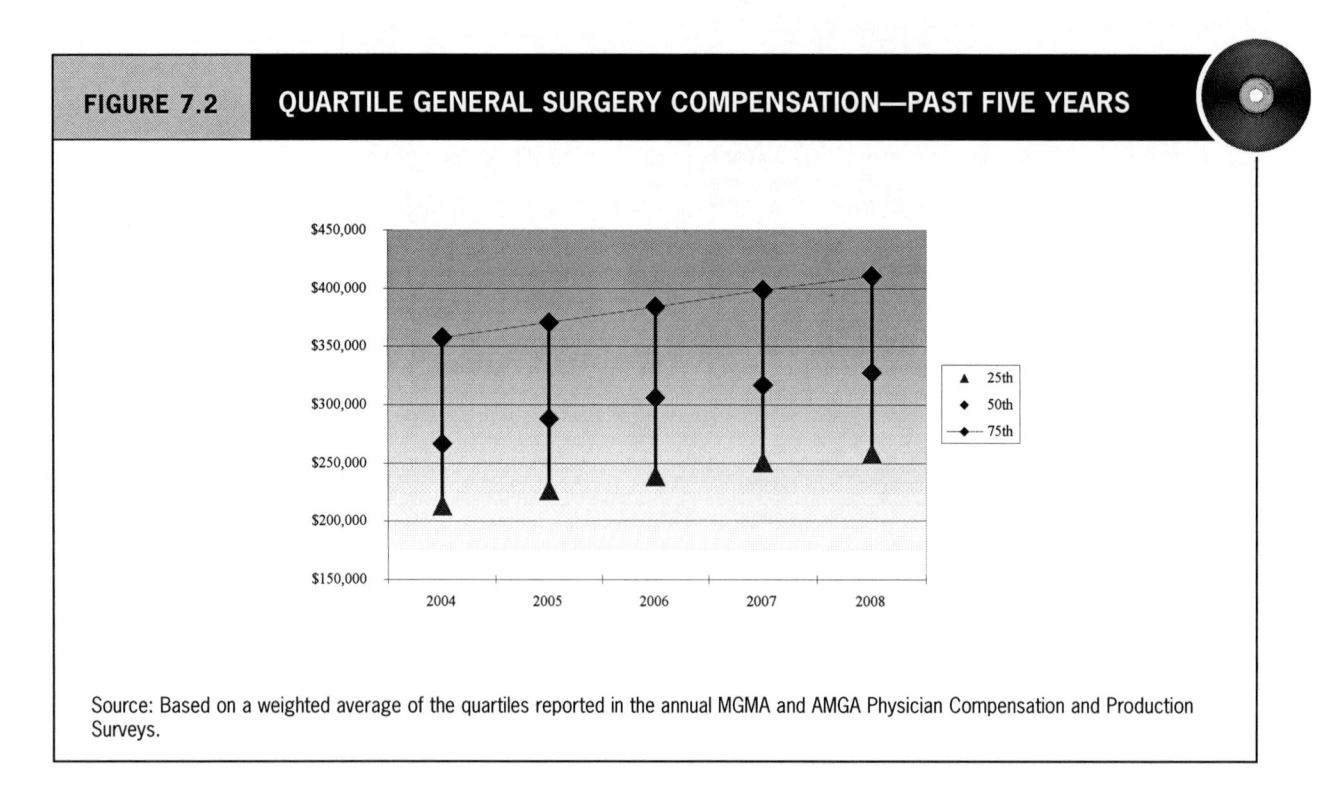

FIGURE 7.2: QUARTILE GENERAL SURGERY COMPENSATION—PAST FIVE YEARS

Source: Based on a weighted average of the quartiles reported in the annual MGMA and AMGA Physician Compensation and Production Surveys.

Although the benchmark data are important to establishing an estimate for market compensation, published survey data will show variation in all of the compensation and production metrics, and, regardless of the source, these data should not serve as the only determinant of appropriate compensation for a particular program. Instead, the benchmark data should serve only as a guide, and adjustments to actual compensation levels should typically be based on local and regional marketplace factors.

For instance, surgeons practicing in a Level III trauma center will typically demand higher compensation than those practicing in a community hospital without a trauma program. Another example may be related to a difficult practice location, wherein higher compensation is necessary to offset the less desirable geographic location. For example, hospitals in the Central Valley of California generally are required to offer compensation packages that surpass hospitals located in major metropolitan areas.

Surgical Hospital Compensation Planning

Compensation levels are rising more quickly than in other physician specialties because of the growing demand for general surgeons and short supply of qualified general surgeons. This imbalance of supply and demand of general surgeons leads to increased productivity of surgeons and heightened competition for candidates, resulting in higher compensation to recruit and retain.

The Association of American Colleges (AAMC) reports that fewer medical school graduates are pursuing careers in general surgery and instead are electing to pursue subspecialty training. There is little indication that the trend in compensation increases for general surgeons will slow anytime in the near future.

The amount of compensation paid to individual physicians varies significantly based on several factors:

- Physician performance

- Physician experience

- Unique demands of the surgical hospitalist program (e.g., trauma center and night coverage)

- Regional recruiting trends

In all but a few situations, compensation levels will fall between the 25th and 75th percentiles of benchmark compensation, with a growing number of surgical hospitalists expecting to earn in the third quartile—approximately $325,000–$410,000 per surgeon, according to the most recent benchmark data.

> **TIP: HOW MUCH TO PAY A SURGEON**
> Most surgical hospitalists expect to earn approximately $325,000 –$410,000.

Figure 7.2 illustrates the compensation range for the most recent five-year period.

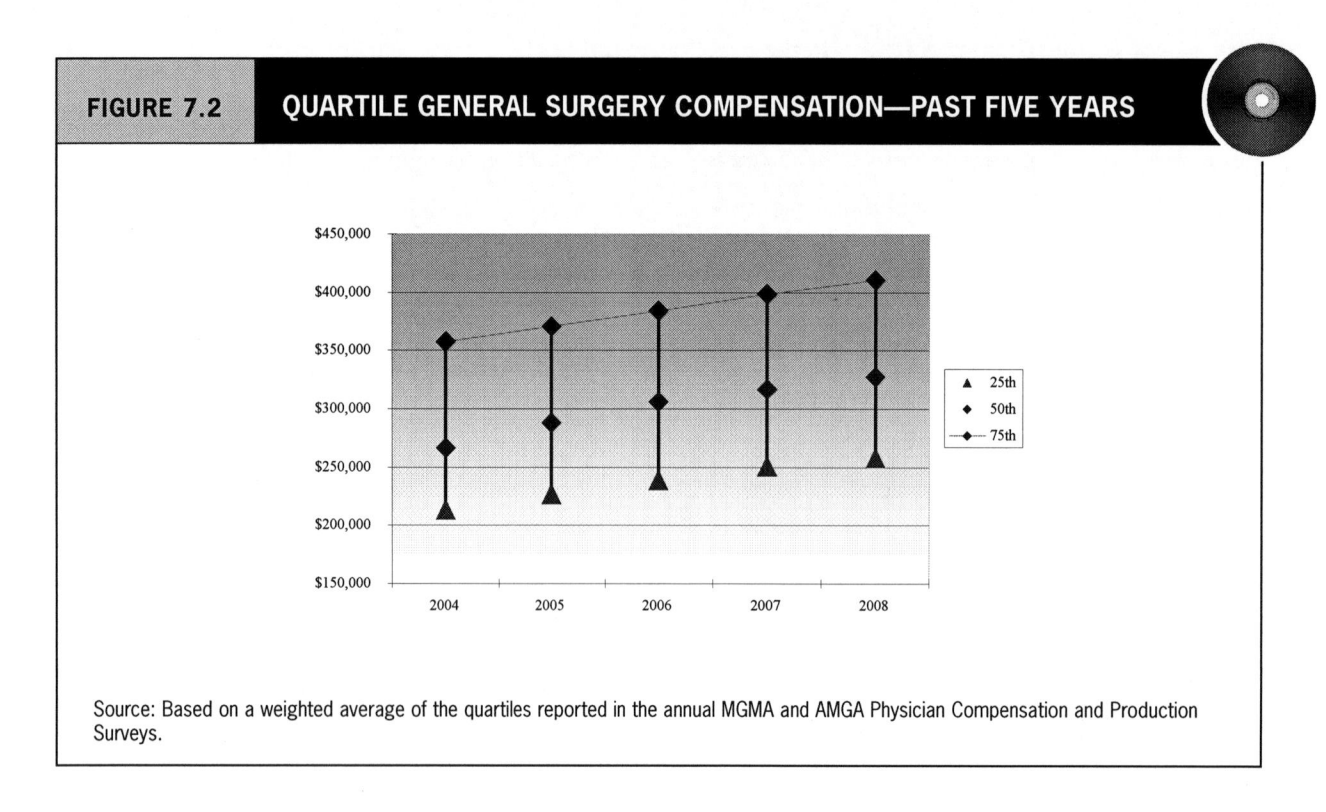

| FIGURE 7.2 | QUARTILE GENERAL SURGERY COMPENSATION—PAST FIVE YEARS |

Source: Based on a weighted average of the quartiles reported in the annual MGMA and AMGA Physician Compensation and Production Surveys.

Although the benchmark data are important to establishing an estimate for market compensation, published survey data will show variation in all of the compensation and production metrics, and, regardless of the source, these data should not serve as the only determinant of appropriate compensation for a particular program. Instead, the benchmark data should serve only as a guide, and adjustments to actual compensation levels should typically be based on local and regional marketplace factors.

For instance, surgeons practicing in a Level III trauma center will typically demand higher compensation than those practicing in a community hospital without a trauma program. Another example may be related to a difficult practice location, wherein higher compensation is necessary to offset the less desirable geographic location. For example, hospitals in the Central Valley of California generally are required to offer compensation packages that surpass hospitals located in major metropolitan areas.

Models of Compensation

Although there is no single best compensation model for surgical hospitalists, several common models exist. The common options can be grouped into three categories: (1) salary-based, (2) productivity- and performance-based, or (3) hybrid salary plus incentives. Each surgical hospitalist program should first determine the goals and objectives of the program and then use this information to develop a compensation model that is tailored to align individual physician behaviors with program goals.

MODELS OF COMPENSATION

- Salary-based compensation
- Productivity- and performance-based compensation
- Hybrid compensation model: Base salary with incentive

Salary-based compensation

Across the healthcare industry, the straight salary-based compensation model is increasingly uncommon except for newly recruited physicians, who generally want a level of financial assurance before relocating. However, it is commonly used when a new surgical hospitalist program requires a base level of clinical coverage, and a fixed salary is required to limit the physicians' downside risk.

Typically, the fixed salary is based on a per-shift compensation rate to give full-time surgeons flexibility, as many practice as part-time surgical hospitalists and spend the remainder of their time in other work such as a private surgical practice. Figure 7.3 illustrates how to calculate the per-shift salary rate.

Chapter 7

FIGURE 7.3 SHIFT-BASED COMPENSATION CALCULATION

Note: Figures may not be exact due to rounding.

Variable		Example
Annual patient care hours per clinical FTE	A	2,000
Patient care coverage hour per shift	B	12
Annual shifts per clinical FTE	C = A ÷ B	167
Annual compensation rate	D	$320,000
Compensation per shift	E = D ÷ C	$1,920

Source: Hypothetical illustration based on ECG Management Consultants, Inc., client experience.

Although the simplicity of offering a fixed salary is advantageous to both the program and the surgeon for budgeting purposes, a fixed salary fails to drive improved performance and does not adjust for increased productivity and demands on the surgeon. Because the model provides the same income regardless of physician productivity levels, it provides little incentive for physicians to maintain or increase productivity. This creates three obvious challenges:

- Increasing shortfalls in professional fee revenue to offset the salary, resulting in growing program financial losses

- Operational and group conflicts over workload and scheduling expectations

- Retention of physicians due to an imbalance in the ratio of compensation to production compared to the market

The discrepancy in paying surgeons market competitive rates is illustrated in Figure 7.4 by comparing a fixed-salary model to market compensation-to-production levels.

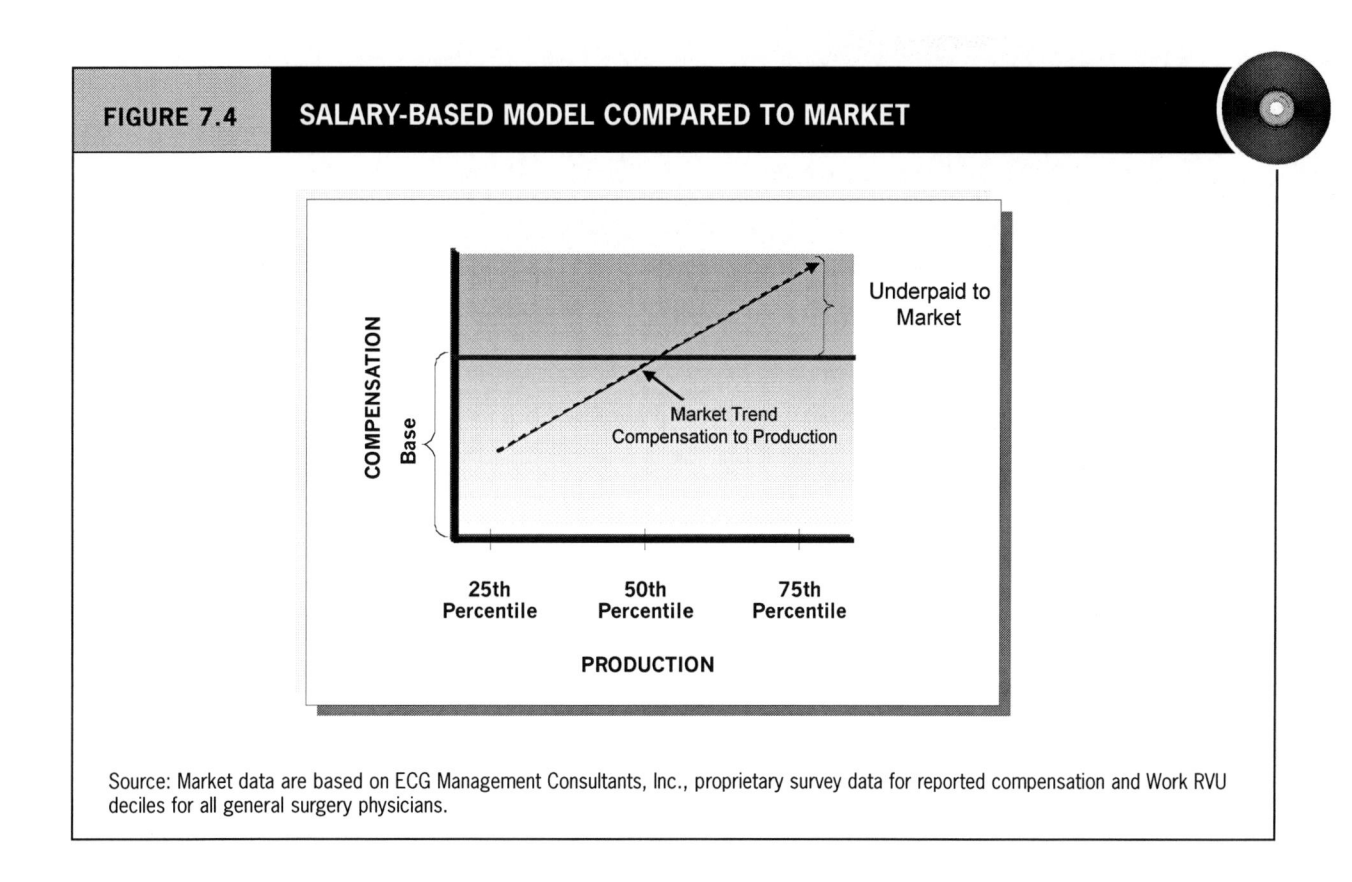

FIGURE 7.4   SALARY-BASED MODEL COMPARED TO MARKET

Source: Market data are based on ECG Management Consultants, Inc., proprietary survey data for reported compensation and Work RVU deciles for all general surgery physicians.

Productivity- and performance-based compensation

Although a majority of general surgeons are paid based on productivity-based compensation models,[1] only a small number of surgical hospitalists are compensated this way. One reason for this difference is the relative lack of historical data and experience in the surgical hospitalist field. Another reason for this difference is that hospital-based programs generally require a minimum amount of clinical coverage and do not allow for the adjustment of physician resources to patient demand that traditional surgical practices do. For instance, in many programs, the surgical hospitalist is on shift to take care of hospital emergency department and unassigned inpatients; the surgical hospitalist should not be encouraged to actively seek elective referrals to increase productivity. Encouraging such behavior would likely incite political challenges with nonhospitalist surgeons at the hospital, if the surgical hospitalist program were not inclusive of all interested surgeons on the medical staff.

However, although compensation based entirely on production is not prevalent, it will likely gain more acceptance as program administrators and surgical hospitalists gain experience and confidence in

Chapter 7

patient volume and physician productivity statistics. If a program administrator has confidence in the data and enough of a historical track record of past performance to forecast future performance, he or she should not be deterred from considering a productivity-based compensation model, as this model presents several key advantages. Foremost, it aligns the economics of the program with individual physicians. In addition, by setting strong productivity incentives, regardless of physicians' current productivity level, this model shifts responsibility for earning potential to the physician.

Several metrics can be used to incentivize productivity, including:

- Work RVUs (wRVU)

- Surgical cases

- Charges

- Net revenue or collections

- Contribution margin

By far, collections or wRVUs are the best metrics for tying compensation to productivity because both incorporate more specificity in financial performance or workload. The advantages and disadvantages for widely used metrics are summarized in Figure 7.5.

Productivity-based systems can be adjusted in several ways to further incentivize certain behaviors. One example is a tiered incentive model that distributes a higher compensation amount per work unit as production passes select thresholds. The benefit is that the compensation model more closely approximates market-level compensation because production levels influence individual effective overhead rates. This model creates greater incentives and more pay to higher-producing physicians. Figure 7.6 illustrates this model.

Surgical Hospital Compensation Planning

FIGURE 7.5 — COMMON PRODUCTIVITY METRICS

Productivity metric	Advantages	Disadvantages
Work RVUs	Most accurate measure of physician work effort	Surgeons may not be in direct control of productivity
Surgical cases/inpatient consults/clinic visits	Most aligned with perceived day-to-day activity of physician	It is difficult to assign relative value or reimbursement between settings
Gross charges	Accurate measure of total surgeon productivity	This metric does not factor in actual reimbursement; benchmarks are irrelevant
Net revenue	True measure of paid value, factoring in payer mix	Physicians at risk for payer mix and collections performance
Contribution	Alignment of practice group net revenue and costs with physician behavior	This metric requires the formation and accounting of small practice groups, or "pods," within the group

Source: Based on ECG Management Consultants, Inc., client experience.

FIGURE 7.6 — TIERED PRODUCTIVITY COMPENSATION PLAN

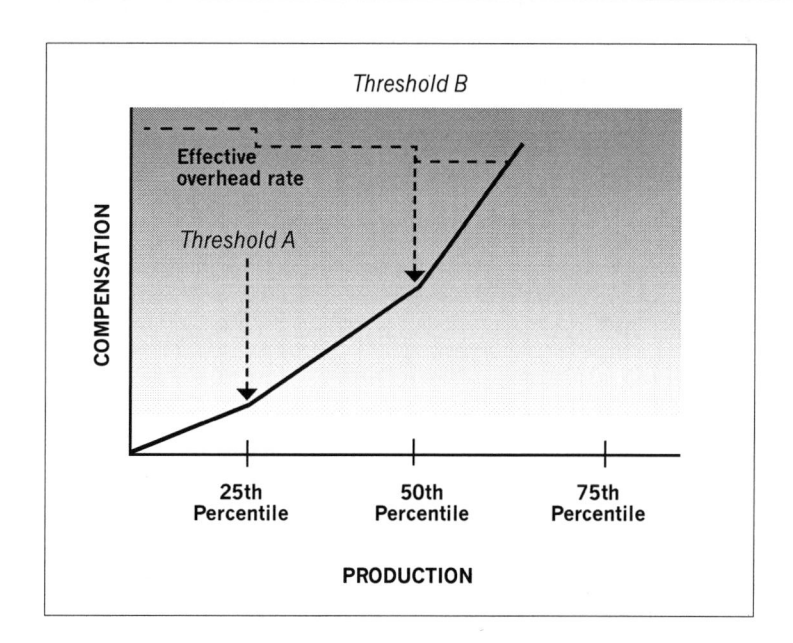

Graph showing COMPENSATION (y-axis) vs. PRODUCTION (x-axis) with markers at 25th Percentile, 50th Percentile, and 75th Percentile. Threshold A is indicated near the 25th percentile, Threshold B near the 50th percentile, with an "Effective overhead rate" labeled between them.

Source: Market data are based on ECG Management Consultants, Inc., proprietary survey data for reported compensation and wRVU deciles for all general surgery physicians.

Chapter 7

Hybrid compensation model: Base salary with incentive

A frequently recommended compensation model is a plan that includes a modest base salary and then introduces a productivity incentive after a certain productivity threshold is attained. Figure 7.7 illustrates how this model limits surgeons' downside risk by placing a floor on compensation levels, while adding an incentive to provide additional income for any productivity that the physician generates above a given threshold. This is a commonly adopted model for surgical hospitalists because it compensates physicians for both coverage and higher performance.

Setting the base and productivity incentive in tandem to reward physicians appropriately requires thorough analysis and financial modeling. Many organizations set the targets at the median benchmarks or percentages of the median (e.g., 90% of median) to accentuate the productivity component. The challenge is first setting the productivity threshold so it is within reach of the surgical hospitalist, as the model may not provide a meaningful incentive if the base salary is set too high. Setting the productivity threshold and compensation per work unit, in turn, affects where the base salary is set. Once implemented, ensure that scheduling and workload distribution between the surgical hospitalists allows each

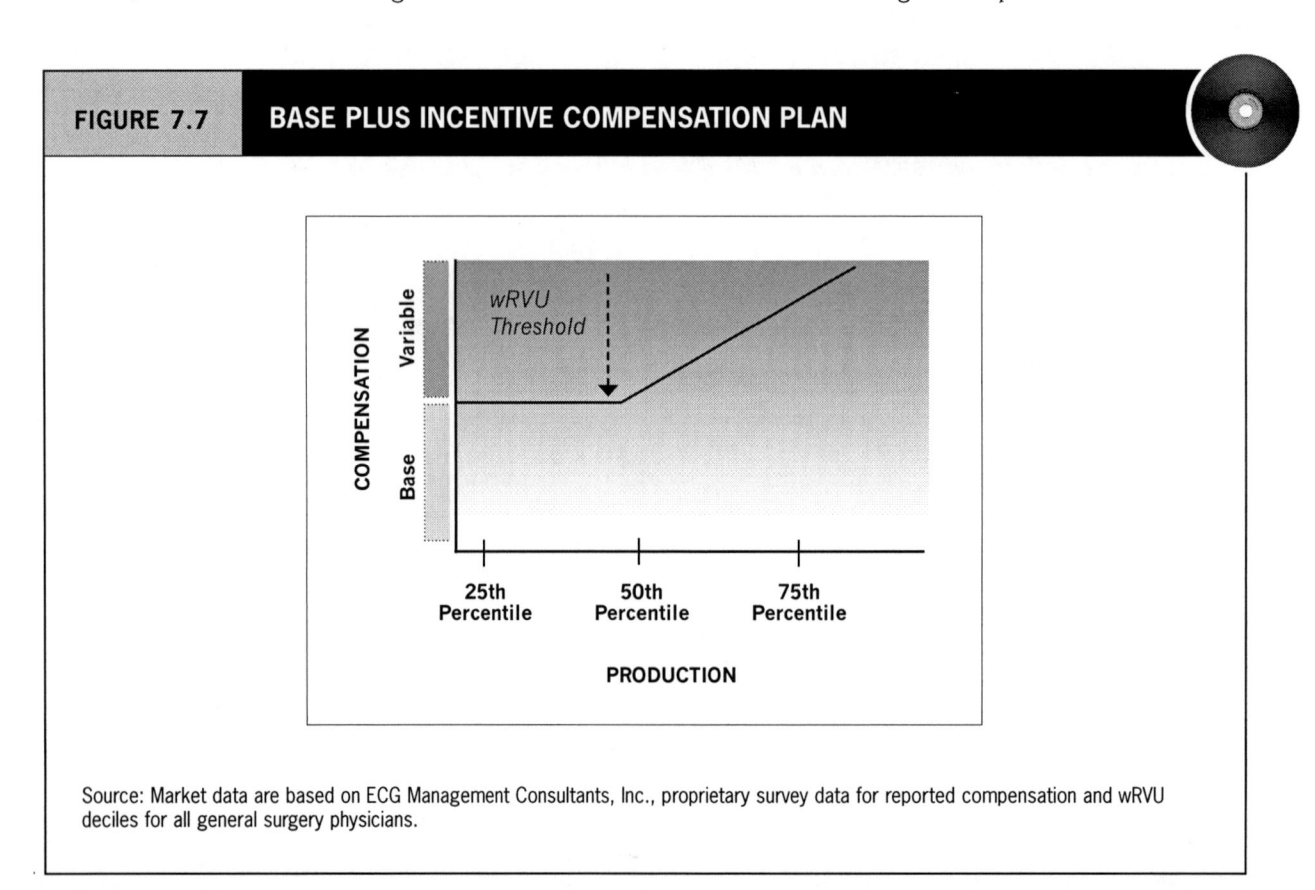

FIGURE 7.7 BASE PLUS INCENTIVE COMPENSATION PLAN

Source: Market data are based on ECG Management Consultants, Inc., proprietary survey data for reported compensation and wRVU deciles for all general surgery physicians.

an equal opportunity for work and income. If distributing the workload fairly among the surgical hospitalists presents a significant concern, the program can evaluate a group-based productivity incentive, in which physicians' aggregate work efforts determine the paid productivity bonus amount.

Other potential features: Bonus pools

A bonus pool can be added to a fixed/productivity compensation model to create non–production-based physician incentives. Bonuses are allocated based on meeting set targets. The bonus pool provides funding for performance incentives such as cost control, citizenship, program development, and clinical quality. The incentives can be based on an endless number of quality- and service-related goals and metrics related to the Surgical Care Improvement Project.

For example, a surgical hospitalist program would define four performance goals and assign $5,000 in bonus compensation if the targets are attained. Establishment of these incentives generally requires that at least 10% of the total compensation be assigned to the aggregate bonus pool to effectively encourage behavior (e.g., four metrics, each of which is paid at 2.5% of total compensation). Adding a bonus requirement to a compensation plan requires management to exercise discipline to avoid bonuses becoming giveaways to physicians.

Example compensation plan

Figure 7.8 summarizes an example of a surgical hospitalist compensation plan. Under the example compensation plan, a full-time surgical hospitalist who produces at the MGMA median level and meets all performance targets would make approximately $340,000 in annual compensation.

FIGURE 7.8 SAMPLE COMPENSATION PLAN

Compensation component	Description/assumptions
Base salary	Base compensation is set at $320,000, based on the MGMA national median for general surgeons
Productivity incentive	• The productivity threshold is set at the MGMA national median level of 7,170 wRVUs • Surgeons will receive a payment of $44.20 per work wRVU above 7,170, based on industry median benchmarks
Performance incentive	• The hospital and the surgeons agree on four quality/performance improvement metrics • Surgeons will receive a maximum of $5,000 in incentive payments for achieving each of the targets

Source: Salary is based on *MGMA Physician Compensation and Production Survey: 2008 Report Based on 2007 Data*. Rounded up to the nearest $10,000 to reflect age of data.

Special Consideration

Modeling the proposed formula

Fear of the unknown is always a major concern when setting physician compensation, as physicians will rightfully want to know, with as much certainty as possible, how their pay will be affected. Therefore, it is absolutely essential to run the numbers on the proposed compensation formula using the most recent available data. Performing a sensitivity analysis, in which different assumptions about variables, such as patient volume and payer mix, will allow physicians to see for themselves how their individual incomes will be affected by any changes. Another important reason to do so is to help ensure that the aggregate amount of physician compensation is appropriate and falls within fair market value standards. Few things could be more upsetting to a group of physicians than to be offered a compensation formula, only to have it be subsequently changed because the organization can no longer afford to pay the promised amount.

Surgical Hospital Compensation Planning

The most important reason for analyzing the projected compensation figures is that it is the only way to ensure that the formula works as intended. Invariably, modifications to the productivity threshold(s) and/or payment rates of the compensation formula may initially produce results that are not entirely predictable or desirable. What follows, then, is an iterative process of adjusting the model and examining the results until they are satisfactory.

If a change is being made to an existing compensation model, keep one caveat in mind: When communicating revised compensation to physicians, convey clearly that future incomes will differ from the projected amount. Specifically, projected amounts are based on historical performance, and because actual performance will vary, compensation levels will also vary. Other changes may likely be required if market data indicate a change in compensation, especially if the compensation model ties certain payment elements to market statistics. It may be helpful to explain the results in terms of showing what the physicians would have made last year if the compensation formula were in effect, as opposed to showing what they should expect to make next year.

Checking the compensation model against the objectives

As the surgical hospitalist program continues to function, consider not only the effect on each surgeon's overall compensation, but also the incentives for increasing productivity, enhancing quality, and meeting other organizational expectations. Focusing solely on total compensation is a common mistake, as income is foremost in physicians' minds. However, there are many ways to redistribute income, and many of them may not be aligned with the broader objectives of the surgical hospitalist program. The compensation model should be continually examined to ensure that physician compensation falls within appropriate ranges and drives the desired outcomes for the surgeon and the hospital.

Keys to success

Physician compensation planning requires a process that ensures that physicians accept the model that can drive the intended outcomes. Some suggestions for guiding the process and ensuring a successful outcome are detailed below.

KEYS TO SUCCESS

Physician direction

- Recruit opinion leaders to assist in the design of the compensation plan

Market relevance

- Pay competitive income for competitive work effort

Flexibility

- Adopt a plan that flexes with the market annually

Transition

- Plan design must include analysis of the effect of the transition to the new structure and may require temporary income protection

Communication

- Communicate fully and frequently to all physicians

Simplicity and objectivity

- Establish understandable, objective, and measurable incentives

Alignment of incentives

- Align physician and organization incentives

Respect for culture

- Respect the differences in the decision-making process and organizational style within the medical group

Resist making special deals

- Once the planning process is complete, stay true to the decisions that the committee made

Creating or modifying a compensation formula is a technical and political challenge because physician compensation is inherently an emotionally charged issue. This necessitates a very rational and fact-based approach to keep emotions from clouding sound decision-making. In surgical hospitalist programs, the effort should be led by a balanced, thoughtful group of representatives that includes surgeons and hospital executives. These leaders should include and be supported by individuals experienced in the type of analysis and process management that this undertaking requires. To achieve consensus, physicians must first understand how their compensation compares to the market benchmarks. They also must understand the changes to their income that are likely to occur and how compensation will compare to the market once the model is implemented. Finally, it is imperative that the compensation model creates incentives that will motivate physicians toward behaviors that are consistent with the greater objectives of the organization.

ENDNOTE

1. ECG 2008 proprietary physician compensation and benefits surveys reported that 78% of general surgeons reported that their total compensation was composed of more than 50% productivity incentive payment.

CHAPTER 8

Surgical Hospitalist Scheduling

John Nelson, MD, FACP

Despite decades of experience, there are no data to prove what is the best schedule for any particular specialty in medicine. Although the work schedule of a resident in training has been the subject of increasing study, conclusions from the residency setting probably have limited application to practicing surgeons/physicians outside of a training environment. Thus, the best ideas regarding a surgical hospitalist's potential work schedule will come from the experience of several groups:

- Existing surgical hospitalist practices

- General surgeons in traditional practice

- Medical hospitalists

All three of these sources provide a framework for thinking about scheduling principles in any particular surgical hospitalist setting. The best way to use this information is to balance it with the needs of the local healthcare system and the preferences of the surgical hospitalists.

Challenges in Developing a Surgical Hospitalist Schedule

There are several challenges to keep in mind when developing a surgical hospitalist schedule, including:

- Unpredictable workloads

- Around-the-clock responsibilities

- Call frequency

- Importance of continuity and timeliness of care

Chapter 8

- Providing for outpatient follow-up

- Influence of operating room (OR) scheduling on the surgical hospitalists' schedule

- Interplay between scheduling and staffing needs

- Surgical hospitalist lifestyle and quality of life

Although general surgeons in a traditional practice and physicians in other specialties share many of these challenges, the challenges can be different for surgical hospitalists.

Unpredictable workloads

Although day-to-day work volume varies in nearly all medical specialties, those without a scheduled portion to their day, such as an outpatient clinic, potentially face more dramatic swings in volume from one day to the next. It is natural to think of surgical hospitalists' work volume in terms of the daily average workload, but there will be relatively few days in which the volume is average. Volume can vary from 50% of average one day to 150% of average the next. Therefore, it is important to build into the schedule a method, such as a backup surgeon, that ensures surge capacity.

Around-the-clock responsibilities

Surgical hospitalists usually take on a greater portion of night responsibility than do surgeons in traditional practices that are responsible for patient care at all hours. On any given night, it is more likely for the surgical hospitalist to be working during hours usually reserved for sleep than it is for most other surgeons. In most surgical hospitalist practices, work volume does not vary according to day of the week; they have the same work volume on weekends and holidays. Therefore, these days should be scheduled just like weekdays (i.e., surgical hospitalists usually won't be able to decrease their scheduled staff members on weekends and holidays).

Call frequency

Surgical hospitalists may fill a deficit in emergency department call coverage. A surgical hospitalist's nights are typically busier than those of other community surgeons; however, their Monday-through-Friday daytime work might be less busy on many days because of their limited scheduled office hours each week, and because their referral volume of hospital patients is low on some days. Because some days are not busy, some surgical hospitalists are willing to take night call more often than are their colleagues in traditional general surgery practice. Even if a surgical hospitalist's schedule leads to more frequent on-call duties than might be typical for other surgeons, some surgical hospitalists might view the total workload as reasonable. However, many surgeons seek the surgical hospitalist role for lifestyle reasons, and they may be unwilling to consider a call frequency that is any greater than typical for the community.

Importance of continuity of care

There is value in scheduling surgical hospitalists in a way that maximizes the portion of patients who see the same surgeon for their surgery and for all of their pre- and postoperative care. Designing such a schedule should reduce errors and increase patient satisfaction. However, such continuity is not possible for every patient, so each practice should carefully consider the tradeoff between continuity and surgeon lifestyle. Some practices are structured so that each surgical hospitalist is regarded as interchangeable for each patient, and whichever doctor is on duty will perform the operation and round on the patient without regard to which surgeon visited the patient previously. This may be the simplest way to ensure that a schedule is easy to create and provides for optimal lifestyle for the surgeons, but it may come at a cost in efficiency, quality, and patient satisfaction.

Providing for outpatient follow-up

Each surgical hospitalist practice should provide a mechanism by which surgeons see postoperative patients in outpatient follow-up for one or more visits. Patients seen by the surgical hospitalist while hospitalized, but who did not have an operation, may or may not be seen in posthospital follow-up by the surgical hospitalist. The best approach will vary depending on local circumstances and the complexity of the patient's condition. In most cases, each surgical hospitalist schedules outpatient office hours roughly half a day per week (e.g., four hours). The practice should ensure that this outpatient work does not result in too much of a disruption to inpatient duties, so the practice may choose to schedule it on days the surgeon has no inpatient responsibility or is serving as back up or second call to a partner surgeon.

Influence of OR scheduling on the surgical hospitalists' schedule

If the OR schedule is so busy that a large portion of the surgical hospitalists' cases need to start as add-ons late in the evening, the schedule should provide for a dedicated night shift staffed by someone who is not the day surgeon and who is rested and able to do the operations. (Refer to the case study from Anne Arundel Medical Center in Chapter 16.) If, instead, the OR can provide guaranteed block time during the daytime hours, it is more reasonable for the surgical hospitalist to work during the day and stay on call by pager many of the nights.

Chapter 8

Interplay between scheduling and staffing needs

The choice of schedule significantly influences an individual surgeon's productivity and how many surgeons will be needed to staff the practice. For example, what appears to be a staffing problem (e.g., the practice seems to require more surgeons) might actually be an issue of poor scheduling. A common problem faced by many practices is whether to have a separate night shift surgeon who has no responsibilities on the day before or after the night shift. Although such dedicated night shift is desirable, it results in a need for more surgeons to staff the practice than if they take night call from home as doctors have done traditionally. Whether it is worthwhile for a small practice to maintain a separate night shift will depend on many local factors, including patient care volume, doctor lifestyle, flexibility, and business operations. Refer to Figure 8.1 for a checklist.

Specific Scheduling Issues

Allocating operative and nonoperative work

At some practices, the patient is seen by whichever surgeon is on duty when the patient needs attention (e.g., at the time of admission or when OR time is available). For example, at 2 p.m. on Monday, one surgeon admits a patient who needs surgery within the next 24 hours. The OR will likely offer one of the following: (1) to schedule a time slot late Tuesday afternoon, or (2) to schedule the case as an add-on case at 9 or 10 p.m. Monday. The admitting surgeon decides whether it is better to wait until late the next afternoon, when he or she can perform the operation him- or herself, or whether the patient can be scheduled for the add-on slot that evening, when another surgical hospitalist would be on duty and perform the operation.

A practice that schedules the surgical hospitalists to work during the daytime and remain on call that night has the same surgeon admit the patient and perform the operation, regardless of whether it takes place that night or the next day. But a practice that has a separate day and night shift surgeon will need to decide whether it is more important to have the operation sooner by a surgeon who has not seen the patient previously or to delay the operation until the next day so the admitting surgeon can perform the surgery.

There are many tradeoffs in deciding which approach is best. One major issue is surgeon compensation. Does the admitting surgeon have a personal economic incentive to perform the surgery him or herself rather than having a partner cover the case? Another issue is the availability of OR time. Is the OR willing to start cases at night that are not truly emergent but that are being done at that time

FIGURE 8.1 — CHECKLIST FOR EVALUATING A SURGICAL HOSPITALIST SCHEDULE

Consider evaluating the schedule model along the following four metrics. These metrics provide assistance in thinking about alternative scheduling. They do not provide a rigid analysis or scoring system that identifies the best schedule.

Patient care: Does the schedule compromise the quality or safety of patient care?

- Does the schedule provide for reasonable patient–surgical hospitalist continuity?
- Does the schedule provide for a reasonable patient load per doctor?*

MD lifestyle

- Does the schedule allow sufficient time off?
- Does the schedule provide for flexibility of time off (i.e., time off when desired rather than only when the schedule provides it)?
- Are worked days/nights routinely too short or too long?
- Does the schedule require a doctor to change from day to night work too often?
- Does the schedule provide for an equitable number of worked weekends?
- How does the group perceive the burnout risk of the schedule?
- Does the schedule have a way to handle sudden absences (e.g., due to illness)?

Flexibility

- Does the schedule allow for adjusting staff resources to varying patient loads?
- Does the schedule anticipate how additional doctors will be added to the schedule?

Business operations

- Does the schedule optimize production capacity of available manpower?
- Does the schedule permit flexibility for nonclinical activity, such as committee work?

*In measuring patient load per doctor, use operative cases and daily encounters over long periods, such as a year, rather than the average daily census or average daily surgical case volume. Also, look at more than the averages—think about how often a doctor's patient load exceeds what is regarded as the maximum safe daily load.

Source: Adapted and used with permission from *Hospitalists: A Guide to Building and Sustaining a Successful Program*, by Joseph A. Miller, John Nelson, and Winthrop F. Whitcomb. (Chicago: Health Administration Press, 2008), p. 135.

because the surgical hospitalist is available then? (Refer to Chapter 6 for more information about the interplay between surgical hospitalist practice and OR scheduling.)

Determining the best approach for a particular practice will require balancing the costs and benefits of continuity (e.g., same surgeon provides operative and nonoperative care) against the risk of surgeon fatigue and sleep deprivation. Unfortunately, there is no research evidence that clearly proves the best approach for a particular practice, and the decision will need to be a product of thoughtful deliberation.

Night and weekend work

Scheduling a night shift surgeon who has no responsibility the day before or after the night shift should reduce surgeon burnout and fatigue-related errors. This may be prohibitively expensive in most small practices, but it becomes more financially viable for larger practices. Hospitals with Level I and II trauma designation must have a trauma surgeon in-house around the clock, and in many cases, the surgical hospitalist will fill this role. In most practices that cover one hospital and have such a dedicated night shift, the night shift doctor is expected to be in the hospital for the entire shift. If the surgical hospitalists cover more than one hospital at night, they are usually on call for each hospital, with the expectation that they will be working most of each night and not trying to sleep at home.

In smaller practices, the surgical hospitalist usually manages night call by pager from outside the hospital. Many of these practices have the surgical hospitalist(s) alternate night call with other local surgeons in traditional practice, since a one- or two-person surgical hospitalist practice may not be able to manage all of the night call without additional help. If there are no other local surgeons available to participate in a shared night coverage arrangement with the surgical hospitalists, there are several options to consider:

- Surgical resident or fellows

- In-hospital medical hospitalists who serve as first responders but call in the surgical hospitalist when needed

- Increase the volume of night work to support increased surgical hospitalist staffing at night

- Nonphysician providers such as nurse practitioners (NP) and physician assistants (PA)

Residents and fellows

Another option is to hire surgical residents or fellows from a nearby training program to provide primary coverage at night (and/or on weekends). Depending on the level of training of the covering trainee, the surgical hospitalist might still need to remain available as backup for more complicated patients. If trainees are hired only for night coverage, they usually do a small volume of billable work, and it may be reasonable to simply have the attending surgical hospitalist bill for services provided starting the next morning and forgo billing for the trainee's work overnight. However, if a resident or fellow provides coverage for a whole weekend, it will usually be best to ensure that person is fully qualified to operate independently and becomes credentialed with payers and submits professional fee charges.

Medical hospitalists

An alternative to investigate is whether the medical hospitalists (or even the emergency department doctors at some very small hospitals) can serve as first call for the surgical hospitalists at night. The surgeons should remain available for emergency surgery and consultation, but the hospitalists could manage many other issues, such as admitting nonurgent patients who can safely wait until the next morning and addressing issues such as pain and fever on the surgical hospitalist's patients.

Add night work to support increased surgical hospitalist staffing

Surgical hospitalists can look for ways to increase the amount of night work they do so that the night shift generates more professional fee revenue. That extra revenue could pay for an additional doctor for the practice to help share the burden of night call, resulting in a more sustainable work schedule. There are few opportunities to increase night work for surgeons, but one example could be for surgical hospitalists who are also board-certified in critical care to share ICU night call with other doctors at a small hospital.

Nonphysician (mid-level) providers

Nonphysician providers (NPs and PAs) could, in some settings, serve as the first responder at night with the surgical hospitalist physician remaining available as backup. The surgeon would always need to be available in person for any surgery or invasive procedure, but the nonphysician provider could potentially do the initial evaluation on new referrals and handle issues that arise for existing patients so that the surgical hospitalist wouldn't have to be the first responder.

Chapter 8

A hospital considering the addition of a dedicated in-house night shift for surgical hospitalists should think carefully about what this addition might mean for OR scheduling. The night shift surgeon will likely be able to perform some nonemergent cases at night. However, increasing OR volume at night requires more than just an available surgeon; it involves other parties, including the OR staff and the anesthesia department, who should be included in the discussions about this. In busy hospitals, it might be cost-effective to increase night OR staffing to support an increase in volume resulting from the night surgical hospitalist.

Outpatient work

Unlike medical hospitalists, surgical hospitalists in nearly all practices will need to spend a portion of their time seeing patients in an outpatient clinic. It is common for each doctor to have outpatient time limited to roughly half a day per week (e.g., four hours) and to see only hospital follow-up patients and no new outpatient elective referrals. This is often done to prevent the surgical hospitalist from building an elective referral practice that would compete with existing surgeons in traditional practice and distract the surgical hospitalist from hospital-focused practice (e.g., care of unassigned emergency patients). Without having constraints on outpatient practice, some surgeons may use the surgical hospitalist role solely to buy time until he or she can build an adequate base of elective referrals that would lead to a resignation from the hospitalist role, resulting in an undesirably high turnover rate for surgical hospitalists. Surgical hospitalists are usually content to limit outpatient practice to hospital follow-ups since many surgeons seek the hospitalist role to avoid developing and managing an outpatient practice.

Small practices with one surgical hospitalist on duty each day will generally use the same doctor to cover the outpatient clinic while also on duty for the hospital. However, in larger practices, the surgeon is in the clinic only during scheduled times, when he or she has no hospital or on-call responsibilities.

Creating the schedule

Important variables in a work schedule include:

- The number of consecutive days worked

- The number of days or nights worked annually

- The typical duration of each worked day

To ensure continuity between surgeon and patient during the hospital stay, surgical hospitalists should work as many consecutive days as are consistent with maintaining a reasonable lifestyle. The number of days or nights, worked annually can vary significantly from one practice to the next. Keep in mind that, as the number of annual days worked decreases, the workload for each day must increase to maintain reasonable annual productivity. And as the average daily workload increases, it becomes more difficult for the surgeon to work many consecutive days, and continuity may suffer. Every practice should make an effort to find the optimal balance between the number of worked days and the workload on the average day.

For some people, the term "hospitalist" has come to have a connotation of shift work in which the doctor has clearly defined hours of responsibility without call or pager coverage outside of those hours. Although that can be a reasonable arrangement in some situations, it has drawbacks and may not be feasible in many practices. A schedule of fixed duration shifts (e.g., 12 hours) means that the practice plans for 12 hours of patient care work during every day shift, but that may happen only on a handful of days each year. Instead, there probably will be many days in which it would have been ideal for the practice to provide significantly more or fewer hours of surgeon staff members. By avoiding shifts of a predetermined fixed duration, surgeons can adjust their daily work effort and duration to more closely match the patient load that day. Figure 8.2 describes some pros and cons of fixed shifts.

A popular scheduling model for medical hospitalists, and for some surgical hospitalists, is the seven-on/seven-off schedule: Each doctor works seven consecutive days, followed by seven consecutive days off. This model is most often coupled with fixed 12-hour shifts (note concerns about fixed shift lengths in the prior paragraph) and requires a total of four full-time doctors. Two doctors work each week, one on day shifts and the other on night shifts, and the other two doctors are off. During the following week, their roles are reversed. Each individual doctor will work seven day shifts, have seven days off, work seven night shifts, have no scheduled work for the next seven days, and then repeat the cycle. This schedule is popular because it provides the doctors with liberal amounts of time off, ensures reasonable doctor-patient continuity, and is easy to keep track of and simple to plot out on the calendar.

These benefits of a seven-on/seven-off schedule are offset, at least partially, by the fact that it requires four full-time doctors to support such a schedule, and many, or even most, surgical hospitalist practices do not have patient volume sufficient to support four surgeons. Another drawback is that it can lead to a systole-diastole segregation of personal and professional time, which might increase burnout,

FIGURE 8.2: PROS & CONS OF ELIMINATING FIXED START/STOP TIMES FOR DAY SHIFT

Pros	Cons

• Adjusts daily manpower to match that day's workload
 	
• Adjusts some working days to be shorter than a fixed-duration shift schedule, thereby:
   – Making it possible to work more consecutive days to maximize continuity of care
   – Potentially preventing burnout, since every worked day is not long (e.g., a 12-hour fixed shift)
   – Making it easier to work more days annually, which may increase productivity and participation in other hospital activities, such as committee work
 	
• Encourages doctors to take more control over the pace of their work (e.g., when they start and stop, for how long they take breaks, etc.)
	• Hospitalist may be out of the building in the afternoon when the patient deteriorates and needs to be seen again
	   – *Note:* This drawback can be partially addressed by requiring all hospitalists to stay on their pagers until the night shift starts and by requiring that at least one doctor stay in the hospital at all times
	
	• Less predictable effect on personal lifestyle (e.g., hard to know exactly when physician will be home each day)
	
	• It is more complicated to create a month's schedule than if all shifts are identical

Source: Adapted and used with permission from *Hospitalists: A Guide to Building and Sustaining a Successful Program*, by Joseph A. Miller, John Nelson, and Winthrop F. Whitcomb. (Chicago: Health Administration Press, 2008), p. 138.

regardless of all the time off it provides. And a schedule of working every other week means that a surgeon will work only 182 shifts annually, half of which might be very low-productivity night shifts. That could lead to low overall annual productivity (most billable work is generated during the seven day shifts out of every 28 days), which may not be financially viable. Lastly, such a schedule gets in the way of each hospitalist being involved in hospital activities that don't follow an alternate week schedule, such as quality improvement and committee work.

There are many scheduling possibilities in addition to a seven-on/seven-off schedule. Many surgical hospitalist practices might start with a single surgical hospitalist who, on most weeks, works a Monday-through-Friday daytime schedule and shares night and weekend call with other community surgeons. As the number of surgical hospitalists in the practice grows, the surgical hospitalists themselves could begin handling more of their night and weekend work and rely less on community surgeons for help at these times. For example, one of the surgical hospitalists in the group might work every weekend, with a community surgeon paid to be on backup if patient volume requires it (e.g., the backup surgeon rounds on half the surgical hospitalist patients Saturday and Sunday and is available in case there are two patients that need surgery at the same time).

A wide variety of scheduling options are reasonable for surgical hospitalists, and opinion and preference govern the choice much more than any hard data or scientific evidence. Each group will need to make their own choices about the schedule that optimally balance the needs of patients and the hospital, while providing for a sustainable and rewarding physician lifestyle.

CHAPTER 9

Communication Issues in Surgical Hospitalist Practice

John Nelson, MD, FACP • John Maa, MD, FACS

This chapter will review important issues related to surgical hospitalists' communication with patients, the patient's primary care physician (PCP), and the referring or consulting physician. Effective communication while providing consults is critical to patient flow, safety, patient satisfaction, and efficient consult care. In addition, it can increase revenue for a surgical hospitalist program: The satisfaction of referring physicians can be key to building a successful practice, whether academic or private. Also recognize that the medical liability for an undesirable outcome can extend to the consulting service, the consultant, and all of those involved in the care of the patient. A safe clinician will always be wary of possible truncations in messages, chart lore, and miscommunications that can occur during shift change. To address these issues, the communication experiences of medical hospitalists provide several ideas and insights useful to a high-functioning surgical hospitalist practice.

Communication with Patients, Families, and Significant Others

Although general surgeons have always met a portion of their patients for the first time during an unplanned hospitalization or emergency surgery, surgical hospitalists will meet essentially all of their patients in this way. Thorough communication is critical to building rapport and providing information, yet time is often limited, and the patient and family are often worried and less able to understand the information presented than they might otherwise be. Thus, surgical hospitalists need to think carefully about how to become efficient and effective communicators; it is integral to their field.

Surgical hospitalists should introduce themselves to each new patient and develop a brief (no more than a minute or so) script to describe their role. It might be reasonable to say, "I am Dr. Smith. I'm a general surgeon with a practice dedicated to the care of hospitalized patients like you. I work with your other doctors in and out of the hospital and will be in communication with your primary care doctor about your illness and my findings."

Chapter 9

The surgical hospitalists and hospital leadership should work continuously to ensure that others at the hospital describe the surgical hospitalist in a similar fashion. Without being provided with such a script, other hospital personnel may tell patients and families that the surgical hospitalist is "our house surgeon" or use other language that may not inspire the patient's confidence. Patients and families want to know that an expert is providing their care, and other staff members may unintentionally give them the impression they've arrived at an expensive restaurant only to be told that the house wine (house surgeon) is their only option, when they perceive that others are receiving something better. Therefore, take the time to prevent this situation—it will usually require repeated conversation with emergency department (ED) physicians, nurses, and others.

There is value in supplementing verbal communication with written information, as seen with the medical hospitalist experience. Every surgical hospitalist practice could benefit from developing a brochure that describes the practice and routinely providing it to each patient seen by surgical hospitalists. Consider keeping copies of the brochures on all nursing units. The unit secretary can also provide a brochure to patients and families. The surgeon may routinely write an order to provide the brochure, perhaps including it in any predetermined order sets. The brochure should include photographs, two- to three-line biographies of the surgeons (e.g., where they trained), and information about how to contact the surgeons while the patient is in the hospital as well as after discharge. Some practices include a three- to five-item patient satisfaction survey that can be detached and mailed back to the practice. See Figure 9.1 for a sample brochure.

If, in addition to a brochure, the surgeons regularly provide business cards to patients and families, include a small color photograph of the surgeon on the card. One small study of medical hospitalists showed that patients were better able to identify their attending medical hospitalist when cards with photographs were provided. One practice enlarged their business cards to the size of bookmarks and reported that they had become as popular as baseball cards, although perhaps a little more difficult for the doctor to carry.

Finally, surgical hospitalists, and perhaps all physicians, should consider providing a copy of the hospital discharge summary and operative report to patients. In some cases, the surgical hospitalist may not know or have accurate information regarding the outpatient doctors a patient sees, in which case it may make sense to ask the patient to provide the hospital records to his or her future caregivers him- or herself. And many patients and their families may benefit from these documents (without having to request them) because the documents can reinforce verbal instructions and provide additional

Communication Issues in Surgical Hospitalist Practice

FIGURE 9.1 — SURGICAL HOSPITALIST BROCHURE

BUSINESS REPLY MAIL
FIRST CLASS PERMIT NO xxx CHICAGO, ILLINOIS

NO POSTAGE NECESSARY IF MAILED IN THE UNITED STATES

SURGICAL HOSPITALIST PRACTICE
Community General Hospital
1234 MAIN STREET
CHICAGO, IL 60000

You have been referred to one of the Community General physicians known as surgical hospitalists.

Hospitalists are doctors who devote their practice to the care of hospitalized patients. The Community General surgical hospitalists are board-certified in General Surgery, and see hospitalized patients who have been referred from community primary care doctors, emergency room doctors or other physicians at the hospital. They do not see new patient referrals outside the hospital (but do provide outpatient follow up for patients they've seen in the hospital).

Who are we?

Dr. A, MD
University of Yale Health, 1999
Residency: State County Medical Systems, Nebraska

Dr. B, MD
Chicago University Medical School, 1983
Residency: Chicago Hospital Center, Illinois

Dr. C, MD
Medical University—New York, 1988
Residency: Medical University Hospitals, New York

Dr. D, MD
Public Academy Medical School, 1990
Residency: University Center, Wisconsin

LOGO
Community General Hospital
(555) 123-456X

Community Surgical Hospitalist Practice

LOGO
Community General Hospital

Why is a surgical hospitalist caring for me?
One of the surgical hospitalists is on duty at the hospital around the clock to manage hospitalized patients who need care by a surgeon. Emergency Room doctors or other physicians, including your primary care doctor, may refer you to a surgical hospitalist. The surgical hospitalists focus their practice on the needs of hospitalized patients including those who need surgery, or need care for traumatic injuries.

How does the surgical hospitalist practice work?
The surgical hospitalist may be in charge of your care or serve as a consultant to another doctor who is caring for you. He or she is available to you and your family to answer questions and discuss your care.

The surgical hospitalists work at the hospital fulltime to provide for your care and attend to any emergencies that may arise. They may consult other doctors to participate in your care as well. He or she will make arrangements for any prescriptions you may need when you are discharged. You may be asked to make an appointment with your primary care doctor, or other doctors, soon after discharge.

The surgical hospitalist may or may not need to see you in outpatient follow up after your hospital stay and will discuss this with you prior to discharge from the hospital.

You may contact the surgical hospitalist after discharge if you have any questions about your hospital stay.

What is the relationship between the surgical hospitalist and my primary care physician?
The two doctors work together. Your primary care physician can provide information about your health history to the surgical hospitalist, and the two doctors can discuss any significant findings or events. At the time of your admission and discharge the hospitalist prepares a detailed report of findings and treatment plans that is sent to your primary care physician.

Your primary care physician asks the hospitalist to be in charge of your care while you are in the hospital, but is welcome to check on you and discuss your care with the hospitalist anytime during your hospital stay.

When you are discharged, you will return to the care of your primary care doctor.

What if I need another specialist while in the hospital?
Consultations from other physicians are necessary in some cases and the surgical hospitalist can arrange for these as necessary. If you have already been seeing other doctors at Community General or elsewhere, be sure to let us know so that we can keep them informed about your hospital stay.

What if I don't have a regular primary care physician?
The Community General surgical hospitalists, and other hospital staff, can assist in finding a doctor for you to see after leaving the hospital. Records from your hospital stay can be sent to this physician.

Your feedback is valuable to us
We would appreciate your opinions about our care. Please fill out the evaluation on the adjacent page and submit it to your nurse, or mail it to us.

How to contact us
If you would like to speak with one of the surgical hospitalists while you or a family member is in the hospital, it is best to ask the attending nurse to page the doctor. Otherwise, you can reach us:

Phone: (555) 123-456X

Billing office: (555) 654-321X

Mailing address:
SURGICAL HOSPITALIST PRACTICE
Community General Hospital
1234 MAIN STREET
CHICAGO, IL 60000

Patient Name (optional) _____

Which hospitalist did you see?
(circle all that apply)
Dr. A
Dr. B
Dr. C
Dr. D

5=Excellent 4=Very Good 3=Good 2=Fair 1=Poor

1. Availability of the doctor when needed — 5 4 3 2 1
2. Skill of the doctor(s) treating you — 5 4 3 2 1
3. Courtesy/respect given by the doctor(s) — 5 4 3 2 1
4. Amount of information the doctor gave you about your illness and treatment — 5 4 3 2 1
5. Your perception of the doctor's assessment and management of your pain while in the hospital — 5 4 3 2 1

Your feedback is valuable to us. If you have a minute, we would appreciate your opinions about our care. You may give the survey to your nurse or mail it back to us at the address at the back of the survey.

Source: Adapted from John Nelson, MD, FACP, Nelson Flores Hospital Medicine Consultants, Bellevue, WA. Adapted from publication and used with permission from *Hospitalists: A Guide to Building a Successful Program* by Joseph A. Miller, John Nelson, Winthrop F. Whitcomb (Chicago: Health Administration Press, 2008), 231-235.

information about findings during the hospital stay and any needed follow-up. Anecdotal experience suggests that even illiterate patients may benefit from this practice, as they can show the records to literate friends, caregivers, or visiting nurses who might be able to use the records to care for the patient more effectively.

Communication with Physicians

Outpatient physicians

The way in which effective general surgeons in traditional practice communicate with other physicians can serve as a good model for surgical hospitalist practice. Such communication usually involves the surgeon providing timely and appropriately detailed records back to the referring, consulting, and PCPs. These records often include a "thank you for the referral," which might be delivered by note or by phone.

However, because community physicians almost never directly refer patients to surgical hospitalists (instead, the ED physician or other inpatient doctor usually makes the referral), the latter may not place as high a value on excellent communication as do doctors outside the hospital. After all, the surgical hospitalist knows that his or her future referral stream does not depend on the recommendations of outpatient doctors. Nevertheless, the surgical hospitalist must communicate well with a patient's other physicians to ensure high-quality care.

An ideal communication protocol is for the surgical hospitalist to dictate admission, operative, and discharge notes at the time of service and never to defer this work until another day. The hospital should ensure that notes are transcribed on a stat basis (e.g., within about four hours) and immediately faxed to outpatient physicians and made available to other inpatient physicians (e.g., via the hospital computer system). The use of computerized templates can facilitate this process.

Many practices may find it valuable to develop routine methods for acquiring records and information from outpatient physician offices and other hospitals. In the absence of a more clearly developed protocol, many surgical hospitalists might forego requesting outside records or simply ask the nearest unit secretary or nurse to retrieve the records, which may have a relatively low rate of success. Instead, a single person, such as the receptionist for the surgical hospitalists or someone else at the hospital, could be responsible for requesting and ensuring the delivery of any needed outside records during business hours. For example, a surgical hospitalist might admit a patient at midnight and leave a voice mail for the receptionist to call XYZ Hospital and ask for the operative report, echo report, and discharge summary from last March. During business hours the next day, the receptionist would ensure that the records are received and placed on the patient's chart.

Inpatient physicians

Careful attention to clear communication is critical to patient safety, as some of the worst mistakes in patient care result from communication breakdown, particularly in the care of complex patients. Surgical hospitalists should have formal meetings with the medical hospitalists, and potentially with other doctors who have high inpatient volumes, to minimize any potential confusion regarding who does what and which doctor will serve as attending physician for which patients. The parties should reach agreement regarding which doctor admits common diagnoses such as bowel obstruction and nonoperative trauma, for example. But all involved should realize that written agreements will never eliminate differences of opinion regarding how a particular patient is handled (e.g., whether the surgeon is attending and medical hospitalist is consultant or vice versa), so an important outcome of meetings between these parties should be to encourage development of collegial relationships that will help future disagreements come to a reasonable resolution. It is always helpful to remind the consulting service at the initial request to make a patient NPO if surgery is being considered.

When the surgical hospitalist is serving in the role of consultant, he or she should try to anticipate issues that may arise. For example, when feasible, he or she should write any follow-up and discharge instructions, such as if/when to return for an outpatient follow-up visit with the surgical hospitalist or instructions for wound care. Such recommendations should be definitive; they should not only specify that a wound dressing should be changed daily but what dressing should be used, etc. Recommendations for any medicines should include dose and frequency. Communication of this type can often occur most effectively via legible chart notes, but direct oral communication is necessary for any complex or unusual situations. Emphasize the quality and clarity of communication, and alert all care providers to any specific family concerns and expectations (especially unhappy family members). The consultant should avoid making pronouncements about prognosis or treatment prematurely and should refrain from making statements that may affect family perceptions or travel plans. Consult notes should be written at least once daily in a timely manner, and careful attention should be paid to the accuracy and completeness of these notes, as they can generate billable revenue. For particularly complex clinical scenarios, a multidisciplinary case conference may aid the discussion. Asking for the second opinion of a more senior person is often beneficial.

Clear communication in the ED can often prove challenging, as the clinical scenarios may be quite stressful, with consults that occur late at night. The surgical hospitalist often will become skilled at interpreting the ED intake/flow sheets and ambulance logs. Particular attention should be paid when asking ED attending physicians to call in new consultants from other disciplines if the clinical problem is in an area outside of the hospitalist's expertise.

In seeking to provide good service to other inpatient physicians who have requested a consult, the surgical hospitalist should keep in mind the "Ten Commandments for Effective Consultation," in Figure 9.2. Although originally published in 1983, they remain relevant today.

FIGURE 9.2   TEN COMMANDMENTS FOR EFFECTIVE CONSULTATION

1. Determine the question
2. Establish urgency
3. See for yourself
4. Be as brief as appropriate
5. Be specific and concise
6. Provide contingency plans
7. Honor thy turf
8. Teach with tact
9. Remember that talk is cheap and effective
10. Follow up

Source: "Ten Commandments for Effective Consultations." Arch Intern Med 1983; 143: 1753–1755. L. Goldman, T. Lee, and P. Rudd.

Communication Between Surgical Hospitalists within the Same Practice

Some scheduling models may mean that surgical hospitalists hand-off and cross cover patients more often than might be typical for general surgeons in traditional practice. For example, a practice may have separately scheduled day and night shifts such that patients who need urgent surgery might be admitted by the day surgeon but not get to the operating room until the night-shift surgeon is on duty. Such frequent handoffs require excellent communication. Several methods have proven successful, including electronic reports, face-to-face sign-out, and the utilization of nurse practitioners.

The Joint Commission *(www.jointcommission.org)* mandates development of and compliance with a formal handoff communication plan to minimize the risk of information loss. An effective plan might require that the admitting surgeon dictate a complete admission history and physical that is transcribed on a stat basis and is available by the beginning of the next shift. This could be accompanied by a verbal sign-out that follows a standard format, such as SBAR (situation, background, assessment, recommendations), with the opportunity for the receiving doctor to get answers to any questions.

CHAPTER 10

Measuring Success

Leslie A. Flores, MHA

A meaningful system for measuring and reporting program performance is one of the most important tools available to ensure the effective functioning of a surgical hospitalist program. The primary purpose of any performance measurement system is to identify opportunities to improve performance. However, performance information can also be a useful for the following:

- Clarification and alignment of the goals and interests of the various stakeholder groups

- Financial support negotiations between the surgeons and the sponsoring organization

- Surgeon incentive compensation plans

- Managed care contract negotiations

- Program marketing

This chapter will address specific metrics and analytical approaches that are useful in monitoring the performance of a surgical hospitalist program and in creating a performance dashboard or report card.

The Performance Measurement Process

The performance monitoring effort may be initiated and led by either the program's organizational sponsor (e.g., hospital administration) or by the surgical hospitalists. However, it will be most successful if all key stakeholders work together to define performance metrics and targets and to determine what will be done with the information collected. The performance monitoring process should be seen as a joint effort of the sponsoring organization and the surgeons to ensure that the surgical hospitalist program is operating as expected and is meeting its stakeholders' needs.

The performance measurement process will consist of the following steps:

1. Decide who will be involved in designing the performance measurement system and convene a project design team. This team may include hospital or medical group administration; the surgical hospitalists; individuals who will obtain, analyze, and present the performance information; and representatives of other stakeholder groups, such as nursing, the emergency department (ED), anesthesia, etc.

2. Agree on the design of the performance monitoring system, including:

    – The metrics to be included in the performance monitoring system
    – Specific performance objectives (i.e., target levels of performance)
    – Where the data will come from and who will obtain and analyze it
    – The frequency of data reporting
    – What the reports will look like and who will prepare them
    – With whom the performance information will be shared
    – Clear expectations regarding how the performance information will be used

For example, will the information be shared only with administration and the surgeons, or will it be disseminated to others? Who is expected to respond to the reports and to develop improvement plans based on the information? Will they be used to determine performance bonuses for the hospitalists, or in negotiation of contract renewals?

Criteria for a Successful Performance Measurement System

The fundamental criteria for a successful performance measurement system for surgical hospitalists include the following:

- The selected metrics are meaningful to the sponsoring organization (e.g., the hospital or medical group) and the surgeons

- The data for the selected metrics are relatively easy to obtain in a consistent, reliable manner

- There is a high degree of confidence in the accuracy of data reporting for the selected metrics

- Data analysis is straightforward, objective, and rigorous

- Performance targets and comparison benchmarks are reasonable and, if obtained from external sources, are credible

- Performance information is presented in a way that is clear, consistent, and easy to understand

- The performance information is shared with the entire surgical hospitalist team and key stakeholders on a regular basis; for most metrics, this should be at least quarterly

- The performance information is actionable (i.e., it can be used by the surgical hospitalists to improve their performance)

- The surgeons and the organization are both held accountable for using the performance information to guide decision-making and improve performance

What Aspects of Performance Should Be Measured?

Keeping these criteria in mind, the designers of the performance monitoring system should start the process by determining what aspects of performance should be monitored for their particular program. The selection of specific metrics will vary significantly from program to program, as well as over time, based on the current issues and concerns of each surgical hospitalist group and its sponsoring organization. These might include financial issues (the finances of the program or of the larger organization), volume and market share concerns, and service issues, such as patient satisfaction, clinical and patient safety issues, etc. Each program should select meaningful metrics, add and delete metrics periodically to ensure that the monitoring process continues to evolve, and address current issues and concerns.

The best surgical hospitalist programs adopt a balanced approach to performance measurement that does not focus exclusively on one or two areas of performance, such as focusing only on financial performance, at the expense of others. A robust performance monitoring system will include one or more metrics to evaluate each of the following aspects of surgical hospitalist program performance:

Chapter 10

> **PERFORMANCE MEASUREMENTS**
> - Descriptive metrics
> - Clinical quality
> - Operational effectiveness
> - Financial performance
> - Customer satisfaction

Descriptive metrics

Descriptive metrics do not measure performance in and of themselves, but they are valuable in understanding the scope and nature of the surgical hospitalist practice, and they help inform the analysis of other types of metrics.

Descriptive metrics include basic information such as patient volume (number of cases), top surgical procedures performed (by CPT code), top diagnosis-related groups (DRG), case-mix index (CMI), number of surgical hospitalist shifts or hours worked, number of full-time equivalents (FTE) payer mix, and similar items. Figure 10.1 lists a variety of sample descriptive metrics for consideration.

A program will not necessarily measure all of these metrics but should select those that are most meaningful for its particular situation. Descriptive metrics do not measure performance in and of themselves, but they are valuable in understanding the scope of the surgical hospitalist practice. Descriptive metrics help inform the analysis of other types of metrics.

FIGURE 10.1 — CHECKLIST FOR EVALUATING A SURGICAL HOSPITALIST SCHEDULE

Descriptive metrics

Number of cases or number of patient encounters by type (e.g., admissions, consultations, surgical procedures, subsequent inpatient visits, follow-up clinic visits, etc.)
- ❏ Total for a defined period
- ❏ Average, high, and low daily volume during the period
- ❏ Average daily starting census for the program

Operating room (OR) minutes
- ❏ Average minutes per case

Average hours on ED or trauma diversion per week or per month

Types of patients cared for by the program
- ❏ Top 25 surgical procedures performed (by CPT code)
- ❏ Top 10 DRGs
- ❏ All DRGs constituting 80% of program volume
- ❏ Proportion of patients with surgeon as attending physician vs. surgeon as consultant
- ❏ Proportion of teaching patients vs. nonteaching patients on the service

Patient source
- ❏ Number of trauma service patients
- ❏ Number of unassigned emergency patient admissions
- ❏ Number of regional transfers
- ❏ Payer mix by volume or revenue

Patient acuity/complexity
- ❏ Medicare CMI for patients managed by surgical hospitalists
- ❏ APR-DRG or other severity-adjusted data, if available

Amount of surgical hospitalist resources deployed
- ❏ Number of shifts or hours worked by shift type (e.g., days vs. nights)
- ❏ Number of surgical hospitalist FTEs
- ❏ Number of clinical and/or nonclinical support staff FTEs

Surgical volume growth over time
- ❏ Trauma service growth
- ❏ Growth in transfers from other hospitals

Source: Leslie A. Flores, MHA, Nelson Flores Hospital Medicine Consultants, La Quinta, CA.

Chapter 10

Clinical quality

Quality metrics will help a surgical hospitalist program and its stakeholders evaluate the quality and clinical efficacy of the patient care it provides. The primary purpose of any surgical hospitalist program is to provide high-quality patient care; thus, quality metrics should be first and foremost in any performance monitoring system. Quality metrics may evaluate whether surgical hospitalists use the right systems and processes (process measures) or whether surgical hospitalists achieve the desired results (outcome measures).

Examples of clinical quality metrics might include frequency of utilization of established clinical protocols or compliance with Medicare surgical infection prevention core measures (process measures), OR surgical site infection rate, DVT rate and other surgery-related never events, in-hospital mortality rate, and 30-day readmission rate (outcome measures). Refer to Figure 10.2 for a sample list. Again, it is not necessary to measure all of the sample metrics below, and there may be other metrics that the program wishes to monitor instead. The important point is that each program should select metrics that are meaningful for its unique situation.

FIGURE 10.2 — SAMPLE CLINICAL QUALITY METRICS

Clinical quality metrics
Utilization of established clinical guidelines, protocols, and standard order sets by surgical hospitalists
Frequency of unplanned return to surgery
Surgical site infection rate
Venous thromboembolism rate
Other surgical errors/near misses
Medication errors
72-hour and 30-day readmission rates
Mortality rates <ul><li>ICU vs. non-ICU</li><li>Full code vs. no-code status</li><li>By DRG</li></ul>
Frequency of unanticipated return to ICU/CCU
Compliance with surgery-related Joint Commission/Medicare core measures and other pay-for-performance criteria

Source: Leslie A. Flores, MHA, Nelson Flores Hospital Medicine Consultants, La Quinta, CA.

Measuring Success

Operational effectiveness

The surgical hospitalist practice and its stakeholders want to ensure not only that the surgeons are providing high-quality care, but also that they have systems and processes in place to ensure the effective management and operation of their practice. Operational effectiveness is a broad category and includes items such as surgeon productivity, response times to pages, clinical documentation and timely chart completion, surgeon job satisfaction and turnover rates, time from initial contact to completion of admitting orders, percent of admission and discharge notes dictated at the time of service, patient wait times, ED diversion, ambulance diversion, and many similar measures. Refer to Figure 10.3 for a sample list.

Financial performance

Because surgical hospitalist practices may require a source of additional financial support beyond professional fee collections, use metrics that track the following:

- The financial performance of the surgical hospitalist program

- The program's contribution to the larger organization's financial performance

These financial metrics are important components of a comprehensive performance monitoring system. Financial performance metrics includes CPT coding, payer mix, professional fee charges and/or collections, days of revenue in accounts receivable, and the degree of variance from the surgical hospitalist cost center budget. Financial performance also includes measures of hospital resource utilization, such as average length of stay (ALOS), hospital cost per case, or ancillary utilization for surgical hospitalist patients. Refer to Figure 10.4 for a sample list.

Surgical hospitalists have a wide variety of stakeholders, or "customers," and should routinely assess the satisfaction of at least these major groups:

- Patient and family satisfaction (e.g., Press-Ganey satisfaction results)

- Medical staff satisfaction (PCPs and consulting specialists)

- Nursing staff satisfaction

Refer to Figure 10.5 for a sample list of customer satisfaction metrics.

Chapter 10

FIGURE 10.3 SAMPLE OPERATIONAL EFFECTIVENESS METRICS

Operational effectiveness metrics

Surgical hospitalist productivity
• Annual surgical cases per FTE (individual and average for the practice)
• Annual nonsurgical billable encounters per FTE (individual and average for the practice)
• Annual wRVUs per FTE (individual and average for the practice)
• Number of surgical cases or patient encounters per shift, by shift type (e.g., days vs. nights)
  – Average by individual
  – Average for the practice

Surgical hospitalist responsiveness • Response time to pages, if available • Frequency of complaints by medical staff or hospital clinical staff regarding surgeon responsiveness • Percent of time that the time from initial surgeon contact to start of surgery exceeds target (e.g., one hour for emergent patients and four hours for nonemergent patients)
Medical record documentation • Utilization of computerized physician order entry (CPOE), if available • Handwriting clarity • Timeliness of chart completion and/or frequency of suspension for medical record completion • Percent of admission notes dictated at the time of service (or within other specified time frame) • Percent of surgical notes dictated at the time of service (or within other specified time frame) • Percent of discharge notes dictated at the time of service (or within other specified time frame) • Quality of clinical documentation to support optimal hospital DRG coding
Surgical hospitalist job satisfaction • Surgeon call-off rate or frequency of uncovered shifts • Surgeon morale survey results • Surgeon turnover rate
Compliance with internal program policies and procedures • Internal sign-out or handoff protocols (change of shift and when rotating off service) • Acceptance of referrals and transfers • Completion of time sheets and other operational documentation • Participation in case management rounds and other meetings • Primary care physician (PCP) communication protocols

Source: Leslie A. Flores, MHA. Nelson Flores Hospital Medicine Consultants, La Quinta, CA.

Measuring Success

FIGURE 10.4 SAMPLE FINANCIAL PERFORMANCE METRICS

Financial performance metrics

Charge capture and CPT coding
• Quality of documentation
    – Does documentation accurately capture services provided?
    – Does documentation support the selected CPT code?
    – Does the selected CPT code fully capture the surgical services performed?
• For nonsurgical services such as consults, evaluation of CPT code distribution by service level
• Charge capture (completeness and timeliness)

Professional fee charges and collections (by individual surgeon and total for the program)
Practice payer mix by financial class
Accounts receivable tracking • Total dollars in accounts receivable • Average day's revenue in accounts receivable
Collection ratio (net collections as a percent of total professional fee charges)
Frequency of rejected claims • Frequency of successful appeal of rejected claims
Surgical hospitalist cost center (revenues and expenses) performance compared to budget
Practice overhead expense as a percent of practice revenues (or of surgical hospitalist compensation)
ALOS (including comparisons to peer group, where applicable) • Overall for the practice • By DRG or service line • ICU vs. non-ICU days

Hospital cost per day or per discharge (including comparisons to peer group, where applicable)
• Subcategories of cost:
    – OR costs per case
    – Direct nursing expense per day or per discharge
    – Supply expense per day or per discharge
    – Ancillary utilization per discharge (pharmacy, lab, radiology, respiratory therapy, physical therapy)
• By DRG and total for the program

Hospital financial performance per surgical hospitalist discharge • Average hospital reimbursement per discharge • Average hospital contribution margin per discharge
Surgical emergency department on-call stipends avoided

Source: Leslie A. Flores, MHA, Nelson Flores Hospital Medicine Consultants, La Quinta, CA.

FIGURE 10.5 SAMPLE CUSTOMER SATISFACTION METRICS

Customer satisfaction metrics
Patient and family satisfaction
PCP satisfaction
Consulting specialist satisfaction
Sponsoring organization administration (hospital, medical group, and/or health plan) satisfaction
Hospital clinical staff satisfaction (nurses, case managers/discharge planners, social workers, clinical pharmacists, respiratory therapists, etc.)

Source: Leslie A. Flores, MHA, Nelson Flores Hospital Medicine Consultants, La Quinta, CA.

There is naturally some overlap among these metric groupings, and many metrics could arguably fall into more than one category. For example, "time from initial contact to start of surgery" might just as easily be considered an indicator of clinical quality as operational effectiveness, and patient satisfaction might be considered an indicator of clinical quality or customer satisfaction.

Setting Performance Objectives

Once the performance measurement metrics for the surgical hospitalist practice have been selected, it is important to set performance objectives or targets against which to assess actual performance. The primary reasons to undertake performance measurement are to determine whether the program is meeting program expectations and to identify opportunities to improve performance. It is not possible to do either unless performance expectations are clearly defined in the form of objectives for the selected metrics.

The performance objective might be expressed as a fixed number or percentage (e.g., "minimum of 1,000 wRVUs per FTE per quarter," or "98% compliance with surgical infection core measures"). Alternatively the performance objective might be expressed in terms of performance relative to a defined baseline period or comparison group (e.g., "ALOS equal to or better than all community [nonhospitalist] surgeons") or an external benchmark (e.g., "professional fee charges per FTE equal to or greater than the Medical Group Management Association (MGMA) median").

Useful questions to ask when setting targets include:

- What is the program's (or the organization's) historical or baseline performance on this metric?

- Is improvement over the baseline performance desired?

- Is there a comparison group against which the practice's performance on this metric should be compared? Consider both internal comparison groups (e.g., nonhospitalist surgeons practicing in the same facility) and external comparison groups (e.g., surgical performance in other similar hospitals available through clinical data repositories such as Premier or Thomson Reuters, or survey data available through the MGMA or other organizations).

- Are there externally validated benchmarks or best practice standards available for this metric?

Analysis Considerations

Once the metrics have been selected and performance objectives have been identified, the task of collecting and analyzing data begins. Here are some factors to consider in analyzing performance information.

Understand the environment

No two surgical hospitalist programs are exactly alike, and each program operates in a unique organizational environment. Understand and account for the values, goals, terminology, and overall culture of the surgical hospitalist group and the organization in which it functions. Using consistent and organizationally accepted analytical methodologies and reporting formats will enhance the credibility of the performance monitoring information. For example, it is helpful to understand that hospital administrators typically define LOS as the number of midnights a patient was in the hospital, whereas doctors often think of LOS as the number of days they saw the patient on their service. The surgical hospitalists' definition of LOS will usually be one day longer than the hospital-defined LOS because the surgeons see the patient the day before the first midnight, as well as the day after the last midnight.

Understand data sources and limitations

The most common sources of data for surgical hospitalist performance measurement are the practice's census management and billing data and the hospital's clinical and financial information systems. Sometimes valuable information is also available from external data repositories in which the hospital may participate, such as Thomson Reuters, Premier, or the University Health System Consortium. In order for the performance monitoring system to be credible, its data sources must be considered

Chapter 10

accurate, complete, and timely. Any data weaknesses or limitations, such as when the hospital information system doesn't reliably capture the attending physician or surgeon, should be clearly understood and accounted for or disclosed.

Assessing individual performance vs. group performance

It is often useful to evaluate the performance of individual surgeons in the group and the aggregate or average performance of the group as a whole. Assessing individual surgical hospitalist performance will support effective physician supervision and performance management by allowing each doctor to see how he or she compares to his or her peers. Assessing group performance, on the other hand, supports assessments of whether the program as a whole is effective in meeting organizational expectations.

However, many of the performance criteria related to patient care do not lend themselves to individual performance assessment. Because more than one surgical hospitalist may be involved in the care of any single inpatient, it is sometimes difficult to assign performance on metrics, such as ALOS, core measure compliance, or patient satisfaction, to an individual surgical hospitalist. Which surgeon would get the credit—the surgeon who admitted the patient and performed the surgery, the surgeon who saw the patient most often during hospitalization, or the surgeon who discharged the patient?

Comparison data: Baseline, comparison group, or benchmark?

When considering what data the surgical hospitalist program's performance should be compared against, the designers of the performance measurement system might choose a baseline period, a comparison group, or an external benchmark. Using a baseline period for comparison is useful if the goal is to evaluate some aspect of performance before and after a certain intervention (e.g., average number of trauma cases per month before and after implementation of a surgical hospitalist program). The greatest danger of using a baseline period is that any changes in the selected metric (e.g., trauma service volume) may be due to other factors than the intervention (e.g., implementation of the surgical hospitalist program) that is assessed. For example, the hospital's trauma service volume may have increased since the "before" period in part because of the closure of a nearby trauma program or a change in trauma criteria or paramedic routing priorities.

When there is a valid comparison group still practicing in the same organization, evaluation against such a group is useful. Probably the best comparison group for a surgical hospitalist program would be other nonhospitalist general surgeons practicing in the hospital. Sometimes, however, many or even all of the surgeons may choose to leave the hospital and practice primarily in an outpatient surgery setting. Therefore, over time, there may no longer be an adequate comparison group.

External benchmarks such as survey data also can provide useful comparisons, as long as the limitations of the survey methodology and results are understood. For example, the annual MGMA Physician Compensation and Production Survey[1] does not yet include a separate category for surgical hospitalists; that survey represents a more traditional surgical practice. Thus, the production data in the MGMA survey will not be directly comparable to a typical full-time surgical hospitalist practice. In many or most settings, surgical hospitalists should anticipate lower overall productivity than general surgeons in traditional practice. Their work may be skewed toward a greater portion of nonoperative patients (e.g., nonoperative trauma), and they may be scheduled to provide 24/7 in-hospital coverage during which not all hours are productive.

Case mix or severity adjustment

Many clinical quality and resource utilization metrics should be adjusted for patient acuity. The most common acuity adjustment uses the CMS CMI to adjust data by DRG. A simple, high-level case-mix adjustment may be accomplished by dividing the data for a given metric by the average CMI for all the patients in the data sample.

$$\frac{\text{Metric data}}{\text{Average CMI}} = \text{High-level case-mix adjustment}$$

For example, if the surgical hospitalists have an ALOS of 4.03 and an average CMI of 1.12, the case mix–adjusted ALOS will be 4.03 / 1.12 = approximately 3.60. If the comparison group of community-based general surgeons has an ALOS of 3.98 but a CMI of 1.06, their case mix–adjusted ALOS will be 3.98 / 1.06 = approximately 3.75. So although the surgical hospitalist may appear, on the surface, to have a longer ALOS, when the data are adjusted for patient acuity, the surgical hospitalists actually show a lower ALOS than do their nonhospitalist peers.

Some hospitals use more sophisticated acuity adjustment methodologies, such as 3M's proprietary "APR-DRG Severity-of-Illness" software or Ingenix's proprietary "APS-DRG" software. Surgical hospitalists should understand what patient acuity adjustment information is available from their hospital and strategize with hospital finance or decision support staff members to reach agreement on how to use this information to adjust performance data.

Chapter 10

Consider outliers

Another analysis problem encountered by many surgical hospitalist practices, particularly small programs, is the effect of outlier patients. One or two unusually sick patients who are in the hospital for an extended period of time can skew performance data on parameters, such as LOS and cost per case, so that the comparison to baseline or benchmark data does not present an accurate picture of the majority of the surgeons' practice. In such cases, it may be useful to delete the "outlier" cases (unusually long or unusually short LOSs) before evaluating the program's performance against the target. To address this issue, one option is to truncate the LOS after two standard deviations beyond the mean LOS.

Trending over time

In addition to providing a current snapshot of surgical hospitalists' performance compared to the performance objective or comparison data, many performance measurement metrics lend themselves to trending over time so that improvement or deterioration in performance can be identified. However, be careful to adjust for factors such as seasonal volume variation. For example, quarterly volume data are probably best compared to volume for the same quarter in the previous year (year-over-year), rather than to the previous calendar quarter, due to seasonal fluctuations in hospital census (e.g., Q1 vs. Q2).

Formatting the information

It is common for requests for surgical hospitalist performance information to result in a substantial amount of data, often consisting of many pages of tables with small numbers. Some of these numbers are applicable to the desired analysis, and many are not. Busy practicing surgeons are unlikely to spend the time and energy to regularly review lengthy reports to find the few key indicators that can help them decide how to improve their practice. Therefore, the designers of the performance measurement system should work with finance, decision support, and information system employees to obtain the desired information in simple, easy-to-understand formats that are not cluttered with significant extraneous information. Performance information also will be more useful if key findings are demonstrated in simple, colorful graphics, such as graphs, pie charts, or scatter diagrams. Finally, a few key performance indicators should be selected and distilled into a one- or two-page dashboard or scorecard that is consistently formatted and presented to all of the surgical hospitalists and the program's stakeholders on a regular basis. A sample dashboard is presented in Figure 10.6.

Measuring Success

FIGURE 10.6 SAMPLE REPORT CARD

XYZ Hospital
Surgical Hospitalist Program
Quarterly Performance Dashboard: Jan-Mar 2009

Descriptive metrics	Target	Actual current quarter	Actual previous quarter	Trend
Total cases	275	268	220	↑
Cases requiring surgery (%)	72%	68%	59%	↑
CMI	1.2	1.18	1.21	↓
ED diversion hours	< 72/qtr	108	87	↑
Clinical quality				
Unplanned return to OR (%)	<= 3.2%	3.3%	2.1%	↑
Core measure compliance (%)	>= 95%	86%	76%	↑
Surgical site infections (%)	<= 2.2%	2.5%	3.4%	↓
VTEs (%)	0%	1%	0%	↑
Operational effectiveness				
Surgical procedures per FTE	50	46	37	↑
wRVUs per FTE	1,400	1,340	1,006	↑
Surgical note dictated at time of service (%)	100%	68%	51%	↑
Uncovered shifts (%)	0%	0%	3%	↓
Financial performance				
Coding accuracy (% per audit)	>= 85%	71%	76%	↓
Charges per FTE	$200,000	$160,800	$125,700	↑
Collection ratio	>= 47%	42%	45%	↓
ALOS (CMI-adjusted)	<= 4.2	4.1	4.6	↓
Customer satisfaction				
Press Ganey (avg. phys. %tile)	>= 89%	78%	66%	↑
Medical staff satisfaction	>= 75%	82%	64%	↑
OR staff satisfaction	>= 80%	81%	55%	↑
Unit nursing staff satisfaction	>= 80%	73%	69%	↑

Source: Leslie A. Flores, MHA, Nelson Flores Hospital Medicine Consultants, La Quinta, CA.

Chapter 10

Conclusion

Healthcare organizations that sponsor surgical hospitalist programs invest significant organizational resources, including financial, human, and political capital, in building their programs. It is incumbent on both the sponsoring organizations and the surgical hospitalists to ensure that these resources are well invested by measuring and reporting program performance on a regular basis and by working to improve program performance continually.

There is no single best performance measurement for surgical hospitalist programs, as programs have different reasons for their existence and operate in unique environments. Robust performance measurement systems ensure that attention is not unduly focused on a single aspect of performance (e.g., financial), but that ongoing performance assessment addresses financial, clinical, operational, and service aspects of the program in a balanced way.

ENDNOTE

Leslie A. Flores, "Measuring Success" chapter is adapted from its original appearance in Kenneth G. Simone, Jeffrey R. Dichter, *The Hospitalist Program Management Guide,* Second Edition (Marblehead: HCPro, Inc., 2008) 13–34.

REFERENCES

1. *Physician Compensation and Production Survey: 2008 Report Based on 2007 Data,* (Englewood, CO: MGMA, 2008).

CHAPTER 11

Trauma Coverage

Paul M. Maggio, MD, MBA • David A. Spain, MD, FACS

The hallmark of trauma care is a thorough and consistent commitment to providing timely treatment to the injured patient. Trauma centers must be ready at a moment's notice to provide complex care 24/7—no matter how inconvenient or disruptive doing so might be to normal work flow. This is not to say that every trauma center must be capable of providing the full range of trauma care to every patient. Instead, this commitment must be consistent with the institution's capabilities.

Thus, if a hospital is considering establishing a trauma center, it must undertake a thorough assessment of its available resources. These resources are usually measured as personnel resources and capital equipment, but they also include the hospital's culture, medical staff, and ability to make and carry out such an undertaking. The hospital also must evaluate the role it may play within the regional system of trauma care relative to other institutions by working with existing facilities and regulatory agencies. The hospital can then pursue a level of commitment consistent with its internal resources and commitment, as well as the system's need. Generally, this goal is accomplished by obtaining a certain trauma level designation through a regulatory agency. The most common systems use Level I, II, and III designations.

The Role of EMS

A handful of states possess well-developed, coordinated, statewide trauma systems; however, in most states, the trauma system is a bit more fragmented. The designating authority for trauma center status varies from state to state, and in general, the designating authority is an emergency medical services (EMS) agency at the city, county, or state level. Once a hospital verifies that it possesses the appropriate resources and commitments to provide trauma care, the hospital undergoes a review and, if confirmed, is designated as a trauma center by EMS. Some counties and states use local or state resources to review trauma centers, whereas others use an external process to verify a trauma center. The most commonly used and established external verification process is through the American College of Surgeons Committee on Trauma (COT). The COT has taken the lead in defining not only the characteristics of a Level I, II, or III trauma center, but also how that trauma center functions within the system of trauma care in a particular region. The COT has outlined its trauma center requirements in *Resources for the Optimal Care of the Injured Patient 2006*.[1] This publication provides a blueprint for obtaining and maintaining trauma center status. The COT also provides a consultation program in which expert trauma surgeons, who are thoroughly familiar with the criteria for trauma center verification, visit a candidate trauma center and help it assess its resources and capabilities. This process can be extremely valuable in gauging a hospital's potential to provide adequate trauma care.

Trauma Center Levels

A Level I trauma center provides a full range of trauma care to all injured patients and acts as a lead coordinating trauma care center for the region. Most Level I trauma centers are located at academic tertiary care medical centers that have a full range of residency training programs. In addition, these centers are required by the COT to have active programs in injury prevention, rehabilitation, education, and research. A core of general surgeons, identified as trauma surgeons, provide most of the trauma care in these hospitals, possessing expertise in trauma care in their academic careers. Most of these trauma surgeons also have qualifications in Surgical Critical Care from the American Board of Surgery, obtained through additional fellowship training. Most of these programs are well established and have dedicated educational and training programs. In the majority of these centers, trauma surgeons function as acute care surgeons providing trauma, emergency surgery, and critical care coverage.

Level II trauma centers are typically medical centers—urban or suburban—that can provide definitive initial trauma care. However, due to lack of resources (personnel and equipment), not all Level II trauma centers can provide comprehensive care to a severely injured patient. Therefore, a small subset of patients may ultimately require transfer to a Level I trauma center for management of more complex injuries, such as traumatic aortic transections, complex pelvic/acetabular fracture, or significant plastic reconstructive cases. Although some are located at academic centers, most Level II trauma centers are in community hospitals that are staffed by private practitioners or hospital-based physicians. Some of these centers have residency and research programs, although such programs are not required as they are in Level I trauma centers. In areas without a Level I trauma center in close geographic proximity, the Level II trauma center must take on the responsibility within the regional system for education, outreach, and leadership.

Level III trauma centers are generally rural hospitals in areas without ready access to Level I or II trauma centers. They provide initial assessment and resuscitation, stabilization, and, occasionally, emergency operations for trauma patients. These hospitals often lack consistent access to specialty care, such as neurosurgery or definitive orthopedic surgery. Thus, most seriously injured patients will require transfer to a Level I or II trauma center for definitive care after initial evaluation and stabilization. Refer to Figure 11.1 for a comparison chart.

FIGURE 11.1 TRAUMA LEVEL COMPARISON CHART

Trauma level	Level I	Level II	Level III
Common location	Urban	Urban or suburban	Rural
Common type of center	Academic tertiary care medical center	Community hospital	Community hospital
Residency program availability	Full range of residency programs	Some possess residency programs	No surgical residency May have family practice
Type of provided care	Full range of care for all cases	Wide range of care; some complicated cases transferred to level I	Initial assessment and stabilization

Source: David A. Spain, MD, FACS, professor of surgery, chief, Section of Trauma, Emergency, and Critical Care Surgery; associate division chief, General Surgery, Stanford (CA) University.

The Role of the Surgical Hospitalist and Acute Care Surgeon

There are several critical elements for a nondesignated hospital to assume providing trauma care. First and foremost is the hospital's institutional commitment to provide the necessary resources and administrative support to tackle this initiative. However, there are two main challenges in Level II and III trauma centers: orthopedic coverage and general surgeon staffing. For example, orthopedic coverage can be problematic, especially in a rural Level III trauma center with a limited number of available orthopedic surgeons.

Chapter 11

Another common stumbling block is maintaining a consistent core of general surgeons to provide trauma coverage. General surgeons are truly the lynchpin of trauma care. Although emergency medicine physicians are important resources during the initial assessment and resuscitation, general surgeons evaluate operative injuries and set priorities. In a community hospital, providing general surgery coverage for trauma can be difficult. Most commonly, the general surgeons providing trauma coverage are in private practice and have multiple obligations. During the day, these surgeons may have patients to see in the office or be busy with elective operations. A busy night of trauma call may make the following day's activities very challenging to complete. Also, a very sick, multiply injured trauma patient may require significant hours of care over several days. All of these factors can be a significant drain and challenge to the private practice surgeon. Thus, many community-based trauma centers have moved to a group of hospital-based surgeons to provide trauma care.

The surgical hospitalist or acute care surgeon plays a major role in advancing a nondesignated hospital to a level III trauma center or moving a Level III trauma center up to Level II status; they provide consistent trauma call coverage. The group of surgical hospitalists typically provides all the daytime trauma coverage and, in smaller practices, may split the nighttime coverage with willing general surgeons. The surgical hospitalist also can make arrangements to take over any complicated trauma patient picked up during a night of trauma call. Thus, the surgical hospitalist can off-load the most onerous aspects of trauma care yet keep the other general surgeons involved by assisting with call. This arrangement meets the needs of multiple contingencies and allows for consistency by keeping the bulk of care in the hands of a dedicated core of surgeons. These situations provide significant opportunities for surgical hospitalists to assume major leadership roles within their institutions.

Benefits of Trauma Status

Obtaining trauma center status can benefit the hospital in many ways. A recent analysis of our efforts to obtain and maintain COT verification at Stanford Hospital has shown multiple salient effects: increased trauma volume, decreased length of hospital stay, better financial performance, and improved survival.[2] Multiple other studies have documented that, with careful planning, attention to detail, and an acceptable payer mix, trauma centers can function as profit centers.[3,4]

Obtaining trauma center status can have many salient effects for the hospital. A recent analysis of the seven-year commitment at Stanford Hospital to obtain and maintain Level I trauma center status documented significantly improved survival for severely injured patients (from 65% to 83%), a 25% decrease in ICU length of stay, increased volume (20%), and an eightfold increase in hospital profits.[2] Stanford Hospital has clearly benefited from a favorable payer mix, which not all hospitals enjoy. Moreover, these improvements occurred without a significant change in patient demographics and suggest a significant improvement in the quality and efficiency of care. In a fixed-cost industry such as healthcare, the most efficient way to increase profits is to improve capacity management and productivity (i.e., increase patient volume, decrease the complication rate, and improve patient throughput). This is exactly what happened at the Stanford trauma center. Although it is a Level I trauma center, these same benefits may apply as well to Level II or III trauma centers.

Richardson et al[5] analyzed two rural hospitals that were roughly equidistant from a Level I trauma center with similar patient demographics. One hospital made a major commitment to become a Level III trauma center, and the other diminished its involvement. The Level III trauma center realized an increase in patient volume. This led to more operations at the Level III center but also more transfers to the Level I trauma center. However, a careful analysis of these patients, found that the appropriateness of these transfers had improved significantly. Transfers from that hospital for possible radiographic abnormalities virtually disappeared, while it became an increasing cause for transfer from the other rural hospital. These results were truly a win-win solution for the trauma centers and their patients. More patients were able to obtain care locally at the Level III trauma center, avoiding the cost and inconvenience of transfer. And when transfer was undertaken, it was much more likely to be appropriate—a benefit for the Level I trauma center. In fact, what truly made this work was a group of committed general surgeons who took it upon themselves to organize the hospital and its medical staff to meet the needs of their community. In most hospitals trying to obtain Level II or III status, this is usually the critical step: finding a group of general surgeons who are willing to make the commitment to provide trauma care and also take the lead in organizing this effort. As a leader in this effort, the general surgeon (or surgical hospitalist) can be a significant benefit. The COT process allows many collaborative arrangements with the trauma surgeons being credentialed for initial evaluation and management of multiply injured patients.[1] This allows for appropriate involvement of the subspecialist without over burdening him or her. In this respect, the hospital-based general surgeon can truly help engage the subspecialist to participate in trauma care.

Chapter 11

The Hospital-Based Surgeon

Over the past decade, numerous trends and influences have caused organized trauma surgery to reexamine its role in the care of all acutely ill surgical patients, not just trauma patients. The training of future general surgeons who will care for these patients also has been an area of major concern. At the same time, there has been a major shift in general surgery as a whole. Most trainees now obtain fellowship training after general surgery and enter practices with a defined scope of care, often with a predominant outpatient practice and little or no involvement in emergency care. In many institutions, this has left a major void in the care of the acutely ill emergency surgical patient. Many trauma surgeons feel that the convergence of these two issues—a group of patients that may be underserved and an opportunity to enhance the training and desirability of caring for these patients—has also created an opportunity leading to the emergence of the hospital-based surgeon.

The hospital-based surgeon may take many forms. The prototype is the trauma surgeon, the hospital-based surgeon dedicated to the care of the injured patient. However, for many reasons, including decreased penetrating injury rate and increased nonoperative management of most blunt injuries, a trauma-exclusive practice has become less feasible except at a few of the busiest trauma centers. In addition, this mode of practice does not address the two needs outlined above. These factors have led the American Association for the Surgery of Trauma (AAST) to put forth a major effort to redefine the next generation trauma surgeon as an "acute care surgeon."

The acute care surgeon will have training and expertise to care for trauma, critically ill, and emergency general surgery patients. A necessary component of this model is formal training in surgical critical care, which allows the acute care surgeon to care for all critically or injured patients through the entire spectrum of care—from the emergency department (ED) to the operating room (OR), through the ICU, and until discharge. We believe that this will be the most highly developed and complete model of the hospital-based surgeon. This surgeon will largely exist at all Level I and some Level II trauma centers. Yet it may not be feasible at all Level II trauma centers, impractical at most Level IIIs, and, by definition, nonexistent at nontrauma centers. These limitations have led to the development of the surgical hospitalist model of surgical practice.

In many Level II trauma centers and most Level IIIs, the general surgeons providing trauma care did not obtain specialized training in surgical critical care. Although general surgeons may be very competent on their specific training and experience, the move to closed ICU models has made it increasingly difficult for these surgeons to provide critical care coverage of their patients. In many institutions, this problem has been solved with collaborative work arrangements between the surgeons and intensivists. The surgeons provide initial evaluation, resuscitation, and operative care when indicated for critical trauma or general surgery patients, while the intensivist assists with ICU care. In recognition of this growing trend, the COT guidelines underwent a major revision acknowledging the value of these relationships. Although surgeons may partner with intensivists to provide ICU care, a major requirement is active and full participation by the surgeon in the care of these patients and not a simple abdication to the intensivists. Together, this collaborative partnership can deliver the full spectrum of care to critically ill or injured patients. In this model, the general surgeon is functioning as the trauma and emergency general surgeon.

The other model that has evolved and that may be most applicable to nontrauma centers has been called the "surgical hospitalist".[6] These surgeons are primarily responsive to the ED for emergency general surgery issues. This most closely resembles the medical hospitalists model in terms of philosophy and practice pattern. It was proposed that medical hospitalists add value by 1) providing measurable quality improvement, 2) providing continuity from inpatient to outpatient care, from ED to floor, and from ICU to floor, 3) doing what others have given up, such as indigent care and hospital committee functions, 4) creating teams to improve care and the working environment, and 5) taking care of acutely ill, complex hospitalized patients.[7] This is exactly what trauma surgeons have been doing for the past 25–30 years.

By accepting the principles of trauma care and applying them to all acutely ill surgical patients, the hospital-based surgeon will have an opportunity to advance care for a group of underserved patients. The key point is not to be too proscriptive in the precise model of surgical care or in the terminology used to describe it. Many practice models may evolve depending on local needs, resources, culture, and politics. However, the hallmark of trauma care is a commitment to provide care to injured patients to the best of your personal and your institution's capabilities. Hospital-based surgeons, by virtue of their dedication and availability, may be in a unique position to help their hospital improve care of acutely ill surgical patients by making a commitment to become a trauma center.

Chapter 11

REFERENCES

1. American College of Surgeons Committee on Trauma, *Resources for Optimal Care of the Injured Patient*, Chicago, American College of Surgeons, (2006).

2. P.M. Maggio, S.I. Brundage, T. Hernandez-Boussard, and D.A. Spain, "Commitment to COT Verification Improves Patient Outcomes and Financial Performance (Abstract)," *J Trauma* (2008).

3. P.A. Taheri, D.A. Butz, C.M. Watts, L.C. Griffes, and L.J. Greenfield, "Trauma Services: A Profit Center?" *J Am Coll Surg* 188 (1999): 349–354.

4. P.A. Taheri, P.M. Maggio, J. Dougherty, et al, "Trauma Center Downstream Revenue: The Impact of Incremental Patients within a Health System," *J Trauma* 62 (2007): 615–619; discussion 619–621.

5. J.D. Richardson, T. Cross, D. Lee, et al, "Impact of Level III Verification on Trauma Admissions and Transfer: Comparisons of Two Rural Hospitals," *J Trauma* 42 (1997): 498–502; discussion 503.

6. J. Maa, J.T. Carter, J.E. Gosnell, R. Wachter, and H.W. Harris, "The Surgical Hospitalist: A New Model for Emergency Surgical Care," *J Am Coll Surg* 205 (2007): 704–711.

7. L. Wellikson, "Hospitalists and Physician Leadership," *Trustee* 61 (2008): 34, 40–41.

CHAPTER 12

Surgical Hospitalist Programs and the Academic Medical Center

John Maa, MD, FACS

Over the past decade, surgical departments at academic medical centers have encountered new obstacles in the traditional academic tripartite missions: (1) education, (2) scientific research, and (3) the provision of high-quality care. Academic medical centers are dedicated to accept all patients as part of their mission and thus tend to have more complex, more highly variable, and more costly cases than community hospitals. The breadth and variety of intraoperative consults parallels the very complex and challenging patients transferred to an academic center from local referring hospitals. Financial pressures to generate clinical revenue have reduced faculty availability for emergency call coverage and for the education of surgical residents and medical students. Shortages of hospital inpatient bed capacity result in an increase in the disease acuity of hospitalized patients, more rapid turnover, and a resultant increase in the need for improved clinical efficiency and care quality. An increasing array of patient safety and quality improvement (QI) efforts require implementation, a task made more challenging by the constant rotation of house staff members as a result of the 80-hour workweek. This chapter will explore the special challenges to surgical hospitalist programs at teaching hospitals, specifically focusing on the education, research, and patient care missions.

Surgical Education of Surgery Residents and Medical Students

Teaching hospitals support residency programs and typically are affiliated with a medical school. In addition to clinical duties, the academic surgical hospitalist also must fulfill important educational and supervisory roles to achieve the mission of surgical education. Time must be allocated to complete these teaching responsibilities, which may include preparing lectures, facilitating teaching conferences, assisting in medical school curriculum workshops and oversight committees, conducting residency interviews, and ensuring compliance with 80-hour ACGME workweek regulations.

Chapter 12

A recent trend is the challenge of carrying out the teaching mission in academic medical centers. Residents are less available to teach due to duty hour limitations and increasing administrative/documentation tasks, and faculty are equally challenged by an increasing need to focus on patient care for revenue and call coverage. These financial pressures have diminished faculty availability for medical student and resident education. The educational community has raised concerns about the medical student's continuity of interaction with the patient and his or her understanding of the natural history of disease, as well as the limited faculty observation of the developing students' clinical skills, professionalism, and communication.

Additionally, at many academic centers, CMS now requires faculty to dedicate more time to ensuring complete and proper documentation of care to fulfill Medicare billing requirements, as patient care notes written or dictated by house staff may be insufficient for billing purposes. Another central challenge is that the teaching mission is often perceived as an underfunded mandate at an academic medical center with insufficient incentives and available resources to fulfill this important educational mission. Often, junior faculty are assigned early in their careers to teaching roles to offset their salary support—with the goal of applying for grant funding for educational research projects.

The key vision of the University of California, San Francisco (UCSF) Surgery Hospitalist program is to address the Department of Surgery's mission of education at the medical student and resident level by improving the quality and perception of the surgical faculty as educators, enhancing professionalism, and providing a new model for surgical education in the context of safe patient care at an academic medical center. By leading daily rounds and minimizing elective procedures and clinics during the on-call week, academic surgical hospitalists are continuously available to supervise and teach, and to provide more consistent, integrated feedback to residents and medical students. The program presents the opportunity to involve medical students in the evaluation of undifferentiated patients and represents a powerful tool for surgical education in the emergency department (ED). A key challenge is to maximize both patient safety and timeliness of care; therefore, the UCSF program assigns students and house staff a time limit in the evaluation of new patients so that delays in care delivery do not result.

Introduction of the surgical hospitalist model at UCSF in 2005 resulted in significant improvement in medical student perceptions of the (1) observation of physical exam skills, (2) adequacy of feedback, (3) faculty clinical teaching, and (4) the clerkship as a whole (advanced communication). In a study, students and residents reported highly valuing the interaction with faculty surgeons and the role-modeling of timely and professional care. The rotation has become one of the most popular for UCSF third-year medical students. Respondents cited teaching as the greatest strength, particularly in the evaluation of undifferentiated patients in the ED and inpatient settings. In house staff evaluations, 42% of respondents cited teaching as the greatest strength of the hospitalist service, similar to the experience with medical hospitalist programs.

In the era of the 80-hour resident workweek, the surgical hospitalist model strengthens the Department of Surgery's commitment to surgical education and maximal patient safety by promoting continuity in student and resident education, providing appropriate supervision to maximize patient safety, and introducing a mentoring relationship for student professional development and feedback.

> **KEY EDUCATIONAL STRENGTHS OF THE SURGICAL HOSPITALIST MODEL INCLUDE:**
>
> - A safer program model to deliver surgical care and teach simultaneously
> - Increased exposure to the undifferentiated patient in the ED with direct practice for the observed history and physical exam of the abdomen
> - More time for residents to educate medical students as their clinical efficiency is promoted
> - Junior residents are accelerated into the role as chief of a surgical service
> - A platform for novel curricular innovations to improve faculty mentoring and patient continuity

Promoting Clear Communication at an Academic Medical Center

Efficient evaluation of consultation requests is critical to patient flow, patient safety, patient satisfaction, and revenue flow at an academic teaching center. Surgical hospitalists develop expertise and confidence while conducting consults that allows them to also teach in a safe and efficient manner. But a surgical hospitalist seeking to provide safe care at an academic medical center also must be careful not to make assumptions prematurely about any patient care data that trainees communicate to them; the data may be critically important, especially in areas outside of the trainee and surgical hospitalist's expertise. The potential for confusion lurks when multiple teams and different levels of team members are involved in care of a single patient, and there are interlinked relationships in the plans for future care. Some of the most challenging errors in patient care are the result of communication breakdowns—particularly in caring for complex consults. The hospitalist should ensure that the attending from other services approves the recommendations by house staff consultants, and that the attending radiologist has reviewed CT scans and x-rays (particularly those upon which the decision to operate is based).

The surgical hospitalist at a teaching hospital should recognize the complexities of working with trainees (residents and fellows), physician extenders, and medical students who may misinterpret information as a result of inexperience, incomplete sign-outs, or insufficient knowledge. Important patient care details are more likely to be overlooked during the change in shift at the end of the day or during the change in attending service staffing at the beginning of the week. It is important to beware of misrepeated messages or truncations in communication to ensure the accuracy of sign-out and recognize the chart lore and other errors that can be easily propagated in an electronic medical record. It can be helpful to alert the consultant to potential unhappy family members, unrealistic expectations, and other complexities in the patient's care. To promote clarity in the written record, the attending hospitalist surgeons perform all documentation for the delivery of inpatient and ED care.

To most effectively promote clear and safe communication at a teaching hospital and overcome the inexperience of trainees, the surgical hospitalist can request a multidisciplinary case conference to aid in the discussion or request a second opinion or involvement of a more senior person. And although it is a wonderful teaching opportunity to observe diseases evolve on a consult service, there are also important reasons why urgent consult requests are not the best scenarios for education. Often, the best time to teach will be during a clinical conference, after care has been delivered and the patient has returned safely home.

Enhancing Resident Supervision and Continuity of Care

Another central intent of a surgical hospitalist program is to address the challenges in fragmentation and continuity of resident education, a result of the introduction of the 80-hour workweek. A central challenge facing surgery nationally in a changing era of patient expectations and ACGME workweek regulations is to define a new surgical education system that also maximizes quality and safety of patient care. Teaching hospitals have experienced the greatest effect of resident work hour restrictions.

The surgical hospitalist program seeks to simultaneously teach and allow residents the ability to learn but also to balance this by ensuring the delivery of high-quality care.

The surgical hospitalist model at an academic medical center depends critically upon the valuable contributions of house staff, fellows, and other trainees. The surgical residents fill an invaluable role as assistants in the operating room (OR) and in the delivery of patient care; most surgeons in academics find it rewarding and fulfilling to teach and mentor house staff and students in the OR and wards. The surgical hospitalist will play an important role in patient safety by supervising the efforts of the house staff in the OR (it is no longer accepted practice for surgical residents to perform operations without attending physicians present).

If the academic medical center is not a Level 1 trauma center, then the availability of residents means that the attending physicians will likely not be required to physically stay in house overnight. Looking to the future, current discussions by the Institute of Medicine raise the possibility that the workweek will be reduced further, perhaps to a 60-hour workweek, which may increase the role for surgical hospitalists at a teaching hospital even further.

Two important questions are: Is there appropriate supervision of the trainee? Do attending physicians on rounds interfere with resident autonomy? In the medical hospitalist experience, some teaching hospitals have created nonteaching services, which function without resident involvement and are instead staffed by nurse practitioners (NP). At UCSF, junior surgical residents staff the surgical hospitalist service, and they regard the opportunity to act in a chief resident capacity while being appropriately supervised by faculty as a key strength of the program. Identifying the balance between resident autonomy and patient safety at a teaching hospital is challenging. At times, when residents are unavailable to achieve compliance with the 80-hour workweek, surgical hospitalist attending physicians at an academic medical center will need to evaluate patients directly without resident involvement to meet the goal of timely consultation. At UCSF, the surgical hospitalist is to see new ED consults within 30 minutes.

A key team member in promoting continuity of care at many academic medical centers is the NP. Nonphysician providers (NP's or physician assistants) can play an invaluable role in the delivery of skilled care, promoting clear communication with patients, families, and other healthcare providers, and helping residents avoid violating the ACGME 80-hour workweek requirements. With appropriate supervision, they are an essential component to the delivery of patient care, and they can help promote projects and protocols in patient safety, quality improvement, and the delivery of evidence-based medicine. In the era of the 80-hour resident workweek, the surgical hospitalist model seeks to enhance the academic commitment to surgical education and maximal patient safety by promoting continuity in patient care and appropriate resident supervision.

Complexity of Care

The care of patients with surgical emergencies is an inherently difficult and unpredictable task, and surgeons at tertiary care centers increasingly encounter challenging clinical scenarios, such as acute cholecystitis in solid organ transplant patients, occult GI bleeding and graft versus host disease from hematologic malignancies, bowel obstructions in morbidly obese patients, typhylitis in stem cell transplant patients, and enterocutaneous fistulas in patients referred from other institutions. The care of these patient populations is time-intensive and associated with prolonged lengths of stay (LOS). The trend toward increasing specialization after fellowship training has left many surgeons less comfortable managing these complex illnesses outside of their areas of expertise, especially when these conditions present emergently.

A surgical hospitalist program at an academic medical center offers advantages to develop expertise in the management of these complex surgical patients and to design protocols that will enhance preoperative assessment and improve efficiency and quality of care. A surgical hospitalist program at an academic medical center will need to anticipate this higher degree of acuity, as well as higher volume (e.g., at a 600-hospital bed facility such as UCSF Medical Center), and should anticipate clinical needs by directing quality improvement efforts and inpatient quality initiatives in the management of complex patients. One example of a complex condition at UCSF Medical Center is typhylitis (neutropenic enterocolitis), which is seen as a complication of bone marrow suppression from chemotherapy.

Transfer requests from the community: Another source of increased complexity of care

As a surgical hospitalist program matures, surgeons will increasingly be recognized by surgeons in the community as a resource to handle particularly challenging clinical cases. The program will need to anticipate this source of increased volume and develop the surge capacity to safely handle this extra patient population. At UCSF, the surgical hospitalist program manages a large fraction of the surgical transfer requests from hospitals throughout Northern California, which also represent a disproportionate share of the underinsured population. A key principle to ensure patient safety and optimal outcomes is to involve other expert surgeons from the nonhospitalist faculty to assist in cases requiring special expertise. The care of these complex patients is associated with a prolonged LOS and high perioperative risk. Many patients and their families will need to travel long distances to seek care.

Once patients have received appropriate care at the academic center and are discharged, clear and consistent communication with the referring physicians and primary care providers is required to ensure continuity of quality care. The surgical hospitalist program leadership will benefit by developing a good relationship with the transfer center at their institution to coordinate transfer requests from the community and to ensure that reciprocal transfer arrangements are established for the subsequent return of the patient to the referring community hospital. A strength of the surgical hospitalist model is the availability of surgeons dedicated to ensuring optimal outcomes for complex patient referrals from the community.

Collaborations

Another key opportunity at an academic medical center is to collaborate with established medical hospitalist departments on quality improvement and patient safety projects. A surgical hospitalist program may serve as the foundation for QI programs, with the intent to transform the surgical delivery system by emphasizing error reduction, patient safety, and evidence-based surgery. Postoperative surgical complications are a marker of poor-quality surgical care, and many studies have demonstrated that patients admitted through the ED are sicker and have increased perioperative morbidity and mortality. Perhaps further analysis of the structure, process, and outcome elements in this challenging patient population will improve the quality of emergency care and, thereby, reduce overall healthcare costs.

At several centers across the country, medical hospitalist programs have collaborated with surgeons on hospitalist comanagement programs. An active area of interest is to determine whether greater coordination of care between medical and surgical hospitalists may improve surgical outcomes in the care of high-risk hospitalized inpatients who are admitted through the ED to undergo emergency surgical procedures. A key tool to assess the quality of surgical outcomes is the National Surgical Quality Improvement Program (NSQIP), a risk-adjusted, validated instrument that can determine whether the morbidity and mortality of patients admitted via the ED requiring surgery is reduced. Other important endpoints to study include perioperative process measures of the Medicare Surgical Infection Prophylaxis and Surgical Care Improvement Project. A logical extension is to then study the effect of surgical-medical comanagement on the morbidity and mortality of patients undergoing elective surgical procedures.

Many admitted patients have prolonged waits in the ED because inpatient beds are unavailable, which results in ED overcrowding, boarding of admitted patients, and ambulance diversion. An important area for further research is to determine whether a coordinated medical-surgical approach to the care of complex inpatients will alleviate the problems of overcrowding in the ED by enhancing the timeliness of evaluation and admission of patients through the ED and increasing inpatient hospital bed availability by shortening hospital LOS and facilitating earlier discharge of inpatients. Key outcome measures will include ED waiting times, ED board rates, and ambulance diversion rates. Perhaps if hospital-based clinicians spent less time deciding which service will admit a patient, EDs would be less overcrowded and important medical clues would not be missed in the workup. A joint medical-surgical hospitalist approach to the care of inpatients would likely allow earlier discharge, shorten LOS, and increase hospital bed capacity. New methods of collaborative admission practices between medicine and surgery also could reduce the time patients spend waiting in the ED for a decision about the need for hospital admission. Such collaboration is likely to have benefits in nearly all types of hospitals, not just academic centers.

As the emphasis of surgical hospitalist programs is placed foremost on the needs of the emergency surgery patient and the broad base of operative emergencies within the discipline of general surgery, the experience of the surgical hospitalist will assist in a better understanding of the current national crisis in emergency care, with the potential to identify ways to better match existing resources with patient needs.

Academic promotion and relationships with nonhospitalist surgical faculty

A central challenge to the success and sustainability of an academic surgical hospitalist program is to ensure that junior faculty are properly mentored and have sufficient dedicated research time to achieve the academic goals that will allow them to be promoted. The requirements for promotion for surgical hospitalists will be similar to their nonhospitalist colleagues and will depend critically on the publication of peer-reviewed manuscripts and success in obtaining grant funding from intra- and extramural sources. Traditionally, maintaining an emergency call schedule was dependent on the goodwill of the surgical faculty to equally contribute to the call schedule, and existing systems offered few incentives to become promoted by taking call. A key intent of the hospitalist model is to allow adequate protected time for the hospitalist faculty to perform research during their weeks not on service. Identifying senior mentors who have succeeded in a research career also will be of great benefit to the junior hospitalist surgeon. One caution is to avoid becoming excessively involved in administrative committee duties.

Another concern is that surgical hospitalists will quickly become recognized by referring doctors at their hospital as being more readily available for surgical care and will likely find themselves being referred an increasing number of urgent and elective cases in inpatient and outpatient settings as their reputation evolves. Thus, they will need to be wary of the demands of an expanding clinical volume that can detract from their research priorities and jeopardize their promotion. Early on in their academic career, a preferable method to support their salaries may be derived from compensation for teaching activities, rather than from professional fees.

Another important strategy is to involve the other nonhospitalist faculty in the care of elective cases that possibly require complex surgical intervention. Coordination with these faculty members who are freed from call coverage duties and who offer specialty expertise and assistance will result in the proper matching of available resources within the department.

The research track record of medical hospitalists highlights one strategy for successful research grant applications in the surgical hospitalist field. The majority of the early research described the medical hospitalist model itself, focusing on hospital LOS, costs, and enhancements in education. The research later evolved to focus upon quality and efficiency improvements in care, implementation of best practices, sign-out safety, and enhancing patient safety. These efforts succeeded through extensive collaborations with other departments and by applying to funding agencies such as the Agency for Healthcare Research and Quality and then the National Institutes of Health. However, a particularly challenging arena to demonstrate significant improvement is in the dimension of quality of care.

Relationships with other academic departments and the medical center

The emergence of surgical hospitalists as key providers of inpatient care will create important opportunities to assume leadership roles within the medical center and to work closely with other hospital leaders, such as the chief medical officer and CEO, and departmental leaders to work toward mutual, institution-specific quality improvement and patient safety goals. Because they will become familiar with the institutional challenges to patient safety, surgical hospitalists will likely be invited by medical center leaders to participate in several hospital committees, such as the patient safety, academic senate, OR, pharmacy and therapeutics, code blue, and medical executive committees.

Another question to consider is whether the surgical hospitalist program should segregate to become a distinct division within the academic center. It is likely that existing programs will need to mature before this can be considered, and in the early growth phase, it is likely wisest not to attempt to form separate units. Another anticipated next step will be the creation of yearlong surgical hospitalist fellowship training programs at academic medical centers, which may also emphasize leadership training and an understanding of the statistical methodology of outcomes research and NSQIP. Ultimately, local hospital factors will likely determine whether the surgical hospitalist program evolves into separate division within an academic medical center or whether it continues to reside within a division of general surgery or the department of surgery.

Conclusion

The surgical hospitalist model can enhance the academic mission of patient care, research, and teaching at an academic medical center, while concurrently providing a foundation for patient safety and quality improvement.

This new paradigm for the organization of surgical departments in academic medical centers seeks to provide professional, quality, and prompt care despite resident 80-hour workweek restrictions and to more effectively match existing emergency surgical resources with patient care needs.

CHAPTER 13

Acute Care Surgery: The Evolution of a Specialty

L.D. Britt, MD, MPH, FACS, FCCM

Excellence in the trauma profession has been well chronicled over the past three decades, including the development of state/regional trauma systems, the endorsement of specific trauma management paradigms and protocols, and the establishment of technology-enhanced trauma bays/ICUs. However, the trauma profession is currently facing a major crisis. The waning interest in trauma as a career has been repeatedly documented. Richardson and Miller highlighted that the overwhelming majority of residents had no desire to pursue a career in traumatology.[2] Such a state of specialty decline comes at a time when all disciplines of surgery are besieged with threats. In fact, there has never been a period in which the field of surgery has faced so many challenges to its basic tenets, including ensuring quality of care for patients, academic excellence, and financial stability. There are few remaining cynics, if any, who question the need to reinvigorate trauma surgery, as there has been a well-documented decline in interest and a steady drop in graduate medical trainees pursuing a career in traumatology.

Some historical perspective is necessary to better understand the environmental and financial dynamics that have been the catalysts for this change. Starting in the mid1990s, there was a noticeable decline in the violent crime rate. Whether this decline has resulted from the creation of stricter laws in many jurisdictions, sentencing criminals to longer prison terms, or the creation of more penal institutions is still speculative. According to the Bureau of Justice Statistics, the drop in the violent crime rate in the mid1990s was the highest decrease since 1973 when the bureau began reporting its annual National Crime Victimization Survey. Although there is a need for more comprehensive prevention programs, credit must be directed to some of the existing programs that address gun control and domestic violence. Regardless of the cause, the decline in violence-related trauma—predominantly penetrating injuries—parallels the decrease in surgical cases. This is compounded by the successful nonoperative management of solid organ injuries. With most trauma services being inundated with blunt injuries that require minimal operative intervention, today's trauma surgeon infrequently participates in major surgical operations and is often relegated to resuscitation/stabilization and critical care management.

It would be very easy to attribute these changes to the waning interest in pursuing trauma as a career. However, this declining interest antedated many of the aforementioned trends. In 1985, the American Board of Surgery surveyed surgeons taking their board-qualifying exam, and only 3% indicated interest in a career in trauma and critical care. Also, Richardson and Miller reported that only 18% of graduating residents were interested in trauma as a major part of their future practices. During this same period, Esposito et al reported that most surgeons in the state of Washington preferred not to treat trauma patients.[3]

Considering that there is a documented improved chance of survival for patients who sustained major trauma if they are treated in a specialized trauma center within regionalized systems of trauma care, a crisis is rapidly developing in which optimal trauma care will be severely jeopardized because of the dwindling number of surgeons who are trained and/or willing to care for the injured. The adverse effect of this becomes even more evident when it is evaluated in the context of optimal trauma experience. Konvolinka et al noted that survival of seriously injured patients is greater in high-volume trauma centers.[5] The study noted that when a surgeon manages 35 or fewer seriously injured patients per year, he or she is unlikely to have unexpected survivors. However, with the management of more than 125 seriously injured patients per year, there should be at least two unexpected survivors per year. In Australia, for example, emergency surgeons are needed particularly in the outback, where 10% of the Australian population resides. As lengthy travel may be required for patients in rural areas to access quality trauma care, some multiply injured patients will only survive if the right surgical procedures are performed at the scene immediately. These may include neurosurgical, general surgery, or orthopedic operations performed often as damage control procedures, followed by the definitive procedure in the hospital to which the patient is transferred later.

More than a century ago, William Halsted, considered by most to be the creator of the residency training system for America, stated that "every important hospital should have on its resident staff of surgeons at least one who is well able to deal with any emergency that may arise."[6] Perhaps this should be the mantra to bring to an end all further discussion about the separation between trauma and nontrauma emergency surgery. Howard Champion astutely highlighted in his presidential address to the membership of the Eastern Association for the Surgery of Trauma at the 1992 annual meeting that trauma should not be separated from general surgery.[7] He stated that efforts should be made to keep trauma and general surgery inseparable. In his 1998 presidential address at the American Association for the Surgery of Trauma, David Richardson asked the question that now demands an answer: "Trauma center and trauma surgeons: Are we too specialized?"[8] The argument could be made that we have become too specialized and that broadening our profession to include other elements of general surgery is not only appropriate, but highly desirable. Spain et al reported the results of an e-mail survey of approximately 60 trauma centers, which found that 65% of the trauma surgeons also performed emergency surgery while on trauma call.[9] Twenty-five percent did not, and 15% performed nontrauma emergency surgery sporadically. The authors concluded that delivery of both emergency and general surgical care by the trauma service provided a necessary buffer for the variations in trauma volume.

Recently, there has been a new initiative to broaden the spectrum of trauma to include, in addition to emergency general surgery, more elements of trauma management (e.g., orthopedic and neurosurgical trauma). This proposed new specialty would be named "acute care surgery." Critical care would need to remain an integral part of this proposed specialty, as the acute care surgeon must remain an essential provider of critical care for injured patients and for patients from other specialists who are unwilling or unable to provide this care. In addition, there should be a logical expansion of the trauma care network to the emergency care system. One caveat needs to be highlighted: There are no guarantees that widening the spectrum of the trauma specialty will improve the overall financial status, as unsponsored acute hospital care continues to increase as reimbursement declines. More than a decade ago, trauma care costs in the Unite States. were estimated to be approximately $13 billion, which included hospitalization and professional fees with a high proportion of uninsured or underinsured patients.

It is unlikely that broadening coverage to include all emergency surgical care will have a substantial effect on this financial disparity. This proposed specialty change from traumatology to acute care surgery will likely draw criticism that such a change is an unnecessary response to a consequence of the times, both socioeconomic and political. However, a more convincing argument can be made that traumatology and emergency surgery, both major components of general surgery, should have never been separated and, therefore, this proposed change would be a natural evolution. Regardless of the debates that ensue, the official unveiling of a new specialist, the acute care surgeon is the best solution to a now nationwide problem—the steady decline in subspecialty coverage in the emergency setting and the recruitment and retention of trauma surgeons. How should this new initiative proceed? Ideally, implementation of this new professional model should not be done under the ruse of trial and error. On the contrary, the trend is well established for the next phase in the evolution of the trauma surgeon. At this point, there should be no reluctance on our part to embrace this specialty change.

Chapter 13

Figure 13.1 depicts the essential components of this new specialty.

FIGURE 13.1 — THE ESSENTIAL ELEMENTS OF A CAREER IN ACUTE CARE SURGERY

- Patient care (including critical care)
- Education
- Research (basic science and clinical)
- Emergency system design
- Prevention
- Health policy advocacy
- Mentorship
- Fellowship

TRAUMA
- Blunt trauma
- Penetrating trauma
- Critical Care
- Burns

+

GENERAL SURGERY OPERATIVE EMERGENCIES
- Refractory intraabdominal sepsis
- Preferated hollow viscus
- Intestinal obstruction
- Refractory gastrointestinal bleeding
- Necrotizing soft tissue infections

=

ACUTE CARE SURGERY

Source: Eastern Virginia Medical School, Department of Surgery, Norfolk, VA.

Trauma surgeons in some countries and provinces already undertake emergency neurosurgical and orthopedic surgery. For example, at the Division of Trauma Surgery in Zurich, Switzerland, trauma surgeons are trained to perform all emergency neurosurgical, general surgical, and musculoskeletal (orthopedic) interventions. The philosophy in this institution is that only a surgeon well trained in different surgical subspecialties, and who has a comprehensive understanding in trauma care, can decide what the optimal treatment is for these patients. Each trauma center will develop its own triage and management structure. When subspecialties are unwilling to cover trauma services, the model of the comprehensive trauma surgeon (i.e., the acute care surgeon) will gain increasing acceptance. Even if this concept is broadly adopted, there are still other threats to or challenges for the profession, including:

- Declining reimbursement

- Nonsurgeon control of the ICU

- Malpractice issues

- Pay-for-coverage subspecialties, the increasing financial burden

The fate of our profession revolves around our ability to embrace change and firmly address each real threat with careful analysis and implementation of a highly focused plan. Many consider the acute care surgeon to be distinct, a unique specialist with expertise in trauma, critical care, and general surgery.

Although a two-year format was chosen as a template for the curriculum for acute care surgery, the following highlights the original proposed formats; refer to Figure 13.2.

FIGURE 13.2 PROPOSED ACUTE CARE SURGERY FORMATS

Proposed formats after four years of core general surgery	
Format A (two years)	**Format B (three years)**
Year one: • 12 months—Trauma/emergency surgery/critical care Year Two: • 3 months—Thoracic • 3 months—Transplant/hepatobiliary • 3 months—Vascular/interventional radiology • 3 months—Elective (orthopedics, neurosurgery, plastics)	Year one: • 12 months—Trauma/emergency surgery Year Two: • 9 months—Critical care (SICU/NICU/CCU/burns/PICU) • 3 months—Vascular/interventional radiology Year Three: • 5 months—Ortho and neurosurgery • 3 months—Thoracic • 2 months—Transplant/hepatobiliary • 2 months—Elective (plastic/ped surg/endosurgery)

Source: Eastern Virginia Medical School, Department of Surgery, Norfolk, VA.

Proposed Formats after Four Years of Core General Surgery

I. General

    A. Prehospital/system management (special input from Dr. Norm McSwain)

    B. Initial assessment and early resuscitation

    C. Diagnostic imaging

    D. Anesthesia in the emergency setting

    E. Fundamental operative approaches

    F. Nutrition

    G. Critical care (the same nine-month curriculum)

II. Organ Systems
   A. Pharyngeal/laryngeal/tracheobronchial
   B. Esophageal
   C. Thoracic
   D. Abdominal wall
   E. Gastroduodenal
   F. Intestinal
   G. Hepatic
   H. Pancreatic
   I. Splenic
   J. Vascular
   K. Urogenital/gynecologic
   L. Orthopedics
   M. Neurosurgical

III. Areas for special emphasis
   A. Acute care surgery in the rural setting
   B. The elderly and acute care surgery
   C. Disaster and mass casualties management
   D. Education: Surgical simulation
   E. Prevention: Principles and methodology
   F. Advanced directives
   G. The nonviable patient and organ procurement

IV. Operative management principles
   A. Management of perforations/injuries
      1. Esophagus
      2. Stomach
      3. Duodenum
      4. Small bowel
      5. Colon/rectum
      6. Bladder
      7. Lung
      8. Cardiac

B. Management of solid organ injuries
   1. Trachea/bronchus
   2. Spleen (splenectomy/splenorrhaphy)
   3. Liver (hepatic resection/hepatorrhaphy)
   4. Pancreas (major resection/debridements)
   5. Kidney (primary repair, nephrectomy/partial repair)

C. Necrotic tissue—debridements principles

D. Abscess—drainage principles

E. Appendectomy

F. Adhesiolysis

G. Cholecystectomy/cholecystostomy

H. Common bile duct exploration

I. Gastrointestinal resections

J. Colostomy

K. Colostomy reversal

L. Hemorrhoidectomy/rectal prolapse management

M. Gynecological emergencies
   1. Ectopic pregnancy
   2. Ovarian cyst
   3. Tubo-ovarian abscess

N. Thoracic
   1. Mediasternotomy
   2. Left/right thoracotomy
   3. Wedge and partial lung resection
   4. Cardiac injury repair
   5. Decortication (open and VATS)
   6. Pleurodesis

O. Orthopedic
   1. Intraoperative washouts
   2. Placement of external fixators
   3. Fasciectomies (upper and lower extremities)
   4. Open reduction and internal fixation

- P. Neurosurgery
    1. ICP monitoring placement (including ventriculostomy)
    2. Burr hole placement
    3. Limited craniotomy
    4. Halo traction
- Q. Plastics
    1. Soft tissues, flap construction
    2. Management of hand injury
    3. Management of facial soft tissue injuries

The curriculum for acute care surgery should be competency based as designed by the Accreditation Council for Graduate Medical Education (ACGME).

REFERENCES

1. LD Britt, DD Trunkey, DV Feliciano. "A Proposed Curriculum: Acute Care Surgery," *Acute Care Surgery* (New York: Springer, 2007) 752–753.

2. JD Richardson, FB Miller. "Will Future Surgeons be Interested in Trauma Care? Results of a Resident Survey." *J Trauma* 1992; 32(2): 229–235.

3. TJ Esposito, RV Maier, FP Rivara, CJ Carrico. "Why Surgeons Prefer Not to Care for Trauma Patients." *Arch Surg* 1991; 126(3): 292–297.

4. JG West, RH Cales, AB Gazzaniga. "Impact of Regionalization: The Orange County Experience." *Arch Surg* 1983; 118(6): 740–744.

5. CW Konvolinka, WS Copes, WJ Sacco. "Institution and Per-Surgeon Volume Versus Survival Outcome in Pennsylvania's Trauma Centers." *Am J Surg* 1995; 170(4): 333–340.

6. WS Halsted. "The Training of the Surgeon." *John Hopkins Hosp. Bull.* 1904; 15: 267–275.

7. HR Champion. "EAST Presidential Address: Reflections on and Directions for Trauma Care." *J Trauma* 1992; 33(2): 270–278.

8. JD Richardson. "Trauma Centers and Trauma Surgeons: Have We Become Too Specialized?" *J Trauma* 2000; 48(1): 1–7.

9. DA Spain, JD Richardson, EH Carrillo, FB Miller, MA Wilson, HC Polk Jr. "Should Trauma Surgeons Do General Surgery." *J Trauma* 2000; 48(3): 433–438.

10. HR Champion, MS Mabee. *An American Crisis in Trauma Care Reimbursement: An Issue Analysis Monograph.* (Washington, DC: Surgical Critical Care Services, 1990).

CHAPTER 14

Documentation, Coding, Billing, and Related Issues

M. Tray Dunaway, MD, FACS, CSP

The most important element in achieving correct reimbursement for hospitalist services is not physician knowledge of documentation, coding, and billing, but rather the establishment of excellent business relationships with knowledgeable experts in your hospital.

As surgical hospitalists, our primary intent is not to be coders, compliance officers, or DRG coordinators. Instead, we want to practice medicine and let somebody else worry about all the paperwork. And with regard to documentation, for most of our patients, the information we need to deliver care could easily fit on a 3x5 index card. However, from a reimbursement perspective, this method is unsustainable. When practicing medicine as a hobby, the "holy trinity" of documentation, coding, and reimbursement is irrelevant. But when practicing medicine to earn a living, a correct compliance approach to the coding conundrum is critical for financial success.

To achieve not only correct reimbursement but also the best reimbursement, hospitalists need to fully comprehend, integrate, and apply expert documentation, coding, billing, reimbursement, and compliance knowledge into their particular practices. This can be achieved in two ways: they can assume a part-time practice and keep up with the constantly changing rules and regulations of the reimbursement process, or they can learn enough about the processes to use willing and able resources in a hospital setting to allow them to practice medicine full-time.

The choice is easy for a hospitalist who elects to practice medicine instead of dedicating valuable time to reimbursement documentation. The hospitalist does not need to hire additional reimbursement personnel, as most private practices already employ them. The hospital is likely to hire the right person for the job simply because the hospital knows it will likely result in a great return on investment for the hospital, as well as benefiting the hospitalist.

Chapter 14

Physicians typically want to minimize their work with documentation, coding, billing, and compliance, but they also want to reap the benefit of full reimbursement, as well as the credit and recognition great physician documentation can deliver. Most of this chapter is not coding/documentation instruction and will not suffice for adequate coding education to make coding practical. The first half is intended to increase awareness of principles of collaboration with others involved in the documentation/coding/billing process, a perspective critical for success. The latter half will feature an overview, an anatomic discourse of basic evaluation and management (E&M) principles that also gives practical, time-tested tips that any physician can use.

Words

Let's start with the basics. Words matter, some more than others. By a linguistic team effort and through alphanumeric codes, our clinical words are translated into the healthcare languages of finance, quality, and regulation. The rules of the game regarding words are fairly straightforward.

Only a physician can write and certify clinical words. The linguistic team consisting of coders, DRG coordinators, compliance officers, discharge planners, and other health information management (HIM) experts can translate the clinical words into code but cannot write clinical words that matter in charts (e.g., $\downarrow$ K ≠ "hypokalemia," "$\downarrow$ Hct" ≠ "blood loss anemia", and "infiltrate on CXR"≠ "pneumonia"). The linguistic team also cannot change the clinical words physicians write down, even if the desired change is more accurate than the words initially chosen by the physician. This is the physician's exclusive power of the pen. So when a hospitalist is approached by a hospital linguistic team expert with a suggestion for a better word to more accurately describe a patient so that the corresponding alpha-numeric code will more accurately be translated to financial, quality, and regulatory languages, it can only be a suggestion. In all likelihood, the suggested words will benefit the hospital and hospitalist because of the linguistic expert's knowledge of financial, quality, and regulatory languages of healthcare. If they could simply change the word themselves, they would. But they cannot because of the rules of the game.

Linguistic team members work at understanding the rules of the game full-time. And, of course, the rules change constantly. October of every year is a particularly exciting month for the linguistic team because it is the month when the coding and word rules change. Fortunately, the linguistic team does keep up with the Medicare changes and helps clinicians use the rules to the best advantage of both the hospital and physicians.

When a clinician learns to trust the linguistic team and vice versa, mutual respect for each other's expertise grows. This translates into improved profitability and regulatory compliance, as well as recognition by third-party payers and the public of provision of better healthcare by physicians and the hospital. The increasingly regulated nature of healthcare and the myriad of changes are too time-consuming for physicians to track without assistance from trusted resources. When setting up a hospitalist practice, most hospitals provide documentation and coding resources, but it is part of the hospitalist's responsibility to help generate a great working relationship with the linguistic team.

Practice leadership should insist that a compliance plan for the hospitalist practice is developed and administered. A compliance plan is simply business-of-medicine malpractice insurance. Compliance refers to numerous regulatory statutes that govern how we run our medical businesses. But most applicable to a practicing physician, it centers on documentation. Compliance officers should consider easing regulation on physicians to become documentation coaches. Compliance people and others on the linguistic team interface between the clinical languages of healthcare and the other languages of healthcare with which clinicians are not as familiar.

With expert assistance from the linguistic team, physicians can become experts at documentation. By listening to this expert advice, physicians can learn which words really matter in clinical documentation and which words are more valuable in a variety of circumstances affecting processes, determinations, and judgments that ultimately affect the hospital and hospitalists in a codependent business alliance. Physicians should take the time to build strong relationships with the hospital linguistic experts who are eager to help doctors, and the hospital, succeed. Each should teach the other the essentials of their business to guarantee mutual success.

Codes

The critical contribution of physicians to the reimbursement process is physician-documented words that ultimately determine the assigned code and presented for reimbursement, as well as to speak the other non-clinical healthcare languages. Integrating suggestions of the linguistic team into documentation will benefit the physician and the hospital.

Chapter 14

Hospitals and physicians use two systems of codes. Hospitals use DRG coding—now transitioning to Medicare Severity (MS) DRG—and physicians use E&M coding. DRGs will transition to MS-DRGs over a two-year phase in fiscal year 2008–2009.

What are the implications of these changing codes, and what can we do about it? Let's first examine the DRG system.

DRG

When the DRG system first was incorporated into hospital billing and reporting of clinical information, a primary diagnosis assigned to a patient classified the group the patient belongs to and, specifically, from a reimbursement perspective, the ballpark fee Medicare would pay through its inpatient prospective payment system (IPPS). Secondary diagnoses and complications and comorbidities (CC) also influenced the classification and reimbursement. It was a piecemeal approach to figuring out how to pay for patients depending on how sick they are. The transition to MS-DRG is even more piecemeal and more bewildering to physicians. As the name implies, the MS-DRG is used to reflect the Medicare severity–adjusted condition of patients and is designed to stratify patients from the "sick" to the "not as sick" to distribute a shrinking reimbursement pool more efficiently—if not more equitably—from Medicare's perspective.

MS-DRGs have ushered in new categorizations. Some of the old CCs have been eliminated, such as COPD, CHF, A-fib, and dehydration, and some old CCs have been changed to major CCs (MCC), such as acute MI, pneumonia, acute renal failure, and sepsis. And some CCs remain unchanged. The former DRGs are split into three categories to more accurately reflect resource utilization and subsequent government payment. The categorization is roughly based on the presence or absence of diagnoses classified as the now familiar MCCs, CCs, or without MCC or CC (i.e., non-CCs).

The words and symbols that clinicians use may or may not function as MCCs or CCs. "↓ Hct" does not translate to "acute blood loss anemia" or "postop anemia." "↓ Na" does not translate to "hyponatremia." An "infiltrate on CXR" that you treat with antibiotics does not translate as "pneumonia." Even though for clinicians they may appear intuitive, symbols are insufficient for accurate coding. To reiterate, words matter. And your linguistic experts are ready to help you make sure that you get all the credit and recognition you deserve with the right words.

The MS-DRG, ultimately, will generate a relative weight for each patient. This relative weight reflects an index of how sick the patient is and, in turn, how much Medicare is likely to pay to the hospital for the patient's care. But the relative weight is not only about the hospital; it is also very much about the attending physician of record. This MS–DRG-derived number, assigned as a relative weight to the patient you treat, reflects how sick your patients are to Medicare and to other interested third-party payers. If Medicare is working so hard to determine the severity of illness of patients to determine how they pay hospitals for inpatient services, might this someday just affect payment physicians receive from Medicare as well?

It is in the mutual interest of hospitals and hospitalists to use words that reflect the most accurate assessment of how sick a patient is to ensure assignment of the most appropriate MS-DRG. Simply put, if the MS-DRG classification is undercoded, physician and hospital reimbursement may be adversely affected, and credit and recognition of taking care of a sicker-than-average patient is overlooked. If an MS-DRG classification is overcoded—misleading third-party payers into believing the patient was sicker than he or she really was—compliance difficulties will ensue that, if proven to be intentional, could lead to fraud and abuse accusations that could ultimately result in civil and criminal prosecution. At best, unintentional overcoding, although not criminal, can lead to stiff fines and penalties. Having a great relationship with hospital coding experts, coupled with an effective and well-administered compliance plan, is a proven way to ensure correct reimbursement, recognition of clinical excellence, and mitigation of civil and criminal repercussions from noncompliance.

So does this mean that, for a hospitalist, it's necessary to understand all about MS-DRG, CCs, MCCs, and myriad alphabet-soup acronyms for the latest machinations foisted upon us by Medicare? Absolutely not. Here's exactly what a savvy hospitalist needs to do: Document your admission history and physical (H&P) consultations, progress notes, and discharge summary for every legitimate diagnosis a patient has that has any clinical significance.

The linguistic team will sort through the diagnoses that only the physician can document. Because of their knowledge in interfacing clinical and nonclinical languages of healthcare and subsequent coding translations, they can select the optimal MS-DRG with or without MCCs or CCs to yield correct and accurate reimbursement and representation of your clinical work. And you can help them achieve optimal coding by simply documenting diagnoses. The role of the surgical hospitalist is to remember to complete the simpler task of providing complete and accurate information about patient diagnoses.

Chapter 14

Present on Admission

If Medicare's objective is to pay more for the sicker patients, what about patients who became sicker once they were admitted to the hospital? Medicare won't pay for some illness that are acquired during the stay at the hospital and not present on admission.

This Medicare initiative is another reason to list every diagnosis on admission. For instance, a surgical hospitalist may admit a patient to the hospital with cholecystitis, and she leaves improved after successful cholecystectomy but with a pressure sore. Medicare will not reimburse for care of the complication sustained under your care. The same principles will apply to hospital-acquired infections and some, but not all, iatrogenic complications. Make it a priority to list every diagnosis that is present on admission, distinguishing present-on-admission conditions from hospital-acquired conditions. That way, third-party payers will not assume that a new diagnosis on discharge was your fault and thus deny payment or otherwise penalize you.

ICD-9, or 10, and 11!

The diagnosis reference ICD is a collection of diseases, signs and symptoms, external causes of injuries or diseases, and social circumstances published by the World Health Organization (WHO). The system was originally developed for worldwide morbidity and mortality statistics and has been subsequently modified for reimbursement purposes. Many hospitals currently use ICD-9, although the most recent version, ICD-10, was developed in 1992. Still yet, hospitals can look forward to another version, ICD-11, scheduled for 2015 release.

So is it necessary for surgeons to understand this? No, not unless they want to be a professional coder. Does it matter? Absolutely. Physicians need to document diseases (diagnoses) as detailed and precisely as possible. Let your hospital experts sort out the coding; if they ask you a question about diagnoses, understand they are fine-tuning the coding to reflect the most accurate diagnosis possible, not only for the hospital's benefit, but for your benefit as well.

There is one very important factor of how ICD lists diagnoses as well as symptoms. The bottom line is that symptoms don't pay well. Given a choice between a symptom and a diagnosis, physicians should document the diagnosis, if possible. "Chest pain" to describe a myocardial infarction or pneumonia is not specific enough and could lead to lowered reimbursement. If a symptom is all that you can document at the time, so be it. But do not document a symptom as a diagnosis if you have a real diagnosis.

Physician documentation of all clinically significant diagnoses is a central theme for documentation purposes, and we will illustrate this for a number of examples. Let's turn for a moment to E&M coding.

E&M Codes

Whereas MS-DRG codes determine hospital reimbursement, E&M codes govern physician reimbursement. Surgical hospitalists may occasionally see patients in an outpatient clinic setting, but payment for most such visits will be bundled with the preceding inpatient procedure. Thus, there are only four categories of E&M codes that they will use regularly:

- Initial hospital care (IH)

- Subsequent hospital care (SH)

- Consultations (CON)

- Hospital observation codes (HOBS)

There are other applicable inpatient E&M codes a surgical hospitalist will use occasionally, but this review is limited to the four main groups.

Knowing which code is applicable and which code is best for specific circumstances is critical. These codes are five digits, the first three of which are 922 for E&M codes. The fourth digit identifies the variety of code, and the fifth digit determines the actual level of code. Each numerical code has a descriptive name that is self-explanatory. The descriptive names and numerical codes can be found in the first section of the AMA's annually published and revised current procedural terminology (CPT) book. It can serve as a useful reference from time to time, but there is usually no need for physicians to buy one as the hospital's linguistic team most likely has more than one copy.

Chapter 14

There is no need to memorize them, since it can lead to coding confusion. Rather, simply remember that there are:

- Three levels of IH codes, low to high 1, 2, 3, corresponding to the fifth-digit level of service

- Three levels of SH codes, low to high 1, 2, 3

- Five levels of CON codes, low to high 1, 2, 3, 4, 5

- Three levels of HOBS codes, low to high 1, 2, 3

Relative Value Unit

Each code is associated with a specific relative value unit (RVU). An RVU is a number published by Medicare to accompany each code. The values assigned to different codes are adjusted periodically. As implied by its name, RVUs state the relative value of each code representing the physician work associated with that code. These are called work RVUs (wRVU). Total RVUs can also factor in other specifics such as where the procedure was done (e.g., office vs. hospital). By changing the RVU on any given code, Medicare enables itself to increase or decrease the reimbursement level of the code.

Again, there is no need to memorize the CPT codes. The intent is to understand and use each code and its associated RVU appropriately. Some physicians find it most useful to simply assign the RVU as though it were a dollar figure. For instance, the wRVU of a level 3 (the highest level) of an initial hospital (IN) inpatient visit (IH 99223) is currently 3.78 wRVUs. To calculate how much actual dollar reimbursement this code represents, Medicare multiplies it by an amount that is determined by the geographic location of the practice. But if you think of the wRVUs in dollars (e.g., $3.78), it is easy to see how it compares to the next lower IH inpatient visit code (IH 99222) of $2.56 (or 2.56 wRVUs).

Hospital Observation

"Doctor, do you want to admit this patient or admit for observation?" This critical question will influence payment to the physician and the hospital. For example, the RVU of a level 3 IH inpatient visit (admission H&P) is 2.99. The same level of documentation, but classified as a hospital observation level 3 in which the admission and discharge is on the same day, is a much higher 4.26 RVUs, yielding a more than 40% increase. That is an important difference.

It is important to know whether a patient should be admitted for observation or for an inpatient admission. Consider using the following algorithm:

> **OBSERVATION VS. ADMISSION ALGORITHM**
>
> Does the patient's condition require treatment or further evaluation that can only be provided in a hospital setting, specifically as an inpatient or an observation?
>
> - **If yes:** Can the patient's condition be evaluated or treated within 24 hours and/or is rapid improvement of the patient's condition anticipated within 24 hours?
>   1. If yes: Admit for observation
>   2. If no: Admit for inpatient admission
> - **If no:** The patient should be treated as an outpatient, by home health, or by an extended care facility.
> - **If unsure:** Keep the patient for additional time in the holding area to determine an ultimate yes or no.

Additionally, if the patient is admitted as an observation patient and it turns out that the patient is admitted and discharged on different calendar days, the observation code level 3 to be used (99220) will have the same RVU (2.99) as an admission at the same level of care.

Consultations

Words matter with consultations too. A consult is not a referral. There is a big difference between the two terms, and it is reflected in coding and subsequent billing. Medicare has rules concerning what a consultation is and what a referral is. To qualify as a consultation, three Rs must be present. Refer to Figure 14.1.

Chapter 14

FIGURE 14.1 — CONSULTATION RULES AND DESCRIPTION

Consultation rule	Description
Request	There is a written request for a consultation made by an initiating (or requesting) physician, and the need for consultation is documented in a patient's medical record. In an inpatient setting, this is not usually a problem. The written order, or a consultation request form from a ward secretary, is sufficient, and progress notes usually reflect the need.
Rendered opinion	The consulting physician evaluates the patient and renders a written opinion in the chart. This does not preclude a phone call back to the initiating physician, an excellent routine to keep the initiating physician relationship strong, but a written opinion must be in the medical record.
Report back to requesting physician	A written report is furnished by the consultant to the initiating physician. The initiating physician now can make an informed decision as to appropriate treatment. The recommended treatment may be followed or ignored by the initiating physician, and treatment may be made by the initiating physician or the consultant.

Source: Healthcare Value, Inc., Camden, SC.

If the initiating physician requests the services of the consultant, then treats the patient (after the consulting physician has completed the consultation, which can be coded and billed separately), and then the consultant assumes responsibility for the complete care of the patient, it becomes a referral. With regard to a consultation followed by treatment, payment for a consultation can be made regardless of which doctor initiates treatment unless a transfer of care occurs. Transfer of care means a referring physician transfers responsibility for the patient's complete care at the time of referral. A patient referral can only happen if the receiving physician documents approval of care in advance. For example, an internist requests a consultation for a patient with abdominal pain. The initiating internist documents the reason and request for the consultation in the chart. The surgical consultant examines the patient and documents a written opinion. The surgical consultant suspects appendicitis and reports back to the initiating physician. The initiating internist, while briefly considering "How difficult could an appendectomy really be?" asks the consulting surgeon to address the problem and then transfers care to the surgeon. The consultant then performs an appendectomy and can legitimately code and bill for not only the appendectomy, but also the consultation.

Alternatively, if the internist calls the surgeon about the referral of a patient who may have appendicitis and, upon dropping by the patient's room and confirming the opinion, the surgeon does the appendectomy and assumes full care postoperatively, no consultation may be billed.

Words matter. For any physician who accepts or requests referrals or consultations (not the same), do not document, "I am referring a patient to you." Rather, write, "I am requesting a consultation," or simply, "I have (or will) asked Dr. Smith to see my patient." This has mutual value to all physicians and should be a common courtesy to allow physicians a choice between referrals and consultations.

ED Codes

Although technically not an inpatient code, emergency department (ED) visits by a hospitalist may be coded and billed several ways. If the hospitalist sees a patient in the ED and essentially functions as the ED doctor, treats the patient as an ED doctor would, and sends the patient home, it is appropriate to use ED billing codes. This is significant because ED visits require less documentation for otherwise similar levels of care. If a hospitalist is called to the ED to render an opinion as a consultant, a consultation code may be used if the patient is subsequently released from the ED or if the patient is admitted to another service. If the hospitalist admits the patient, an admission code (admission or observation) would be appropriate. However, if the evaluation leads to the decision to proceed with surgery, both the admission code (E&M decision-making component) and the surgical procedure code can be billed.

Procedural Codes

E&M codes are listed in CPT manuals but occupy only the first few pages of this ever-expanding publication. The rest of the CPT book is devoted primarily to procedural codes, such as those used for surgery or bedside procedures.

As with all coding, rules constantly change; codes are dropped, bundled, or added every October. It is a coder's job to stay current, but it is the job of the surgical hospitalist to meet with the coder on a

Chapter 14

regular basis, especially every November, to make sure that applicable code changes are reviewed and efficiently used. From this meeting, the coder and hospitalist can develop a one-page print or electronic checklist form. This checklist includes the most commonly billed codes; the checklist can then be recorded and sent to the coder for billing purposes. For uncommon procedures or services, the form can include a fill-in-the-blank space to record details to help the coder assign the right code for the event. These should be completed and sent to the coder immediately after the procedure to ensure quick coding and subsequent billing

A healthy working business relationship between surgeons and coders is key to successful, correct coding and subsequent billing. Questions to a surgeon from a coder are intended to clarify and ensure accuracy rather than to represent a threat to autonomy or professionalism.

Coding Education

Although physicians need not become coding experts, they should become documentation experts. That said, a basic understanding of E&M coding is essential if for no other reason than to understand what information a coder must have to comply with third-party payer rules and regulations. This understanding ensures accuracy for correct billing and improved reimbursement. Mutual understanding goes a long way in mutual respect.

Before delving into books and coding courses, a physician should consult his or her own coder. If the practice has such a person, he or she may be the best point person to provide the applicable education. Ideally, doctors should learn enough to make it easier for the coder to help the physicians and the practice. And the coder should learn enough about the surgical hospitalists' job to know how to help most effectively.

All physicians should know which category of code is most appropriate for an E&M encounter, what level of code is most appropriate, and specifically what documentation is required to support the code. Physicians who are aware of these critical elements and incorporate these basic coding elements into their documentation enable coders to focus on the more arcane issues. For almost all other coding needs, physician documentation of the most accurate and specific patient diagnoses will suffice.

Documentation, Coding, Billing, and Related Issues

E&M Coding Anatomy

There are some essential bits of information to consider when documenting for an E&M code. The three key components of any E&M code: history, physical examination, and medical decision-making. Documentation for any E&M code must include at least two of the three key components. Generally, new patients, hospital admissions, or an established patient with a new consultation require all three, whereas an established patient or follow-up patient requires full completion of two, with a mention of the third.

Think of each of these components as individual checklists for specific bits of information. Individual E&M codes have variable minimal documentation requirements from each of the three key components. Medical decision-making (MDM) has three subcomponents: data, diagnosis, and risk.

Medical decision-making

MDM, in conjunction with the H&P, is a way to ensure that the problem a patient presents with warrants the level of code billed. Most physicians already unknowingly document MDM during the H&P. The level of MDM (straightforward, low, moderate, or high) is determined by a combination of risk, amount/complexity of data, and diagnoses/management options. And each of these components has its own checklists of information bits in which a specific number of details are required for the various levels of risk, data, and diagnosis classifications.

Data

Briefly, points are assigned to the amount/complexity of data we review or order, such as a lab, an x-ray, or a medical diagnostic test. Extra points are assigned if we personally look at an x-ray or a urinalysis specimen, for example, (and not simply rely on the radiologist or lab interpretation of the study) or have a conversation with the interpreting physician about the findings.

Diagnosis or management options

Similarly, points are assigned for diagnoses/management options to new problems. And there is a difference between a new problem requiring a workup, or alternatively, not requiring a workup. For the purpose of CPT coding, there is a distinction between established problems that are stable and those that are unstable or out of control. Even chronic self-limited or minor problems may be assigned some points.

Chapter 14

Risk

A series of hypothetical patient descriptions separate a specific patient into four risk categories: minimum, low, moderate, and high. Although most physicians have not seen these hypothetical descriptions, a coder will have experience in differentiating these conditions.

Putting MDM together

The level of risk is established when the points for data and diagnoses are tallied to determine risk, and the level of MDM is derived from the individual scores. Risk is key in this process because it's independent of decisions by less-than-honest physicians who order unnecessary tests or add inconsequential diagnoses to drive up points. Third-party payers, particularly Medicare, will deny the use of points or scorecards when auditing. However, auditors often use these scorecards for private third-party payers who also administer CMS programs.

History

The history component is more familiar territory for physicians, but there are some esoteric elements. The minimal documentation required in the history depends on the level of the code. However, the anatomy of the history is described in specific categories.

- **Chief complaint:** All E&M documentation must contain a patient's chief complaint. Even if it never changes, it must be documented for every encounter.

    - *Tip:* Never omit the chief complaint from any E&M documentation

- **History of present illness (HPI):** No matter what you document, an auditor is looking for a variable number of elements in the HPI. Location, severity, duration, quality, timing, context, modifying factors, associated signs and symptoms, associated comorbidities, or even the status of three or more chronic or inactive conditions are all bits of information that can score points. Depending on the level of code, one to four of these categories must be included.

    - *Tip:* Include as many of the following elements into the first line of your HPI as possible: location, severity, duration, quality, timing, context, modifying factors, associated signs and symptoms, associated comorbidities, or status of chronic or inactive conditions. No matter what the code level, try to document at least four in every H&P.

Documentation, Coding, Billing, and Related Issues

- **Review of systems (ROS):** Depending on the specific code, the number of items required in an ROS will vary. But only specific categories of ROS are recognized for E&M coding: constitutional, eyes, ENT/mouth, cardiovascular, respiratory, gastrointestinal, genitourinary, musculoskeletal, endocrine, skin and/or breast hematologic/lymphatic, allergy/immunology, neurologic, and psychiatric.

    - *Tip:* Whenever feasible, have someone other than the surgical hospitalist collect data for the ROS. It is acceptable for a physician to review a ROS taken by an assistant, or even completed by a patient or family member, and have the physician simply initial and date the ROS to acknowledge acceptance of the information. In the ROS, it is acceptable to simply state "negative" or even write "–" to complete a category. This is not the case for physical exam findings.

- **Past medical history (PMH), family history (FH), social history (SH):** Most codes require two or three elements of PMH, FH, or SH. For most hospital documentation, all three are required. Documenting only "noncontributory" for any one (or all) of these elements does not count as having completed that element for the purpose of selecting the CPT code.

    - *Tip:* As a hospitalist, always document a PMH, FH, and SH. This can be done as briefly as may be clinically appropriate. Only one subject is required for each of these categories. Although physicians recommend a complete PMH with previous medical-surgical history, current medications, and allergies, auditors are not as interested in the past medical, family, and social history documentation. For example, an entry of "no known allergies" for PMH will suffice. "Mother alive" works for FH. "Graduated high school" is sufficient for SH.

ULTIMATE HISTORY TIP

A physician must personally complete the history of present illness. However, other information presented in the medical history may be completed by assistants, as long as the physician reviews and approves the history of present illness. And assistants may gather all history information; only the physician must personally complete the HPI. Working in a hospital setting where nursing has its own intake paperwork can be a significant physician advantage. Modifying the nursing intake form to concentrate the information critical to physician E&M documentation can serve as a significant physician time-saver. This is applicable to a paper-based system or with an electronic healthcare record format.

Chapter 14

Physical Examination

Required content in the physical exam is similar to that of ROS: constitutional, eyes, ENT/mouth, neck, respiratory, cardiovascular, chest (breasts), gastrointestinal (abdominal), genitourinary (male), genitourinary (female), lymphatic, musculoskeletal, skin, neurologic, and psychiatric. Each category is composed of bullet points, further subdividing each topic into specific required areas of documentation.

There are two types of physical exams that may be documented: the general multisystem exam or a variety of single-system exams. These single systems include cardiovascular, ENT, genitourinary, eye, hematologic/lymphatic/immunologic, musculoskeletal, neurologic, psychiatric, respiratory, and skin. You do not need to be a specialty physician to use a single-system exam. For the purposes of CPT coding, any physician can perform and document any exam they choose. (This is not to suggest that this is always reasonable or good for patient care, but simply to point out that CPT coding regulations do not specify which physical exam components can be done by which specialties.)

Each type of exam has its own requirements for the different E&M level of code. Most surgical hospitalists and nonhospitalist general surgeons will do the general multisystem exam.

TIPS FOR PHYSICAL EXAM DOCUMENTATION

- For physical exam documentation, indications of "negative" for the main exam division categories are not sufficient. You must specify the negative findings. For example, "Resp – negative" is not enough. Rather, the documentation should state "Resp – Normal resp. effort, normal to auscultation and percussion. Normal tactile fremitus," for example.

- Rather than criticize the bullet points, doctors should simply use them as a negative template from which to dictate or write.

- It is tempting, and certainly permissible, to create a checklist template from the physical exam bullet points. But be careful not to accidentally run through the checkoff boxes and create a negative finding when there is a positive. A fill-in-the-blank modification of a similar checklist is usually a more accurate methodology that requires more than a passive checkmark.

Critical Care and Time-Based Services

There will be opportunities to bill for time-based services. In general, using time-based rules for the basic E&M codes discussed so far is not efficient. Most physicians take considerably less time to do an evaluation and to document it using standard E&M guidelines than the time-based requirements would allow. That said, critical care is a time-based code that is often underutilized to a physician's detriment.

Critical care is simply a time-driven code that can occur anywhere in the hospital—that is, in or out of the ICU. The measurement of the time is cumulative, not consecutive. That means that your taximeter is running for a patient who requires bedside attendance. In settings in which multiple patients require your bedside presence simultaneously, start, stop, and restart the meters (time documented) as you go from one bed to another. Then tally up each bed's meter when your patients do not require bedside presence. Critical care time expires at midnight and another day starts. Other than for neonates or infants, there are only two codes to bill for critical care. Code 99291 allows you to bill for the first hour of critical care. To do this, you must spend at least 31 minutes with the patient at bedside. After the first hour of critical care, each additional 30 minutes is billed under code 99292.

The Coding Bottom Line

Many physicians say, "This is too complex, I give up; I'll just downcode to avoid auditor problems." Unfortunately, this is a solution that many physicians choose, a solution that leaves a lot of unbilled revenue to be quietly gathered up by third-party payers. The components are not complex. They are very simple and easy to understand. The complexity is in the application of the knowledge in a practical and reproducible way that ensures compliance and appropriate maximal benefit for the physician.

Developing a coding guru physician in your hospitalist practice is a good start. This individual can coach other physicians and interface effectively with coders and other documentation experts to simplify the process for your practice. As such, this physician should be compensated for time attending educational programs to help the practice. After all, this will require attending coding seminars and spending enough time on task to become expert. But it's an investment that will pay dividends for years to come. Imagine even a 10%–20% increase in practice revenue, an easily achievable objective for many practices.

Chapter 14

With knowledge of exactly what must be documented to support a code, physicians can document more efficiently. Documentation must not be used to justify a code, which can lead to potential accusations of fraud. The justification of a code is in the MDM determination. When documentation follows the selection of a correct (compliant with regulations) E&M code, rather than preceding the code selection, the actual amount of documentation and time spent documenting is minimized. In some cases, a comprehensive history can be done in as few as 30 words. Although this may be entertaining to demonstrate when teaching, it is not how we should document for a patient's sake. But knowing which 30 words are critical to be compliant and ensure proper payment is essential. By taking a systematic approach to streamline the process to maximize appropriate reimbursement and reduce the time needed to complete documentation, the physician's time is optimized.

Whether using the systematic approach described here or using a different approach, the practice will realize significant benefits in ensuring compliance and appropriate reimbursement.

In this increasingly challenging healthcare environment in which diminished physician reimbursement is commonplace, physicians should ask whether they must work harder or more intelligently. Changing our approach to something as ingrained as how we document an H&P, consults, and progress notes requires effort. But the reward, compounded over years of future practice, is certainly worth the investment in time and effort.

CHAPTER 15

CASE STUDY
Shady Grove Adventist Hospital, Rockville, MD

Joshua J. Felsher, MD, FACS • Jason A. Brodsky, MD, FACS

PROFILE

Established:	2003
Number of FTE surgeons:	3
Employer:	Private practice
Setting:	Community
Status:	Non-profit
Bed size:	296

Declining inpatient volumes for individual primary care physicians (PCPs), combined with inpatient care becoming less financially attractive, were significant forces leading to the development of medical hospitalist programs during the past two decades. More recently, these same economic pressures, combined with the proliferation of ambulatory surgery centers, an aging surgeon population, and an increased emphasis on physician quality of life, have engendered an environment ripe for the development of surgical hospitalist programs. This case study examines the factors integral to the development and operation of a successful surgical hospitalist program from the standpoint of the hospital, hospitalist surgeons, and the medical staff.

The Hospital

Hospital characteristics that favor the development of a surgical hospitalist program include a commitment to the program, problems with covering emergency department (ED) call, and patient volume. Shady Grove Adventist Hospital in Rockville, MD, faced all of these issues, and community general surgeons were increasingly unwilling to take ED call despite being paid to do so. Hospital executives believed the call stipends paid to community surgeons could be more effectively invested in the development of a surgical hospitalist program, as it could ensure uninterrupted coverage.

Chapter 15

Support

All levels of the host institution, the hospital, must support any hospitalist program, surgical or otherwise, for the program to succeed. The program requires financial support in the setup and operational phases of the program. Nonfinancial support is just as important; it will ultimately determine the viability of the program. Examples include the provision of a significant amount, if not all, of the ED general surgery call immediately upon inception of a hospitalist program, operating room (OR) block time, and/or creation of a designated emergency OR, if feasible. Our practice has one clerical staff person and office space provided by the hospital.

Surgical coverage

Hospitals nationwide are having increasing difficulty finding general surgeons to cover ED call. Although our hospital is home to several practicing general surgeons, it still could not sufficiently fill the monthly call schedule via traditional voluntary means. Reasons for this at our hospital include:

- An aging local general surgeon population

- Many solo practitioners, privileged at multiple hospitals

- An increasing emphasis on quality-of-life issues

- Proliferation of ambulatory surgery centers, combined with busy outpatient schedules, pulling surgeons away from the hospital

- Busy on-call nights

- A disproportionate uninsured population encountered on call

Volume

A surgeon needs to operate to generate billing. A hospitalist program will have a better return on investment in a busy environment. The hospital should commission a study early in the program's development to establish an expectation of ongoing support that the program will need.

Our program is based at the hospital with the second busiest ED in the state of Maryland. Shady Grove Adventist Hospital sees more than 105,000 ED visits per year. The ED generates four to five general surgery consults per day, and ED consults generate two to three operative cases per day.

Case Study: Shady Grove Adventist Hospital, Rockville, MD

The Surgical Hospitalist

Candidates for the position of surgical hospitalist must all be general surgeons by training. However, a variety of subspecialty-trained surgeons may be suitable for the position, depending on the nature of the program. These may include:

- **Surgical critical care**—if the hospital has a surgical or "mixed" ICU and there is not adequate coverage provided by medical intensivists
- **Trauma**—if the hospital is a trauma center
- **Advanced laparoscopy**—broadens the coverage of general surgery that may be covered by the program
- **Vascular**—broadens the range of coverage by the program suitably by incorporating a field of surgery that is often emergent in nature

Our program uses surgical hospitalists who are fellowship trained in advanced laparoscopic surgery. Because of the volume of general surgery, the fact that the hospital is not a trauma center, and the presence of a strong medical intensivist program, this level of training is most suitable for our program.

Although case volume obviously affects the staffing and scheduling of the program, we believe that a three-surgeon program is the minimum number of surgeons recommended in all but extremely low-volume settings. A busy program with fewer than three surgeons will have significant quality-of-life issues due to the frequency and unpredictability of call coverage. Any number over three surgeons must be justified by patient volume and caseload. Due to the frequency and unpredictable nature of call in a surgical hospitalist program, a variety of scheduling patterns may be employed. For our practice, reasonable options are outlined in Figure 15.1.

Our program uses surgical hospitalists who work two out of every three weeks, such that two surgeons are available at any given time. The first week of the rotation is lighter in overnight call (two nights), the second week heavier (five nights), and the third devoid of clinical responsibilities.

> **TIP**
>
> Be mindful that continuity of care in the surgical hospitalist program, as with the medical hospitalist, is of extreme importance. Good continuity supports the high-quality care that is vital to the program's integrity.

Chapter 15

FIGURE 15.1 PROS & CONS OF TRADITIONAL VS. BLOCK SCHEDULES

Schedule model	Description	Pros	Cons
Traditional Q3 call	Each surgeon works many consecutive days and takes night call via pager every third night	Simplicity and ease of continuity of care	Monotony/possibility of early burnout, and whether overall volume supports the presence of three surgeons per day
Block call	Five or 10 days on at a time, followed by segment of time off	Improved quality of life for the surgical hospitalist	Quality-of-care issues if there is frequent change of duty

Source: Shady Grove Adventist Hospital, Rockville, MD.

A surgical hospitalist program improves the overall quality of a hospital's surgical care in several tangible and intangible ways:

- Involvement in hospital committees, including the OR committee, the surgical review committee, quality assurance/improvement, and medical staff leadership

- Attendance and participation in weekly meetings, such as hospital grand rounds and tumor board

- Involvement in the implementation of institutional directives resulting from governing bodies, such as the Surgical Care Improvement Project recommendations mandated by Medicare addressing prophylactic antibiotic use in surgery and DVT prophylaxis

- Education of hospital staff members including nursing, surgical and physician's assistants, and fellow physicians in a variety of settings

At our program, surgical hospitalists are involved in all of the above committees, in addition to being faculty at a local school of medicine. Our program also serves as a rotation site for students.

Other General Surgeons on the Medical Staff

In order for the program to succeed, the surgical hospitalist must peacefully coexist with the other general surgeons, some of whom have been on the medical staff for several years. Boundaries, written or understood, must be established from day one. Our practice has found that call coverage, follow-up, and inpatient, outpatient, and intraoperative referrals are particularly important areas to work out between hospitalist and nonhospitalist surgeons.

Call

Taking over the majority of ED call may not seem like it would be an issue or there would be no need for the program in the first place. However, some surgeons may have a desire to continue to take some call. The question of whether the surgical hospitalist program will take all of the call should be decided on a case-by-case basis by the hospital, the hospitalist, and the local surgeon.

Although it is in the hospital's interest for the hospitalist to take all of the call for financial and quality-of-care reasons, the hospital must respect the desire of the local general surgeon to participate in the call schedule or risk losing elective cases from them. The hospitalist must expect to take all of the call if necessary and needs to take the majority of the call to have a viable program. Nonhospitalist general surgeons may be relieved by the presence of the program and may happily depart the call schedule, or they may wish to retain one or several calls depending on personal or financial factors.

At our program, the surgical hospitalists cover 25–27 days per month, and nonhospitalist surgeons voluntarily cover the remaining days.

Other Physicians on the Medical Staff

Other hospitalist physicians

Most hospitals developing a surgical hospitalist program have already had success with a medical hospitalist program. Cooperation between the surgical and medical hospitalist programs improves the quality of patient care at both. As with the call schedule, it is likely that most, if not all, of the inpatient surgery referrals (e.g., surgical consults requested by doctors in other specialties) will immediately be shifted to the surgical hospitalist. Although physicians at our hospital are free to request general surgery consults from any surgeon on staff, they nearly always request the surgical hospitalist unless the patient has a preexisting relationship with another surgeon. The nonhospitalist surgeons are generally satisfied with this approach.

Other surgical subspecialists

OB/GYN surgeons and other surgical specialists benefit from 24-hour availability for intraoperative consultation. The surgical hospitalist is the natural consultant for all intraoperative general surgery issues in patients undergoing intra-abdominal subspecialty surgery. Due to the disruptive nature of such consultations, it is unlikely that the local general surgeon will miss this type of referral. Surgical hospitalists attend to nearly all of the intraoperative consultations at our hospital.

Nonhospitalist referring doctors

Other referring doctors know that hospitalist availability means that a single phone call will get a general surgeon to take care of their patient's problems.

Follow-up and Outpatient Referrals

A major difference between the medical hospitalist and the surgical hospitalist is that the acute care surgeon needs an office to follow up with patients postoperatively. The ideal location for an office is within an adjacent medical office building. Office proximity to the hospital is important due to the nature of this type of practice, as opposed to a traditional practice. Although an office is necessary, the patient population treated by the surgical hospitalist may be open to scrutiny by the local general surgeon who does not want the surgical hospitalist infringing on his or her patient cohort. Our program limits surgical hospitalist outpatient visits to patients in the following categories:

- Patients operated on by the surgical hospitalist (postops)

- Patients managed or consulted on by the surgical hospitalist during a recent hospital stay but who have not undergone surgery (e.g., in a case of diverticulitis)

- Patients seen in the ED but not admitted (e.g., hernia or gallbladder disease)

Postoperative patients should be followed by those who performed their surgery; however, the remaining categories of patients could potentially visit the surgical hospitalist or the local general surgeon in the elective setting. These distinctions need to be made early on in the development of the program.

Conclusion

These considerations are an overview of a successful surgical hospitalist program. In contrast to the medical hospitalist program, each individual surgical program may be vastly different, depending on any or all of the above. However, in general, a perfect storm of significant financial/nonfinancial hospital support, intrinsic poor call coverage, large general surgical volume, appropriately selected surgical hospitalists, and peaceful coexistence with the preexisting surgeon population is required in any setting for a viable program.

CHAPTER 16

CASE STUDY
Anne Arundel Medical Center, Annapolis, MD

David Matteson, MD

PROFILE

Established:	Summer 2005
Number of FTE surgeons:	5
Employer:	Private practice
Setting:	Community hospital
Status:	Nonprofit
Bed size:	278

Starting the Program

Anne Arundel Medical Center is a 278-bed private community hospital located in Annapolis, MD. The approximately 15-year-old program already had a thriving, successful, mature medical hospitalist program in place. The hospital had witnessed a gradual decline in the number of general surgeons on staff and an increasingly busy emergency department (ED) that resulted in an ever-increasing burden on each remaining general surgeon. Despite being in a favorable location, recruiting new general surgeons was a problem, partly because of the low rate of reimbursement in Maryland and the high cost of living in the community.

The hospital decided to take the proactive step to establish a surgical hospitalist program to bring new general surgeons into the area and to relieve the six remaining private surgeons of the significant burden of ED call. The intent was to provide in-house coverage for emergency general surgery patients. The initial surgical hospitalist was responsible for providing consultations for the ED and for inpatients with general surgery problems. Because the program was aimed primarily at providing emergency services, ED patients who did not require admission to the hospital were referred to private surgeons

Chapter 16

to follow up in their offices. If a patient waiting to be seen in the ED had an established relationship or a preference for a private surgeon, he or she could request that private surgeon. Patients within their immediate postoperative periods were referred to their treating physicians for care related to the recent surgery. Most of the time, the private surgeons preferred to concentrate on their elective practices to maximize efficiency and quality of life. Almost all new cases were and continue to be cared for by the surgical hospitalist service. This largely reflects that the surgical hospitalist is in-house and, therefore, able to see new patients more promptly.

Anne Arundel Medical Center now serves a population of about 1 million people. There are about 750 medical staff members. In the fiscal year ending in June 2007, there were more than 22,000 admissions, more than 72,000 ED visits, and more than 22,500 total surgical procedures.

Initially, three surgeons were hired in July 2005. As the original surgical hospitalist of the first three, I had been on staff at Anne Arundel Medical Center as a general surgeon for 18 years at a private practice. Although I relinquished autonomy by becoming an employee of the hospital, I hoped to gain financial security and improve quality of life. I had grown weary of continually negotiating with insurance companies for reimbursement and witnessing the steady decline of reimbursement. Likewise, because the contract with the hospital stated that I would have a 50-hour workweek on average and minimal out-of-hospital call responsibilities, I anticipated an improved quality of life. The other two surgeons were recruited from outside the hospital, one from a nearby hospital and the other from Norfolk, VA. They were both experienced surgeons as well, each being in practice for about 15 years. The search included professional headhunters, ads in surgical journals, and word of mouth.

Scheduling for Continuity of Care

Because this was a new concept at our hospital, the surgical hospitalist position has evolved over time as our service has grown. An important challenge and goal was to provide continuity of care, especially with our team approach and frequent patient handoffs. We wanted the same surgeon to round on patients for several days in a row, instead of a different surgeon seeing the patients each day.

To provide continuity of care, the cornerstone of the work schedule was established, as it remains today. The schedule consists of one surgeon (Dr. A) who works seven days in a row during the daytime. Dr. A is responsible for rounding on the patients, including the care and decision-making for the

Case Study: Anne Arundel Medical Center, Annapolis, MD

patients. To make the schedule work, Dr. A works seven consecutive days, from 7 a.m. to 8 p.m. The second surgeon (Dr. B) works four nights in a row, Monday through Thursday, from 7 p.m. to 8 a.m. The third surgeon (Dr. C) has seven days off following his week on the A shift, prior to returning to work nights. Each week, the individuals rotate to a different shift.

Because we did not possess the staff resources to cover the hospital 24/7, we needed to incorporate the private surgeons into the call schedule. They were responsible for covering the hospital for new consults and admissions Friday, Saturday, and Sunday nights. Any patients that the private surgeons consulted upon during these shifts remained their patients. The private surgeons covered the patients already on the surgical hospitalist service from home these three nights each week.

One year after its inception, we added a fourth surgeon. Almost two years later, we added a fifth surgeon. With these additional surgical hospitalists, the call responsibilities for the private surgeons were reduced to Saturday nights only. In other words, each of the seven private surgeons currently on staff is now only on call for the ED about 12 hours every two months. The rationale to keep them on call for this token amount is that if they are relieved of all of their call responsibilities, it will be difficult to encourage them to take call again if the need arises.

With the addition of the fourth surgeon, the shifts were changed slightly. We added a second backup surgeon to the daytime shift for more complete coverage. With the addition of the fifth surgeon, the schedule was modified again to improve continuity of care, decrease the number of sign-offs during the course of the day, and improve quality-of-life issues for the surgeons.

As in the pervious schedule, Dr. A continues to work seven consecutive days, usually 11 to 12 hours each day. That surgeon remains responsible for rounding on the patients each day, with the subsequent decisions regarding care, management, and possible surgery. Currently, we round on an average 16–20 patients per day. However, our service has been as large as 35 patients on the whole service, with Dr. A primarily responsible for rounding. That surgeon is also responsible for ensuring that patients are ready for surgery and postoperative care. Medical hospitalists comanage medical problems.

The other two surgeons' shifts are combined into a single 23-hour shift that runs from 9 a.m. until 8 a.m. the next day. Instead of working several days or nights in a row, this person now has two to three days off before returning for another 23-hour shift. All surgeons not working the A shift rotate through this B shift. Every Monday, a different person becomes the A surgeon, and the rest of the surgeons rotate through the B shift. We changed the B shift because of a chronic problem; many nights at about 8 p.m., the change of shift was a busy time to perform add-on emergency surgeries. It was never certain whether the person coming or the person leaving would be the best person to perform a surgery when an OR became available. Because of this uncertainty, there was inefficient use of OR time; delays tended to occur in starting cases and in completing add-on surgeries. The current 23-hour shift eliminates the change-of-shift problem, completing add-on cases more efficiently by removing any confusion about who would be performing these surgeries.

Secondly, eliminating the change in shift reduced sign-outs from three to two times per day, once at 7 a.m. when Dr. A arrives in the morning and once at about 6 p.m. before Dr. A goes home for the night. The result is less time signing out patients to the next shift and less potential for errors in handoffs and patient care. Eliminating the change in shift also improves quality of life; working five nights in a row was extremely tiring, and adjusting to changing sleep times with night shifts was difficult. By working only one night at a time, we are able to maintain our normal circadian rhythm.

Finally, eliminating the 8 p.m. change of shift means only one of us won't have dinner with our family that night instead of two of us.

Dr. B has clinics Monday through Thursday from 9 a.m. until 1 p.m. On Monday, we see patients in the wound care clinic. On the remainder of the days, we see postoperative patients in the office. No new patients are seen in the office, but there is an occasional patient who we saw in the hospital but did not operate on, as in the case of diverticulitis or a small bowel obstruction, who we see for follow-up in the office. After Dr. B completes his or her clinic schedule, he or she helps out Dr. A in the hospital. This is usually the time of day when we receive the highest number of new consults and OR rooms start to become available for add-on surgeries.

We usually perform four to six add-on or emergency surgeries each day. Dr. B usually performs these procedures, even though another member of the group may have admitted and evaluated the patient. Postoperatively, surgeon A will manage the care, and surgeon B may never see that patient again. This is especially true for patients who have limited stays, such as those with uncomplicated appendicitis. We try to schedule postoperative follow-up visits in the office with the surgeon who performed the surgery, but this is not always possible. This division of labor generally works fairly well, and everybody understands that they have the opportunity to be the operating surgeon.

Case Study: Anne Arundel Medical Center, Annapolis, MD

We have found that the fewer times a patient is passed off to another physician, the fewer mistakes are made, and the fewer details fall between the cracks. New consults that we receive while both surgeons are working are assigned by Dr. A to be seen by the most appropriate doctor. We average about six to eight new consults or new patient encounters in every 24-hour period, but this amount can vary widely. Dr. B usually sees patients who we anticipate will need immediate surgery, such as those with acute appendicitis or perforated viscus, since it is likely that he or she will be the one performing the surgery. Dr. B also usually takes care of simple, straightforward consults that require limited decision-making time and that will not be followed by our group for an extended period. This includes insertion of central lines, incision and drainage of abscesses, and debridement of decubitus ulcers.

For patients who are not as straightforward or who do not require surgery within the next 24 hours, Dr. A consults with them to promote better continuity of care. Such cases include small bowel obstruction and abdominal pain of unknown etiology. Some complex consults, after their initial evaluation and stabilization by the surgical hospitalist, are referred to one of the private surgeons with specialized expertise who would potentially be able to better handle that patient's condition. Such conditions include complicated colorectal conditions, which are referred to the colorectal surgeon, and nonemergent tumors (especially involving the liver or pancreas), which are generally referred to the surgical oncologists. The surgical hospitalists have been able to establish and maintain a mutual level of cooperation with the nonhospitalist private surgeons by minimizing their performance of elective surgeries.

Outcomes

In 2007, the surgical hospitalist group saw in consultation or admitted approximately 2,200 patients. We performed nearly 900 surgeries during this same period of time. Our daily census and number of surgical procedures performed has steadily increased since that time. Our most common surgery performed is laparoscopic appendectomy. This is followed by laparoscopic cholecystectomy, incision and drainage of abscess, lysis of adhesions for small bowel obstruction, and exploratory laporotomy for the following conditions: perforated viscus, gastrointestinal bleeding, ischemic bowel, and colon obstruction. We are frequently asked to consult and help manage critically ill patients in the ICU because we are readily available in house.

Our group has filled an essential need by providing in-house coverage for general surgery emergencies, improving patient care as well as efficiency of care. We are more readily available to evaluate patients promptly and to operate on patients, filling last-minute holes in the OR schedules. The private surgeons

Chapter 16

are pleased because the amount of call they perform has been significantly decreased. This has allowed them to concentrate on their elective practices and market their areas of expertise without worrying as much about being interrupted by emergencies. As a result, the volume of elective surgeries at the hospital has increased. The total number of general surgeons on staff has increased to 12, with the addition of five hospitalists and, because of the decreased on-call time, two surgical oncologists.

The gradual evolution of our program has worked well. Communication is extremely important because we share patients. A patient potentially has several surgeons involved with his or her care during the course of hospitalization. One surgeon may admit the patient and make the decision regarding surgery, a second surgeon may perform the surgery, and a third surgeon may manage his or her postoperative care. We perform sign-outs twice per day to improve communication.

Although our present work schedule is demanding (alternating between working seven days in a row of 12-hour shifts and working 23-hour shifts), the advantage lies in continuity of care because one doctor is responsible for all care and decision-making for seven days in a row. There is increased stress associated with our job because, most of the time, we are taking care of a large number of severe, acutely ill patients. Because we have no control over the number of patients that are referred to us, it can be challenging to staff the shifts adequately—that is, not to be overwhelmed with a sudden influx of sick patients without having staff members sitting around when it is less busy.

Thus far, the present schedule has worked well the majority of the time. Stress is alleviated when we leave the hospital, can transfer patient care over to a trusted partner, and don't have to worry about getting called back into the hospital. Due to the nature of the patient population, the number of emergencies we take care of, and the difficulty in establishing relationships with patients and their families in this type of practice, one might anticipate increased problems such as potential liability, but thus far, this has not been a problem.

Our goal is to transform the surgical hospitalist position into a career. In our experience at the hospital, most of the physicians who are interested in this job are older surgeons who have grown tired of private practice and are looking for another position for a few years before retirement. We have been fortunate to hire surgeons who typically plan to work for at least several more years. We would like to identify some younger individuals to balance out these more mature surgeons, particularly those who would like to make surgical hospitalist medicine their career. This would provide more stability to the program with lower turnover. The younger surgeons would benefit from the experience and mentorship of the older surgeons. The older surgeons would benefit from the more recent training and techniques of their younger counterparts—although we have been hesitant to hire surgeons who have recently graduated from residency because they may not possess the experience to safely handle the wide variety of possible procedures during the night. Nevertheless, it is beneficial to have surgeons in the group who are open to new ideas and not overly established in their ways.

Conformity and standardization of practice patterns will allow the practice to run more smoothly. It is not practical for individuals to specialize because all surgeons must have the same set of basic skills. At Anne Arundel Medical Center, we feel that the growth of the surgical hospitalist profession will help alleviate the shortage of general surgeons while simultaneously improving the quality of life of those surgeons.

CHAPTER 17

CASE STUDY

University of California at San Francisco, Department of Surgery

John Maa, MD, FACS

PROFILE

Established:	July 2005
Number of FTE surgeons:	4 as of July 2007, 6 as of 2009
Employer:	University of California, San Francisco
Setting:	Academic teaching hospital
Status:	Nonprofit
Bed size:	600-bed tertiary academic medical center

The UCSF Surgical Hospitalist Program was introduced in July 2005, with the primary intent of improving patient access to high-quality and timely hospital-based emergency surgical care. Since its inception in 2005, the UCSF Surgical Hospitalist Program has sought to explore new solutions to the major national challenge of inadequate surgical coverage for a growing patient population. We describe in this chapter an innovation in access to emergency general surgery that strengthens the commitment to the delivery of timely, safe, and optimal patient-centered care.

UCSF Surgery Hospitalist Mission Statement

The mission of the UCSF Surgery Hospitalist Program is to provide high-quality, timely, and efficient care to patients with emergency surgical conditions at UCSF Medical Center while also educating medical students and residents.

Chapter 17

Vision

- To promote evidence-based guidelines for the safe, timely, and comprehensive care of patients with general surgery diagnoses

- To provide appropriate medical student and resident teaching and supervision

- To provide a platform for surgical quality improvement research focusing on patient safety and high-quality surgical outcomes, particularly in perioperative processes of care

- To improve communication and professionalism between inpatient services in the coordination of inpatient patient care

- To propose a new solution to the crisis in access to emergency department ED care and to alleviate the crisis of ED crowding, boarding, and ambulance diversion

- To enhance the resource utilization of ED, operating room (OR), and medical center resources

Introduction

Caring for patients with surgical emergencies, an inherently difficult and unpredictable task, has become even more challenging due to a confluence of pressures. As a result, surgical departments at teaching hospitals across the country increasingly face challenges to fulfill the three traditional missions of patient care, teaching, and research. Financial pressures have pushed all but the sickest patients into the outpatient setting and accelerated the pace and volume of the remaining patients who require hospitalization. Surgeons at tertiary care centers increasingly encounter acute cholecystitis in solid organ transplant patients, bowel obstructions in morbidly obese patients, typhylitis in stem cell transplant patients, and enterocutaneous fistulas in patients referred from other institutions. An increasing array of patient safety and quality improvement (QI) efforts for surgical care require implementation, a task made more challenging by the constant turnover of house staff due to the 80-hour workweek. Decreased academic surgeon availability for call is exacerbated by the need to increase productivity, both academic and clinical, with the perception that taking call doesn't advance surgeons toward promotion. Additionally, the trend toward increasing specialization has left many surgeons less comfortable in managing illnesses outside of their areas of expertise, especially when these conditions present emergently. Lost is the availability of a surgeon capable of caring for and operating on patients with a wide range of surgical emergencies.

The Institute of Medicine has pronounced emergency medical care in the United States to be on the verge of collapse, citing "dangerous overcrowding and an inability to treat patients in a safe, timely, and efficient manner" as the main reasons.[1] Given the critical shortage of surgeons available and willing to take emergency call and to provide emergency and trauma consultation, it is clear that new models are necessary to address growing public demand and to preserve the availability of timely, high-quality, and cost-effective patient care.

Prior to July 2005, emergency general surgical care at UCSF was provided by a diverse faculty spread across two campuses, each surgeon taking call on a 24-hour basis. This system of care was problematic for several reasons. First, daytime consultations disrupted the elective procedures and clinics of on-call surgeons. Patients in the ED or acute care ward would sometimes wait hours until the on-call surgeon was available to evaluate them. Second, the diversity of surgical conditions left many surgeons uncomfortable caring for diseases outside their expertise, especially in emergent cases. Third, the 24-hour structure of the call schedule and separate campuses disrupted continuity of care, particularly for those patients treated by surgeons at the more remote site who would need subsequent care in the ED at the main hospital. Fourth, surgical house staff provided the only continuity, which was further constrained by the 80-hour ACGME workweek. Finally, there was little economic incentive for taking call; the only benefit to a surgeon or the department was revenue generated from the minority of consultations that resulted in a surgical procedure.

To address these challenges, we introduced a new innovation in emergency surgical care at the UCSF Medical Center—the surgical hospitalist—to strengthen the commitment to the delivery of the best patient-centered care, while concurrently fulfilling the educational mission. We place the foremost emphasis on the needs of the emergency surgery patient and the broad base of operative emergencies within the discipline of general surgery. Rather than seeking to expand into the wider domain of neurosurgical or orthopedic procedures, our central intent is to propose solutions to the national crisis in access to emergency care; we suggest ways for academic centers to provide professional, quality, and prompt care in spite of resident 80-hour workweek restrictions.

UCSF pioneered and instituted the medical hospitalist model of care in the 1990s, which resulted in reduced lengths of stay (LOS) and improved quality of care.[2] The UCSF Surgical Hospitalist Program was designed with a parallel intent, introduced in July 2005.[3] Under the surgical hospitalist model, full-time board-certified general surgeons provide coverage on a rotating weekly basis, dedicating all of their time to ED and inpatient consults, with the goal of timely consultation within 30 minutes. Elective procedures and clinics are minimized during the on-call weeks. Surgical hospitalists lead rounds each day to maximize continuity of care and are, thereby, more readily available to supervise and teach residents, nurse practitioners, and medical students. Surgical hospitalist attending physicians provide documentation of daily care, which increases revenue collection and also improves the quality of written communication with consulting healthcare providers. Hospitalists also manage most surgical transfer requests from hospitals throughout Northern California. For patients who may require complex surgical intervention (e.g., advanced hepatobiliary, foregut, thoracic, or endocrine procedures), the surgical hospitalist first assesses and stabilizes the patient and then consults an expert surgeon with skills that match specific patients' needs. The program has since expanded and, as of 2009, has seven faculty members. Since the program's founding in 2005, we have tracked several outcomes and measures of the program's quality of care, including patient and disease characteristics, operative volume and triage of complex cases to senior surgeons, time to consultation, and revenue generation.

Findings from the Surgical Hospitalist Model in Year 1

Patient and disease characteristics

Three surgical hospitalists cared for 853 patients in the initial year, averaging 2.3 new consults per day. Patients averaged 53 years of age (range of 17–100) and were racially diverse. Most presented with acute abdominal pain (63%), soft-tissue infections (18%), malignancy (6%), or hernia (4%). Most consultations originated from the ED (57%), although general medicine (20%) and medical specialists (7%), including critical care physicians, accounted for large numbers. Interestingly, other surgeons were responsible for 8% of the total consult volume; these were generally from surgical specialists such as neurosurgeons or urologists. Because our center is a Level II trauma center and most trauma cases are regionalized to San Francisco General Hospital, trauma accounted for only 3% of consultations. Transfers of patients from other institutions accounted for 6%.

Surgical procedures performed, and triage to specialty surgeons

Forty-two percent of consults (n = 359) resulted in an operation, most commonly appendectomy (29%), incision and drainage of abscess (19%), exploratory laparotomy for intestinal resection or lysis of adhesions (19%), cholecystectomy (11%), and complex liver/spleen/pancreas procedures (7%). We involved surgeons with advanced expertise in 9% (37/853) of cases. Surgical intervention was necessary in 29 of these cases, and surgery hospitalists performed the remaining 92%.

Time-to-consultation and ED provider satisfaction

The average time-to-consult from request to bedside evaluation averaged 16 minutes, and most patients (85%) were seen within five to 10 minutes. In a survey of ED providers six months after the start of the program (response rate 76% [13 of 17]), all providers felt that the surgical hospitalist program had improved timeliness of care, supervision of house staff, patient satisfaction, professionalism of the surgical staff, and reduced ED LOS. In addition, 84% felt the quality of care was either the same (38%) or better (46%). We also compared the wait time for patients undergoing appendectomy in a six-month period before and after the start of our program and found that it decreased 50%, from 16 ± 10 hours to 8 ± 4 hours ($p < 0.05$).

Revenue generation

Financial data from the Division of Finance of the Department of Surgery at UCSF demonstrated a 190% increase in requested consults from the ED and inpatient wards in the first year of the program. That increase was sustained in the second year of the program. We also observed a 415% increase in financial revenue that increased to 591% in the second year, as a result of more thorough and complex documentation of care by attending surgeons. The greatest increase was observed in the area of subsequent care and follow-up, where a 24-fold increase in revenue was achieved through improved documentation and billing. Fifty-one percent of patients treated were insured under capitated care plans, 44% had Medicare/Medicaid, and 4% were uninsured. The revenue from nonoperative care and follow-up notes in particular can be substantial, and it ultimately yielded approximately 20% of the overall revenue to support the program.

Surgical education

The surgical hospitalist model also strengthens the department of surgery's commitment to surgical education by promoting continuity in student education, providing appropriate supervision to maximize patient safety, and introducing a mentoring relationship for student professional development and feedback. Introduction of the hospitalist model resulted in significant improvement in medical student perceptions of the following: observation of physical exam skills, adequacy of feedback, faculty clinical teaching, and clerkship as a whole. Students value the interaction with faculty surgeons and the role-modeling of timely and professional care, particularly in the evaluation of undifferentiated patients in the ED and inpatient settings.

Enhanced Efficiency and Value of Surgical Hospitalist Program

Our preliminary findings suggest that the UCSF Surgery Hospitalist Program is a new and effective way to provide safe, high-quality care in an era of fewer house staff hours, increasing patient volume and disease complexity, and increasing fragmentation in the practice of general surgery. Although other medical centers have combined emergency surgical care with trauma care, or into acute care surgery programs, in an effort to improve quality of care and reduce costs, we believe that our system of care is the first true surgical hospitalist model for general surgical care in the United States. The primary focus of our program is on improving access and the processes of care for general surgical patients, with a lesser emphasis on trauma surgery and without attempting to extend into the domains of neurosurgical or orthopedic procedures. We propose this new model as an alternative to the acute care surgery programs being discussed nationally.

The hallmark is the availability and experience of dedicated on-site faculty who are continuously available for a weeklong period to enhance continuity of care, promote timely evaluation of consults, educate house staff and students, appropriately triage patients with high acuity, and implement patient safety measures essential to the delivery of high-quality and cost-effective care. The success of the surgical hospitalist program is grounded in the following key principles:

- Timeliness

- Triage

- Documentation

- Team-based group practice

- Resident supervision and strengthening the department of surgery commitment to surgical education

- Generating institutional support for surgical hospitalists

- Improving access to emergency care through collaborations between surgical and medical hospitalists

- Enhancing patient safety and quality of surgical care nationally

Timeliness

One of our most important findings was that the average wait time for a patient to be seen by the surgical hospitalist service was 20 minutes. This would often require that attending surgeons evaluate patients directly, before the house staff could see the patients. This increased timeliness of care served to improve relationships with other departments and the OR, and it formed the foundation of other hospital-based quality and efficiency improvement efforts.

Triage

Some cases required specialized expertise—surgical hospitalists performed the initial stabilization and assessment, after which patient needs were matched to the appropriate expert among the remainder of the surgical faculty. The triage system provided a way for junior faculty to become more proficient in the care of patients with complex and challenging conditions, with the assistance of senior experienced surgeons as necessary.

Documentation

In an era of declining reimbursement, new strategies to address suboptimal reimbursement rates by maximizing nonoperative revenue are essential. Surgical hospitalists improved documentation for billing purposes, particularly of nonoperative care. Historically, surgeons have not focused on revenue generation from the delivery of care that does not result in an operation. In this study, 58% of consultations did not result in a procedure. One of the primary aims of the hospitalist program was to enhance collections from subsequent follow-up care, which had previously been poorly documented and billed. This eventually yielded approximately 20% of the overall revenue to support the service. Surgical hospitalist attending physicians documented the initial consultation and daily progress notes, resulting in an overall 415% increase in revenue generation after the creation of the program.

Team-based group practice

Surgical hospitalists freely transferred the care of inpatients at the end of the on-call week. This required a willingness to share in the care of patients and to adopt a team approach to perioperative care, which represents a major departure from the general surgical tradition of a solo practitioner. Our preliminary data suggest that perhaps the greatest beneficiaries of the surgical hospitalist model were the surgeons. Under the new system, most general surgeons at our center were relieved of emergency call and could therefore focus on elective patient care, research, and teaching. Likewise, the three surgical hospitalists found their one week of continuous call, free from elective clinics and procedures, preferable to the combination of a traditional 24-hour call schedule with an elective practice. A critical element for hospitalist surgeon satisfaction was protected research time, free from clinical activities, when they were not on service.

Resident supervision and strengthening the department of surgery commitment to surgical education

An important benefit was increased resident supervision on the wards and in the OR. The program also addressed the challenges in fragmentation and continuity of resident education after the introduction of the 80-hour workweek. Our impression was that house staff valued the real-time contact with faculty surgeons and the role-modeling of timely and professional care, and 42% of house staff cited teaching as the greatest strength of the hospitalist service.

Generating institutional support for surgical hospitalists

A key task is to convince hospital leaders to support the new surgical hospitalist model of care by demonstrating value through savings and reduced healthcare costs. Although our preliminary findings show that substantial resources can be generated by the hospitalist service, we need to determine the level of external support appropriate to sustain the surgical hospitalist program. The medical hospitalist field has been nationally supported by medical centers that have recognized the value added by the hospitalists and the need for institutional support to make up for shortfalls in clinical revenue generation that occur due to time spent coordinating care, often for an unfavorable payer mix. As important as support is for the physicians, medical centers will not reap the full benefits of surgical hospitalists until they deploy resources such as weekend social workers or a dedicated emergency OR suite.

Improving access to emergency care through collaborations between surgical and medical hospitalists

Another key task is to develop collaborations between hospitalist programs in surgery and medicine to improve access to emergency care by maximizing hospital efficiencies and achieving hospital-based patient safety initiatives. The track record of the UCSF Medical Hospitalist Program provides the national visibility and foundation to develop strong and productive collaborations with an emphasis on error reduction, improved sign-outs, and evidence-based surgery.

Enhancing patient safety and quality of surgical care nationally

Our long-term goal is to integrate existing surgical QI efforts nationally to enhance patient safety and the quality of surgical care. We view the surgical hospitalist model as a stepping-stone toward hospital-based patient safety initiatives, such as perioperative wound infection prevention, deep venous thrombosis prophylaxis, and myocardial infarction prevention. An unanticipated benefit of our program was that the surgical hospitalists became recognized as institutional leaders in surgical QI projects. When on-site surgeons are dedicated to emergency care, they can better understand and address problems with the institutional healthcare delivery system that need to be addressed through systems improvements and reengineering. We anticipate that increasing expertise in the delivery of care in an emergency setting can lead to improvements in the care of elective patients as well.

Our efforts to redefine the field of emergency general surgery are paralleled by those of our colleagues nationally to transform and reinvigorate the future of trauma surgery. Changing the way trauma care is organized through regionalization may be part of the solution. However, particularly for the approximately 3,500 nontrauma EDs and hospitals across America[4], the surgical hospitalist model may be an alternative to the acute care surgeon model proposed by others. The emphasis at UCSF also has been to develop hospitalist programs that can support our orthopedic and neurosurgical colleagues to improve the timeliness and quality of care for their patients. Implementation of the surgical hospitalist model can improve the quality and efficiency of hospital-based surgical care and provide a foundation for surgical QI efforts to enhance the structure and processes of emergency surgical care in teaching hospitals. We believe that this model potentially can be used to improve care in every type of surgical practice setting, thereby achieving the Institute of Medicine's call to "point the way toward a future emergency care system that ensures high-quality, efficient, and reliable care for all Americans."[5]

The generalizability of our pilot study is limited by its being retrospective and descriptive, as well as by its being the experience of a single tertiary academic medical center, in which trauma represents a low percentage of patients and the patient population has a relatively favorable payer mix.

Conclusion

As a new paradigm for organizing surgical departments in academic medical centers, the surgical hospitalist model offers a strategy to address the crisis in access to emergency surgical care in the United States. Its creation recognizes the evidence that on-site availability is critical to the provision of high-quality, cost-effective emergency care, and it recognizes the need for academic centers to provide quality and prompt care despite resident 80-hour workweek restrictions. Its implementation can improve the quality, efficiency, safety, and timeliness of hospital-based emergency surgical care, while enhancing professionalism, respect for patient autonomy, and equal access to medical care. Finally, surgical hospitalist programs are an important step to integrating existing surgical QI efforts nationally to enhance patient safety and the quality of surgical care.

REFERENCES

1. Institute of Medicine, *Hospital-Based Emergency Care: At the Breaking Point* (Washington, DC: National Academy Press, 2006).

2. R.M. Wachter and L. Goldman, "The Hospitalist Movement 5 Years Later," *JAMA* 287 (2002): 487–494.

3. J. Maa, J.T. Carter, J.E. Gosnell, R.M. Wachter, and H.W. Harris, "The surgical hospitalist: A New Model for Emergency Surgical Care," *J Am Coll Surg* (2007); 205(5): 704-711.

4. E.J. Mackenzie, D.B. Hoyt, J.C. Sacra, G.J. Jurkovich, A.R. Carlini, S.D. Teitelbaum, and H. Teter. "National Inventory of Hospital Trauma Centers," *JAMA* 289 (2003): 1515–1522.

5. Institute of Medicine, *Hospital-Based Emergency Care: At the Breaking Point* (Washington, DC: National Academy Press, 2006).

CHAPTER 18

CASE STUDY
Thomas Memorial Hospital, South Charleston, WV —an affiliate of the Thomas Health System

Robert J. Gray, FACHE

PROFILE

Established:	2003
Number of FTE surgeons:	2
Employer:	Delphi Healthcare Partners (by contract)
Setting:	Community hospital
Status:	Nonprofit
Bed size:	260

As a senior executive of a hospital system, my objective is to make sure that the emergency department (ED) call schedule is covered without paying medical staff for taking call. Thomas Memorial Hospital came up with another way to address the problem we faced with general surgery ED call. To those of us in administration, paying for call was like handing out candy: Once we started, we wouldn't be able to stop.

Obviously, not every hospital in every market is the same, but for a community hospital in the capitol of West Virginia, a surgical hospitalist practice was a good solution to the ED call problem for us.

Thomas Memorial is a 260-bed community hospital with the highest ED volume of the five hospital EDs in the immediate service area. The hospital has a volume of 45,000 visits, in which a new patient presents every 12 minutes of every day of the year. Fifty-two percent of the hospital's admissions come through the ED, and 15% of all ED visits are admitted (i.e., one in every 6.5 patients).

Chapter 18

West Virginia is a very active place to be in the hospital business, it has a high incidence of obesity, smoking, sedentary lifestyle, diabetes[1], and heart disease[2]. As for age of the population, West Virginia has the second oldest median age of the 50 states, second only to Maine (who overtook West Virginia in 2006).[3]

The Problem with West Virginia

In 2000, West Virginia was one of six states (including New Jersey, Florida, Pennsylvania, Mississippi, and Illinois)[4] with a full-blown malpractice crisis. Runaway malpractice premiums, fueled by a national frenzy to sue, forced West Virginia into a financial crisis. The American Tort Reform Association dubbed the state of West Virginia as a "Judicial Hell Hole."[5]

The medical community found itself in malpractice purgatory. Rates were rising so quickly that the state began to lose doctors, particularly general surgeons. Surgeons were leaving West Virginia because malpractice premiums were rising more quickly than they could pay for them. ED call at Thomas Memorial was down to one in four, from one in eight, and the workload was too demanding for the remaining surgeons. We were one general surgeon away from losing our ED call schedule. General surgery is the backbone of any hospital, as many general surgeons would say.

In 2001 and again in 2003, Gov. Bob Wise urged the state legislature to aggressively reform tort laws, which led to the legislation that capped medical malpractice suits at a maximum of $500,000. After that point, malpractice rates began to drop in direct correlation to suits filed.

Now What?

As the litigious environment began to settle, Thomas Memorial addressed the shortage of ED general surgery call, since the demands of call had become onerous for the remaining surgeons. The remaining surgeons demanded to be paid for call since there were so few of them left to take it. As administrators trying to balance competing interests, we wondered, "How do we pay general surgeons and not pay orthopedists, OBs, ENTs, thoracic surgeons, and others?"

We met numerous times with the general surgeons to try to solve this problem without paying them for call, but it seemed that they were quite unsympathetic to the political problem of how to handle the rest of the medical staff members, who were not going to be paid.

To alleviate the demands of call for the surgeons, we solicited the help of a contract staffing firm, Delphi Healthcare Partners, which recruited two general surgeons to take the unassigned ED call. Delphi said that the two groups to recruit from would be:

- Very young, newly trained surgeons who were undecided on their career paths

- Older physicians (>55) who were weary of running an office and arguing with insurance companies

We got two of the latter.

Both surgeons were 58 years old. Currently, only one of these surgeons covers call at a time, with a rotating schedule of one half month on and one half month off. The surgeon is on call and available day and night during the time he works but is not required to stay in the hospital. Remember, this is possible because they have no office practice.

Why the Surgical Hospitalist Model Works

The program includes two surgeons who each work 26 weeks per year and perform a combined caseload of 600 surgeries annually, plus another 1,400 procedures and consultations on inpatients. They accomplished this without any formal referral patterns from primary care physicians. In the first full year since their arrival, the program generated $1.2 million in gross charges and collected nearly $300,000 (this number is low because of the payer mix of unassigned ED patients). The hospital subsidized the program with an additional $300,000 to keep it solvent.

Implementing the surgical hospitalist program meant that the other general surgeons did not have to leave their office in the middle of the day to come to the ED and then cancel the rest of their office hours for that day. The program reduced their exposure to ED liability. It let them sleep at night. Instituting this program also improved the payer mix for the private general surgeons, since the surgical hospitalists were taking the unassigned ED patients, most of whom were underinsured or uninsured.

Chapter 18

Once the program started, every private general surgeon's volume increased. This was an unexpected positive result. Prior to the program, we experienced a significant decline in the volume of performed surgeries. Within 18 months, however, the volume has all returned, with an additional 10% increase.

The existence of the surgical hospitalist program has made recruiting additional surgeons easier since they are not required to take ED call. The start of the surgical hospitalist program, combined with the recent tort reform in the state, allowed us to recruit an additional six general surgeons into private practice.

Keys to Success

There are five keys to success for such a program:

- Communicate

- Communicate

- Communicate

- Recruit the right physicians

- Communicate some more

The first, second, and third keys to success are to communicate with anybody and everybody who will listen, including physicians, staff members, nurses, referring doctors, hospitalists, etc. Tell them what you are doing, why, how it will work, and what it will mean for them, and keep talking.

The fourth key is to recruit the right physicians. A program's success or failure depends on the performance and demeanor of the physicians you bring into your hospital. For administrative efficiency, a contract service should work for any size hospital, whether urban or rural. Even though you are bringing in new surgeons to take ED call and to solve a big problem, the private surgeons will likely view them as competitors—competitors for patients they didn't want, perhaps, but still competitors. The wrong physicians will kill the program. You get only one opportunity to make it work correctly. The right physicians are critical.

And finally, the fifth key to success is to communicate some more, even after the program starts. Follow up to see how it is being received, and address any issues on the table before they become problems. (The surgeon's lounge is a great place to hang out.)

Postscript

The program has become a casualty of its own success. Because of the positive effects of the surgical hospitalist program, there are several new young physicians who want to take ED call (and, I might add, for no pay), and the need for surgical hospitalists has decreased. Subsequently, the program has been reduced to two weeks' coverage by the surgical hospitalists and two weeks' coverage by the private general surgeons as a three-month phase-out of the program.

REFERENCES

1. "Average Annual Incidence Rates of Diagnosed Diabetes Among Adults, 2005–2007," Kaiser Family Foundation *http://www.statehealthfacts.org/comparemaptable.jsp?cat=2&ind=650&typ=3&gsa=1* (accessed Dec. 15, 2008).

2. MMWR Weekly, "Prevalence of Heart Disease–United States, 2005," Center for Disease Control and Prevention, *www.cdc.gov/mmwr/preview/mmwrhtml/mm5606a2.htm* (accessed Dec. 15, 2008).

3. American Community Survey, "Demographic Profiles, R0101: Median Age of the Total Population: 2005," US Census Bureau, *www.census.gov* (accessed Dec. 15, 2008).

4. Michelle M. Mello, David M. Studdert, Troyen A. Brennan. "The New Medical Malpractice Crisis." *New England Journal of Medicine* 348 (2003): 912.

5. American Tort Reform Association, "Bringing Justice to America's Judicial Hellholes 2002," *www.atra.org/reports/hellholes/2002/hellholes_report_2002.pdf* (accessed Dec. 15, 2008).

CHAPTER 19

CASE STUDY
University of California, Irvine

Michael E. Lekawa, MD, FACS • David B. Hoyt, MD, FACS

PROFILE

Established:	2007
Number of FTE surgeons:	6 full-time and 1 part-time faculty
Employer:	University of California, Irvine
Setting:	Academic medical center
Status:	Nonprofit
Bed size:	462

Background

The Acute Care Surgery (ACS) program at UC Irvine Medical Center developed out of the Division of Trauma, Burns and Critical Care in 2007. UC Irvine is the only academic medical center in Orange County, CA, a geographically small county with a dense population of 3 million people. There are 26 emergency departments (ED) in our county, with our own ED seeing approximately 35,000 patients each year. The medical center is a 462-bed facility with an average occupancy of 93%.

UC Irvine has been a designated Level I American College of Surgeons–verified trauma center since 1982. For the past 15 years, the trauma division has managed the trauma center, the burn center, the surgical ICU, the burn ICU, and the critical care management of the neuroscience ICU. Prior to creating the ACS program, approximately 40% of general surgery call was taken by the trauma division faculty. Inpatient surgery consults were called directly to the most appropriate division throughout the department of surgery at the discretion of the consultant; however, the go-to service for critically ill patients was usually the trauma service. This reputation resulted from our policy of rapid response, reliable availability 24/7, a willingness to perform definitive procedures on short notice and during the same hospitalization, and an indifference to payer mix. These characteristics were a direct extension from our commitment to our trauma and burn patients. The trauma division at UC Irvine was essentially practicing acute care surgery; however, it lacked universal application throughout the medical center, formalized organization, treatment algorithms, and appropriate recognition.

Stimulus to Create an ACS Program

There were many factors that contributed to our decision to further develop a formal ACS program at UC Irvine. We felt that the existing infrastructure of our Level I trauma center, within both the medical center and the department of surgery, could be expanded to sustain an ACS service. By replicating the trauma care model, we could improve resource utilization, patient care, and resident education, while expanding our division's product line.

Although we are an active trauma center with more than 2,500 trauma activations each year, our trauma faculty has noted a decrease in each surgeon's individual operative experience. This has resulted from the profound rise in nonoperative management of solid organ injury, the increase in less-invasive surgical and interventional radiology procedures, and a decrease in operations for penetrating trauma. One of our intents in developing an ACS program was to attract more surgical consults and operative cases. Operative cases are critical in maintaining the interest and surgical skills of our trauma surgeons; we had two of our trauma/critical care surgeons leave in 2006, in great part, due to their desire to operate more. A greater operative experience would also make the field of trauma surgery more appealing to our residents and fellows.

UC Irvine is a tertiary center for several surgical subspecialties, including oncologic, minimally invasive, hepatobiliary, and colorectal surgery. To maintain successful programs in these disciplines, it is optimal for the specialty surgeon to serve large outpatient practices that may not be amenable to interruptions for daytime emergency procedures. And as these subspecialists narrowed the scope of their practice, they may not retain the experience or expertise to manage the wide variety of surgical problems that would present in the ED or medical ICU. For example, there is an increasing reluctance on the part of our breast surgeons, melanoma surgeons, and even minimally invasive surgeons to participate in the call system. Whether due to lack of confidence, interest, or desire, we found it increasingly difficult to distribute general surgery call throughout the department. The cadre of surgeons who were available and willing to take general surgery call was made up mostly of trauma surgeons and recent graduates from the residency program.

Case Study: University of California, Irvine

Outside of the trauma division, there were few generalists in our academic center. As an academic tertiary center, we had witnessed a diminishing volume of primary care patients. And as our primary care patient population migrated away, the primary care residency programs integrated into the community hospitals where community general surgeons provided the bread-and-butter surgical care. Ultimately, the patients who continued to present at UC Irvine Medical Center with elective surgical issues often expected to be managed by the subspecialists in that area, leaving an inadequate volume of work for many general surgeons. Ultimately, all of the surgeons in our department became focused on their subspecialty. We felt that optimal care would be better provided by a smaller group of surgeons who remained available and proficient in treating a wide array of urgent surgical diseases.

Perhaps the most significant stimulus to develop this program was the perception of a growing need for quality urgent surgical care, both in the medical center and in the community. As with many major medical centers, our ED suffers from long waits and prolonged ED stays. One of the many causes of these long ED stays was unnecessary delays for initial surgical consultation and delays in definitive attending participation and decision-making. By institutionalizing an in-house surgeon with the background and experience to perform rapid evaluations, we anticipated that the throughput would improve significantly. The close relationship between our trauma service leadership and the local emergency medical system highlighted the crisis that some local EDs were having maintaining their on-call panel of surgeons. By developing a service dedicated to the care of difficult acute surgery patients, particularly during off hours, we could provide another critical tertiary service to the community. Finally, by providing appropriate and rapid consultation and early operative intervention, our patients would benefit from shorter stays, lower costs, and better outcomes.

Prior to formalizing the ACS program, the trauma division staffed approximately one-third of the general surgery call. As noted above, there are obvious benefits for the surgeon's operative experience that made this the ideal group to provide the staff resources for this endeavor. Superimposing the trauma schedule on the ACS schedule simplified the line of responsibility. By incorporating the trauma and acute care surgeons into a single defined service, the in-house surgical residents were better organized into one organizational scheme, allowing a more efficient deployment based on the triaged needs of trauma and acute general surgery.

Chapter 19

Lessons Learned

Since assuming all general surgery call, more attending physicians became substantially more involved to provide ACS care and trauma care. Whereas residents can provide much of the trauma care in the acute setting, operative intervention requires attending presence in the immediate operating room (OR) area. This makes the individual effect of a night on call more substantial and should be accounted for in the scheduling process. It not only affects the amount of sleep a surgeon can expect to get when in-house, but it also increasingly demands more in-house time when covering with a fellow. The likelihood of having multiple surgical or critical interventions at once also increases, in which case the backup schedule would need to be activated. The ACS division faculty now regards backup call much more seriously, as it recognizes the greater likelihood of its need. All of these issues substantially affect the amount of commitment needed from the on-call surgeons, which must be accounted for in terms of time or financial compensation.

In terms of marketing to other EDs, the results have been mixed. As we have found with trauma, we now receive requests to consult for conditions that would historically have been primarily managed by our subspecialist partners, particularly vascular surgery, neurosurgery, and plastics. It is important that a marketing strategy include as many other willing surgical divisions and departments that provide emergency surgical care as possible.

Perhaps the most important lesson learned to accommodate these above issues was the need for reserved OR time. OR time not only requires the somewhat inefficient reservation of an OR that may sit unutilized for substantial periods of time, but it also requires a commitment from anesthesia and OR nursing to provide appropriate staffing. Coordinating these resources has been our most consistently recurring challenge to date. A 24/7 available OR allows a more rapid delivery of operative care to the patient. However, it also is important for ACS surgeons to have access to ORs during mornings and afternoons. If procedures are routinely deferred until the evening hours, the ACS surgeons will likely find themselves occupied in the OR when trauma activations are more common and the surgeons and staff members to support them are scarcer. We have added an urgent room to the OR schedule to address this problem.

Case Study: University of California, Irvine

What Is the Turf of the ACS Service?

The interaction of ACS and non-ACS surgeons has generally been positive. Initially, the non-ACS surgeons were concerned about a potential loss of case volume and revenue, as well as a potential shift of residents to the ACS service. However, soon after we established the program, the immediate benefit of diminished off-hour interruptions became evident. We have not seen a noticeable decline in any other division's level of clinical work or operating income. Our intent is that all surgical consults be coordinated through the ACS service, although it is difficult to confirm compliance on this matter. The ACS service will involve the subspecialty service, as appropriate, or transfer the patient to another service at the optimal time. Consults for patients who have ongoing relationships with other treating surgeons may still be directed immediately to other services, although the ACS team is always available to assist as needed. There are circumstances in which a patient on the ACS service may have a diagnosis best managed by an alternative subspecialist. As a unified department, we have found our entire faculty very willing to provide assistance to our division to ensure that a surgeon with optimal expertise is present to manage the problem. This may involve secondary consultation or transfer to another service. A team-oriented department allows us to access the best possible minimally invasive, hepatobiliary, oncologic, colorectal, or vascular surgical expertise. It was fortunate that our department has an excellent level of friendly, professional interaction. Strong leadership and cooperation from the department chair and the trauma division was very important in creating the program. Otherwise, concern or distrust from other divisions may have prevented the program from moving forward. The motto "When you see one of us, you see all of us" was coined by our chair to illustrate this concept.

Staffing

Our ACS service provides management of a 2,500 activation/yr trauma program and complete general surgery coverage for the entire hospital and ED. It works parallel to two other services that are staffed by our division, the SICU service and the burn service. The SICU service manages our 16-bed SICU and provides support for the eight-bed NSICU and the pediatric ICU. The burn program operates an ACS-accredited burn center, with nearly 300 inpatient and 1,700 outpatient visits annually. Our division has six full-time and one part-time faculty. Administratively, this includes a department chair, a division chief/trauma director, a residency director, a burn director, and an SICU director. The four core ACS/trauma clinical surgeons perform approximately one in four weeks on the ACS service and one in four weeks in the SICU. Each surgeon provides approximately two to three in-house ACS calls and four additional night calls shared with the critical care fellow.

The ACS, burn, and SICU services are staffed as illustrated below. It is essential to have an adequate number of surgeons and fellows to manage the in-house call. We currently manage two critical care fellows who are able to provide approximately 40% of this coverage. By using a part-time surgeon from one of our community trauma centers, we limit the call exposure of our full-time surgeons. As a result, they are more available for daytime activities, including teaching and administrative responsibilities. Refer to Figure 19.1.

FIGURE 19.1 — TEACHING AND ADMINISTRATIVE RESPONSIBILITIES

Service	ACS	SICU	Burn
Attending	1 plus backup	1	1
Fellow	1	1	
Resident	R5, R4, R2, R1, R1, R1, ED1	R3,R2 Anesth or Gyn	R2 plus backup
Students	2–4	1–4	1
NPs	3		1

Source: University of California, Irvine.

The important contributions of the surgical residents is necessary to provide comprehensive support to this large clinical program, maintain a strong didactic program, provide depth of coverage for spikes in clinical activity, cover the vast majority of night resident call coverage, and comply with ACGME hours and call limitations.

Cost and Caseload

The direct costs to develop the program have been minimal. Essentially, the vast hospital resources (including OR and radiology) available for trauma have been applied to the entire ACS service. The wide array of other surgical subspecialists is already accustomed to providing care to trauma patients that are comprehensively managed by the ACS service. The on-call stipend was increased by a modest 10%, although we did have an additional hospital-supported nurse practitioner (NP) added to the service. We feel that midlevel practitioners provide an indispensable amount of depth to allow efficient care and throughput to the service. The hospital is the obvious source to fund this for two reasons.

Case Study: University of California, Irvine

First, improved care provides better patient satisfaction, a lower risk for litigation due to staffing resources, and faster patient throughput to prevent ED overcrowding. These factors are a direct benefit to hospitals more than to individual physicians. Second, professional compensation lags behind hospital compensation, and our group could not afford this investment despite its critical value.

In our first year (2007), our service performed 525 nontrauma/nonburn/non-ICU surgical procedures. This volume has increased by 42%, to 745 operative interventions in the second year. The compensation per RVU for 2008 is comparable to our trauma compensation per RVU.

The creation of a formal ACS service at UC Irvine illustrates the natural evolution and growth of the trauma service. Our program continues to mature as we develop more protocols, increase our referral base, track our outcomes, and publish our results. If we can demonstrate more cost-effective care with better outcomes and greater patient satisfaction, we will be well positioned to obtain more business and more hospital investment. Our experience is that of a mature, academic Level I trauma center and may illustrate differences from nontertiary centers.

CHAPTER 20

CASE STUDY
Surgical Specialists of Spokane, Spokane, WA

Paul Lin, MD, FACS

PROFILE

Established:	2007
Employer:	Private practice that contracts with 2 hospital systems (4 hospitals)
Setting, status, bed size:	• Sacred Heart Medical Center (nonprofit, 624 beds)
	• Holy Family Hospital (nonprofit, 272 beds)
	• Deaconess Medical Center (for-profit, 388 beds)
	• Valley Hospital and Medical Center (for-profit, 123 beds)

The current model of surgical hospitalists in Spokane, WA has evolved over the course of several years, since October 2007. This has been due to trends in general surgery in the city of Spokane that have mirrored the rest of the country. More than 10 years ago, the two hospital systems in metropolitan Spokane, started a joint Level II trauma service.

The Spokane model is a very loose and informal system of surgical hospitalists. However, this model has many advantages that work well with the unique attributes of this medical community. The main driver to implement this program was to provide adequate 24/7/365 emergency department (ED) call for general surgery for all of the hospitals in town. Spokane has the appropriate number of general surgeons to meet the need for our catchments area, but it does not have enough to provide general surgery coverage at four hospitals every day while trying to run a busy elective practice. However, with the national trend of more and more general surgeons entering specialty practice, there are too few general surgeons to cover four hospitals every day, assuming that the surgical specialists would not want to take general surgery call.

Chapter 20

There is also no question that general surgery call has become increasingly busy. For example, the ED volumes for Sacred Heart Medical Center, the busiest hospital in Spokane, had 47,711 visits in 2004. In 2008, it had approximately 70,000 visits. About 20% of these ED patients end up being admitted. Additionally, Spokane is the major referral center for Eastern Washington, Northern Idaho, Western Montana, and Northeast Oregon. Because of Spokane's ability to provide specialists in areas, such as cardiology, nephrology, cardiothoracic surgery, and neurosurgery, we regularly receive transfers from our extended region. We also have several smaller communities and hospitals surrounding us. There is a de facto regionalization as more and more of these smaller hospitals are unable to provide full-time general surgery coverage for their communities. In 2003, 13% of general surgery admissions came through the ED. In 2008, almost 19% of general surgery admissions came through the ED. These numbers do not reflect the increased acuity of medical patients that require general surgical evaluations as well. It is now impractical to have a full elective practice on the days that we are trying to cover two EDs, let alone covering a Level II trauma service.

These stresses on our private practice led to a system in which surgeons were essentially being paid to take trauma call, although it was in a convoluted way that avoided the pay-for-call label. Also during this time, there has been an influx of general surgery subspecialists who did not want to take ED call. The vast majority of general surgeons who have come to Spokane in the past few years have been fellowship-trained specialists. Because of this effect on the general surgery call roster, the hospitals instituted a rule that required one to take ED call in his or her board-certified specialty. This meant vascular surgeons, pediatric surgeons, and colorectal surgeons, who have their own board certification, were not required to take ED call for general surgery.

However, surgical oncologists, laparoscopic surgeons, breast surgeons, and bariatric surgeons were required to take general surgery ED call, since these specialists did not have their own American Board of Surgery (ABS) board certifications. This caused some problems among some of the specialists, such as breast surgeons, who did not feel comfortable taking care of major general surgical emergencies. One breast surgeon went as far as to pay another general surgeon to take her ED call.

The main stimulus for the current Spokane model was the 2005 merger of three practices. Our resultant group of 13 general surgeons practiced at all four of the hospitals in town. When counting all general surgeons, including those with subspecialty certification, our 13-person group represented less than half of the general surgeons in town. However, since we practiced at multiple hospitals, we were

Case Study: Surgical Specialists of Spokane, Spokane, WA

taking essentially 75% of the ED call throughout the town. Subsequently, each person in our group restricted our primary practice to one hospital. This caused a marked shortage of general surgeons taking ED call in three of the four hospitals. To fill the gap in the ED call roster, the hospitals began to pay surgeons to take extra call to provide 24/7/365 general surgery call at each of the four hospitals. From there, it was a short jump to our current model.

Spokane has two hospital systems, with two hospitals each. The systems also share a joint Level II trauma system. The surgeon on call functions as a surgical hospitalist for that day and does not have any scheduled office time or elective surgeries. He or she covers two hospitals at a time, which includes trauma call and inpatient consults. The two surgeons on call that day are paid a daily stipend by the hospitals, and the work done by the surgeon on call is billed fee-for-service, as normal. The stipend figure is the difference between the average daily elective collections and the average on-call collections with a small premium added. One of the hospitals worked with an outside consultant to arrive at its stipend figure, which is about two-thirds of the daily professional fee collections from the work.

FORMULA FOR ON-CALL SURGEON PAYMENT

Average daily elective collections − Average on-call collections + Small premium = Daily stipend

When the surgeon is not on call, he or she resumes normal elective practice. Our group of 13 surgeons takes the bulk of the ED call at the four hospitals in town. However, any of the other general surgeons in town may choose to participate in this arrangement; currently, eight from outside of our group have chosen to do so. The specific call rotation is different for each hospital and is based on the number of surgeons taking call at that hospital and the frequency that they wish to take call. The hospitals have left the call schedule entirely up to the surgeons.

Because our system is so informal, the individual surgeon decides how the patients are managed. Within my group, we generally follow the patients we admit or consult when on call as we have in the past. We have several fellowship-trained surgeons in our group, and we ask them to take over certain patients when appropriate. However, any urgent surgeries that need to be done the following day are frequently passed on to the on-call surgeon for that day to avoid interfering with our elective practice on the post-call days. The disruption of a surgeon's schedule the day after call is probably a bigger burden to the private practice surgeon taking ED call than is performing emergent surgeries in the middle of the night.

Chapter 20

The main benefit of this model is that we were able to implement it very quickly; all of the participating surgeons were already practicing in Spokane. Had each hospital attempted to implement a more formal surgical hospitalist program, it would have required the time to recruit four or five general surgeons to get off the ground. With fewer and fewer general surgeons available, recruiting has become difficult. The U.S. Department of Health and Human Services has forecasted a 25% shortage of surgical specialists in the next 15 years.

The other option would have been to hire locum tenens surgeons, which would have been prohibitively expensive in the long run and would not ensure the quality of physician being provided. During this transition period to a hospital-based surgical hospitalist program, there would have been a real danger of alienating the surgeons who were already practicing in the community. Despite all the grumblings from general surgeons regarding call, cholecystitis, appendicitis, diverticulitis, bowel obstructions, and perforations—the cases associated with call—still make up a sizable portion of surgeries performed by our practice.

In summary, the system for emergency general surgery coverage that has evolved in Spokane has many attractive features that used the existing resources available in the community. It can be described as a rotating surgical hospitalist system. Although none of the surgeons is a full-time surgical hospitalist, each rotates into that role periodically.

Given how busy general surgery call has become, the greatest benefit of the program for participating surgeons is having the financial resources to close their outpatient and elective surgery schedule while on call. This provides protected time for urgent and emergent patients. It prevents us from being overwhelmed with the combination of our elective patients and the urgent and emergent patients. It also turns a historically burdensome, financially unattractive, and practice-disrupting situation into one that improves revenue and provides a more reasonable lifestyle.

For the community, this arrangement makes the hospitals in town much more attractive places for surgical specialists to practice, as they are not required to take ED call. In fact, since our system was established, recruitment of surgical specialists seems to have accelerated, which benefits patients and the hospitals. We have a faster response time to inpatient and ED consults than before, and we typically do not have to wait until the end of the day to take someone to the operating room. So far, all parties seem to be satisfied with the current arrangement, and we recently renewed our contracts with the hospitals.

Resources

HCPro: *www.hcpro.com*

HCPro's mission is to meet the specialized information, advisory, and education needs of the healthcare industry and to learn from and respond to our customers with services that meet or exceed the quality that they expect. Visit HCPro's Web site at *www.hcpro.com* to take advantage of our new Internet resources.

At *www.hcpro.com*, you will find the following:

- The latest news, advice, and how-to information in the world of healthcare

- Free e-mail newsletters covering everything from survey preparation and Joint Commission standards to healthcare credentialing and health information management

- Your healthcare questions, answered by HCPro's experts

- Weekly tips about how to perform your job at your best

- In-depth, how-to stories in our premium newsletters, including **Briefings on The Joint Commission, Medical Staff Briefing,** and the **Credentialing Resource Center** (paid subscriptions or pay-per-view required to read premium newsletter content)

- The most comprehensive products and services (available through our online store, HCPro's Healthcare Marketplace at *www.hcmarketplace.com*) to help you tackle the tough issues that you face on the job every day

- All of the information and resources that you need about the following topics:

Resources

- Accreditation
- Case management
- Corporate compliance
- Credentialing/privileging
- Executive leadership
- Finance
- Health information management
- Hospital pharmacy
- Infection control
- Long-term care
- Marketing
- Medical staff
- Nursing
- Pharmaceutical
- Physician practice
- Quality/patient safety
- Rehab
- Residency
- Safety

HCPro continues to offer the expert advice and practical guidance on which you've come to rely to meet your daily challenges. This valuable information will be available to you 24 hours a day, seven days a week, via the Internet.

The Greeley Company, a division of HCPro: www.greeley.com

Get connected with leading healthcare consultants and educators at The Greeley Company's Web site at *www.greeley.com*. This online service provides the fastest, most convenient, and most up-to-date information about our quality consulting and national training offerings for healthcare leaders. The Greeley Web site offers a complete listing of all of our products and services, including consulting services, seminars, conferences, and links to other HCPro offerings.

At *www.greeley.com*, you will find the following:

- Detailed descriptions of all of The Greeley Company's consulting services

- A catalog and calendar of Greeley's national seminars and conferences, as well as available CMEs

- Faculty and consultant biographies that introduce our senior-level clinicians, administrators, and faculty, who are ready to assist your organization with your consulting needs and seminars

- An "Ask the Expert" Q&A

- A list of Greeley clients

- A link to free e-mail newsletters

HCPro's Healthcare Marketplace: www.hcmarketplace.com

Looking for even more resources? You can shop for the healthcare management tools you need at HCPro's Healthcare Marketplace (*www.hcmarketplace.com*). Our online store makes it easy to find what you need, when you need it, in one secure and user-friendly e-commerce site.

At HCPro's Healthcare Marketplace, you'll find all of the newsletters, books, videos, audio conferences, online learning, special reports, and training handbooks that HCPro has to offer.

Shopping is secure, and purchasing is easy with a speedy checkout process.

FREE HEALTHCARE COMPLIANCE AND MANAGEMENT RESOURCES!

Need to control expenses yet stay current with critical issues?

Get timely help with FREE e-mail newsletters from HCPro, Inc., the leader in healthcare compliance education. Offering numerous free electronic publications covering a wide variety of essential topics, you'll find just the right e-newsletter to help you stay current, informed, and effective. All you have to do is sign up!

With your FREE subscriptions, you'll also receive the following:

- Timely information, to be read when convenient with your schedule
- Expert analysis you can count on
- Focused and relevant commentary
- Tips to make your daily tasks easier

And here's the best part—there's no further obligation—just a complimentary resource to help you get through your daily challenges.

It's easy. Visit *www.hcmarketplace.com/free/e-newsletters/* to register for as many free e-newsletters as you'd like, and let us do the rest.

HCPro | Insight for healthcare compliance and management